T0115373

THE STRUGGLE FOR LIBYA

Miral Sabry AlAshry

authorHOUSE

AuthorHouse™
1663 Liberty Drive
Bloomington, IN 47403
www.authorhouse.com
Phone: 833-262-8899

Published by AuthorHouse 04/26/2021

ISBN: 978-1-6655-2435-3 (sc)
ISBN: 978-1-6655-2438-4 (e)

Print information available on the last page.

Miral AlAshry

I came to write this book on Libya out of a growing interest in my second county of the region, following 2011 decried the war which I lived before and after the Arab Spring revolutions. In the beginning, I was on vacation in Egypt, January 2011, and the revolution occurred, and I found terror in the streets, so my family and I decided to go to Libya to find safety. After two days the revolution broke out and it was the ugliest coup in the Middle East.

I decided to work in the newspapers to cover the revolution and I published many academic kinds of research about the change of the constitution and democratic developments in Libya. I attended many conferences to talk about the conflict facing Libyan journalists in places of conflict Libyan journalists suffered from sexual harassment, killing, rape, and torture.

I draw my analysis of the struggle over Libya from my in-depth and direct observations, of my close contacts with international and local media professionals as well as my dangerous personal travels to Libya. I am working as an editor covering the conflict in Libya, so this book is acclamation from my experience and the articles I wrote in the newspapers since the beginning of the revolution until now. Hence, you will feel that I am using her scalpel for the anatomy of Libya's crisis.

Finally, the word of a struggle means that every Libyan is fighting for freedom.

Acknowledgements

I would like to thank my supervisor and my Dean, Prof. Abdul-Monem Al-Mashat, for the patient guidance, encouragement, and advice he has provided throughout my time as a colleague.

I have been extremely lucky to have him as a supervisor and dean who cared so much about my work, and who responded to my questions and queries so promptly. You are like my father; I love you so much. I have never seen in my life a person like you.

I must express my gratitude to Mohamed Alatrash, my husband, for his continued support and encouragement and as he gives me his experience as a citizen from Libya.

Finally, I would like to thank my lovely boys who experienced all of the ups and downs of my book.

What did I do to you?

Last words of Libya's Muammar Gaddafi to rebels just before he was killed

Ruled Libya before the revolution

The fallen Libyan leader, Muammar Gaddafi, entered the world in 1942, near Sirte. A son of an itinerant Bedouin farmer, Gaddafi was brilliant in School and soon graduated from the University of Libya in 1963. He graduated from the Libyan military academy in 1965.

On September 1, 1969, Gaddafi and his men took over the country in a bloodless coup, then he formed the Libyan Arab Republic, with the motto "freedom, socialism and unity. By 1973 he had nationalized all foreign-owned petroleum assets in the country, move western countries never forgave him for. He put his own strict Islamic principles by outlawed alcoholic beverages and gambling.

The government initiated a process of directing funds toward providing education, health care, and housing for all. Public education in the country became free and primary education compulsory for both sexes. Medical care became available to the public at no cost,

The per capita income in the country rose to more than the US $11,000, the fifth-highest in Africa. He established the Green Book as his political philosophy, first published in 1975.

Libya has largely a desert, there was a need to have a robust irrigation system to sustain life. Gaddafi's government funded the largest irrigation system in the world-man made rivers to supply water to citizens.

In the past, there was free electricity, cheap petrol and state bank which provided loans to citizens at zero per cent and then there was no external debt, a rarity for an African state. African states are often saddled with loans with steep interest from the IMF and World Bank.

Ruling for 42 years until his demise in October 2011, Gaddafi chalked impressive feats to improve the lives of his people.

Preface

Since NATO intervened militarily in Libya and got rid of Gaddafi, the sole ruler of Libya for over four decades, hopes were raised to see a democratic transformation, socio-economic development, and stability in the country, on the country and from the outset, internal and external struggle for Libya took place among agents of conflicting parties.

This struggle transformed the conflict into a protracted social conflict with complexities and dangers beyond anyone's control. This protracted social conflict manifested itself intensifying socio-political disorder and total instability. State institutions, as limited it was, failed to cope with a spiral of tension, violence, and deadly wars. The whole country turned into a vast battleground for all types of weapons, terrorist groups, militias, mercenaries, remnants of Al Queda, and fled Muslim Brotherhood as well as for foreign military forces. These developments led to state failure where Libya presents a typical case of a failed state.

The Struggle for Libya presents the reader with the most accurate knowledge about the conflict in Libya, draws the map of violence, and analyses the interests of all actors whether are local, regional, or international. In ten chapters, covering the conflict and war in Libya, this book navigates through the bloody waters of a rich oil-producing country. It reiterates that the struggle for Libya is a multidimensional, weapons trade, oil, territory, geostrategic location, and influence.

This book does only provide a deep analysis of the struggle for Libya between competing actors, but it also presents first-hand information and knowledge about the nature, dynamics and severeness of the struggle. The word struggle means that there are forces competing for the soul of Libya on one hand while Libyans are struggling for freedom and democracy.

This book analyses the political issues in Libya which developed into three stages:

First, from October 2011 to July 2012 this period focused on identifying interim leaders and recovery conflict;

Second, from July 2012 to May 2014 this period focused on a transitional period legitimizing and testing the viability of interim institutions.

Third, from May 2014 to the present, (The second Libyan civil war) this period focused on who wants the power using tension and violence among loose political-military coalitions, a multifaceted conflict between their members and violent Islamist extremist groups, and enhanced efforts by third parties to promote reconciliation(Blanchard, 2018).

Contents

Introduction

This book discusses the Libyan conflict during the period of 2011 to 2020, Libya's 2011 uprising and conflict brought Muammar al Qadhafi's authoritarian rule to an end. Competing factions and alliances—organized along local, regional, ideological, tribal, and personal lines—have jockeyed for influence and power in post-Qadhafi Libya, on February 2011 the revolts in other Arab countries, especially neighbouring Egypt and Tunisia, violent protests break out in Benghazi, spread to other cities, on March - UN Security Council authorizes a no-fly zone over Libya and airstrikes to protect civilians, by using NATO assumes command. Ending on July the international Contact Group on Libya formally recognizes the National Transitional Council (NTC), as the legitimate government of Libya, African Union joins 60 countries to support this decision in August. by 20 October - Col Gaddafi is captured and killed from his hometown Sirte then they captured the fugitive son of former Libyan leader Muammar Gaddafi in November. The first months of 2012 clashes erupt between former rebel forces in Benghazi in a sign of discontent with the NTC this increasing tension with the NTC in Tripoli.

In August the transitional government hands the power to the General National Congress. in September storm the consulate in Benghazi, the US ambassador and three other Americans are killed when Islamist militants control the consulate.

The next year the struggle inside Libya increased to control oil on 2013 August the Petroleum Facilities Guard militia begins a blockade of oil and gas export terminals.

At the beginning of 2014, the civil war started in Libya, in February - protests erupt in response to the General National Congress refusal to disband after the mandate expires these protests take two months and the Petroleum Facilities Guard militia lifts closure two oil terminals.

This year, the strongman Haftar appeared he launched a military assault including airstrikes against militant Islamist groups in Benghazi; his objective tries to seize parliament building, accusing Prime Minister Ahmed Maiteg of being in thrall to Islamist groups he used Libyan National Army.

Libya's government fractured in two so that it gives opportunities to jihadist fighters progressively embedded themselves in many of the country's key militias. in the middle of 2014 jihadist groups chose to indirectly support the Tripoli faction by engaging in violent conflict with forces aligned with the Tobruq government and General Khalifa Haftar.

According to that on June Prime Minister Maiteg resigns after Supreme Court rules his appointment illegal. They were chosen a new parliament for elections by a low turn-out attributed to security fears and boycotts; then the fighting breaks out between forces loyal to the outgoing GNC and the parliament.

In July Tripoli international airport destroyed by fighting due to that the UN staff pull out, embassies shut down. At the end of the year 2014, 100,000s displaced by clashes and there is international cooperation to stop fighting by UN-brokered talks between the new parliament and government based in Tobruk and Islamist Libya Dawn militias holding Tripoli.

In the first month of 2015 Libyan army and Tripoli-based militia, alliance declares partial ceasefire after UN-sponsored talks in Geneva. The ISIS group released a video showing the beheading of 21 Egyptian Christians on February Egyptian jets bomb to the Islamic State targets in Derna. ISIS control over port-city of Sirte, halfway along the coast between Tripoli and Benghazi.

With an unannounced and fabricated international trial in July, a Tripoli court sentences Gaddafi's sons Saif al-Islam and eight other former officials to death for crimes committed during the 2011 uprising against his father, on the other hand, Gaddafi's sons freed by an armed group.

According to the situation of the Libyan conflict in 2016 January, the UN announces a new government based in Tunisia, but neither Tobruk nor Tripoli parliaments agree to recognise the authority. The next month the Islamic State group attacks Ras Lanuf oil terminal, and they move on to Brega and Tobruk.

2016 March, opposing forces block airspace by a new UN-backed Government of National Accord arrives in Tripoli by boat. Then UN staff returns to Tripoli after nearly two years to solve the situation. Haftar seizes key oil export terminals in the east in September to expand his power and full control. At the end of December, Pro-government forces oust Islamic State ISIS from Sirte.

In 2017 the government succeeded to eject the Islamic State group from Benghazi after three years of fighting. in July - Haftar succeeded full control of Derna, the last Islamist stronghold in the east. Then, he movies in 2019 April with the Libyan National Army in Tripoli, sparking clashes with the forces of the internationally recognized Government of National Accord.

In the first year of the 2020 Berlin conference the first step from war to peace held on January 19th to protect Libya this conference is one in a series of international meetings on Libya, which have taken place in Paris, Palermo, Abu Dhabi, and Moscow. This conference has been the most important, due to several considerations.

Four international organizations and twelve countries participated in the conference, including the five permanent members of the Security Council. Nine of them were represented by heads of state and government. Also, it's the first time that President Putin's participation was a key factor that encouraged other leaders to attend.

Berlin conference into an "international summit" in Libya. This helped facilitate a consensus among the different parties and the convergence of conflicting positions, even within European countries like France and Italy. But attempts failed. in June, the UN-backed government drives Haftar forces out of Tarhouna, their last stronghold in the west of the country near Tripoli.

The escalation continues and the war does not end

Libya Background
Geographical Information

Libya is fourth in size among the countries of Africa and seventeenth among the countries of the world. It is on the Mediterranean between Egypt and Tunisia, with Niger and Chad to the south and Sudan to the southeast (Libya, 2021, January 28).

Libya - Population

The North African country of Libya lies along the Mediterranean Sea and shares its borders with Egypt, Sudan, Chad, Niger, Algeria, and Tunisia. The country covers 679,363 square miles (1,759,540 square kilometres) surface area which is the fourth largest country in Africa and the 17th largest in the world. The country of Libya unites North Africa with the Middle East. The geography of the land is relatively flat, and the Sahara desert (most of which is uninhabitable) and the Mediterranean Coast are the best-known features in the area. The sparsely populated nation of Libya was 6,848,400 million as of 2020, which ranks 188th in the world in terms of population density. Over 80% of the people in Libya live in or around urban areas, also most of the life in Tripoli, and the other life in the second and third largest cities are Benghazi (pop around 650,000) and Misrata (pop around 300,000), which are the economic and entrepreneurial headquarters of the nation. Three other cities in Libya with populations in excess of 200,000 include Tarhuna, Al Khums, and Az Zāwīyah (Libya Population, 2021)

Arab Ethnicity

Arab ethnicity is a dominant part of Libyan life and identity. The Arab ethnic group is native to the Arabian Peninsula, arriving in Libya during Islamic military campaigns of the 7th century CE. Since Arab ethnicity has historically been tightly connected to the religion of Islam, the Islamic leaders of Libya have often emphasized Arab heritage for the nation over the centuries.

Berber Ethnicity

The other major ethnic group in Libya is the Berbers or Amazigh with 97%. The Amazigh are ancestrally native to Northern Africa, the Amazigh did not historically share a single cultural or ethnic identity the way Arabs did. Instead, Amazigh identity was defined by clan or tribal association (Muscato,)

In February 2014, Al-Ahram weekly newspaper published a report providing a description of the tribal nature of Libyan society. Libyan society is primarily structured along tribal lines, It is also an entirely Muslim country, which subscribes to the Maleki School of jurisprudence. The vast majority of the populace is Arab in origin, while five per cent is Amazigh, three per cent African, and one per cent Tuareg. In addition, the Libyan Jewish minority left the country in 1967 and the Italians that had remained by the time that Gaddafi took power were expelled in 1970 (Fabbrini, 2014).

The International Crisis Group notes that Libya is estimated to have around 140 tribes and clans, when Gaddafi took power he attempted to downplay the tribal system, which he saw as both backward and associated with the monarchy's reactionary practices.

According to that he altered administrative boundaries based on tribal delineations and removed all officials who had been appointed by the king due to their tribe.

Gaddafi continued to use tribal divisions and loyalties as instruments of power, by courting tribal leaders and allocating political posts to dominant tribes. In the 1990s, Gaddafi implemented a collective punishment law, "according to which a criminal's family or tribe can be stripped of its civil rights and social services for failure to denounce one of its member's illegal activities"(The International Crisis Group, 2019).

Oil & Gas in Libya

In 1915 Italians found in a deepwater well drilled natural gas, but natural gas was not a prime commodity at that time. In 1935 a professor from Milan University who was in charge of a water well drilling program made it a point to watch for petroleum. A couple of years later petroleum was detected in a water well drilled near Tripoli. This find was enough to prompt a geological survey in Tripolitania. In 1940 a program of exploration was initiated but the available equipment was inadequate to deal with the severe conditions of the Saharan Desert. Shortly thereafter war came to Libya and all exploration stopped.

Libya became an independent kingdom in 1951. The new kingdom developed mineral rights law through consultation with international petroleum companies. In 1953 Libya granted prospecting permits to eleven petroleum companies. Geologic surveys were undertaken by those companies. In 1955 a petroleum well was successfully drilled under desert conditions just across the border in Algeria.

In 1957 there were about a dozen companies operating in Libya on about sixty different concessions. The companies from French para-statal Compagnie França;aise des Pétroles. In

1957 Esso decided to drill in the area across Algerian. In 1959 Esso drilled in the Siritica region he found six major oil fields(Watkins, Alley, & Valley,1982).

Why conflict in Libya?

Libya's oil reserves are the ninth-largest in the world and are managed by the National Oil Corporation (NOC). Almost the entirety of Libya's public budget(95 per cent) is financed by oil revenues, putting the country at 55 out of 58 countries with significant oil, gas (Shaarawy,2020). In Libya, there is a lack of safeguards and oversight within the sector, with no access to information law, public disclosure on most aspects of Libya's petroleum industry is absent oil contracts and permits are not published and under Gaddafi (Benstead & Kjærum, 2019).

The Public sector with the reputation of being the most corrupt institution in Libya course there is an 'accountability vacuum' between the public sector and the general population. after the revolution, the poor performance of public institutions, the state's inability to provide security and citizens' mistrust in the state leaves a vacuum, This led to armed militias entering the country and controlling oil. The fighting between various militias increased and the executive effectively lost control of most ministries as well as other government facilities in Tripoli.

Libya Crude Oil Production

The war around Tripoli that erupted in April 2019 between the two main political rivals reversed the momentum of the relative economic recovery over 2017. in April 2019 Oil production declined by 0.1 million BPD at the end of July 2019. Within this dynamic, GDP growth is expected to slow down to around 5.5% in 2019 (down from an average of 17.3% over 2017-2018), mainly driven by higher average oil production (1.05 million BPD vs. 0.96 million BPD in 2018) and steady domestic demand (Libya Crude Oil Production, 2020).

In 2020 (minus 0.6%) and stabilize around 1.4% over 2021-22, resulting in a GDP per capita at 61% of its 2010 level. Disinflation is expected to persist over the forecast period (minus 2.8% on average) as parallel market rates converge further towards the official one. Budget deficits will remain high, averaging 10% of GDP. The CBL is expected to continue rationing imports, but current account surpluses will steadily decline from 7.3% of GDP in 2020 to 1.4% in 2022. Consequently, reserves will stabilize around US$ 91 billion over 2020-22 (Libya's Economic Update. October 2019).

The Libyan Armed Forces

The history of the army beaning with King Idris, he trained the army by the United Kingdom and the United States. Second with Gaddafi rose to power in 1969, the army received military assistance from the Soviet Union. The Libyan military fought in several wars with Italy and in

1977 they fought Libyan–Egyptian War. Also, they fought with the Chadian–Libyan conflict (1978–1987) (Tarkowski & Omar, 2015, January 12).

Khalifa Haftar was appointed in 2015 by the Libyan parliament in Tobruk as the supreme commander of the armed forces, he unified many militias into a regular hierarchical structure in the eastern part of Libya that became known as the core of the Libyan National Army (LNA) (Crisis Group, 2016).

After the Qadhafi regime fell down in 2011, the National Transitional Council began the difficult process of restructuring the army, with National Liberation Army forming the basis of the new Libyan Army. Haftar was chosen as the overall commander of the new Libyan Army, and arms depots were looted from militia groups there were between 100 to 300 armed militia groups, and that the number of fighters at the time was estimated to 125,000 individuals (Mangan& Murtaugh, 2014).

The situation was different in Benghazi being a traditional base for anti-regime activity provided army defectors a secure area of operations. Army defectors held their positions at the eastern frontier, passively observing as events unfolded in the rest of the country. However, tensions arose between the Islamist camp, which has a stronghold in Benghazi and Darna (Lacher, 2012).

The southern governorate Fezzan joined the uprising this region has experienced tense ongoing fighting after the fall of the regime, between ethnic tribes of Arabs and Tubus, a tribe of indigenous black African nomads ranging through the eastern Sahara, Ethnic tribes are now competing with Arab tribes over control of the abundant resources with natural resources (water and oil) (McGregor, 2014).

Under an agreement reached at the Lough Erne G8 summit in June 2013, NATO countries and the United States undertook to help train up to 15,000 personnel from Libyan National Army units over a two-year period. As a result of disorder and sexual assaults by some Libyan army cadets, the UK cancelled the programme in November 2014. all of the trainees sent back to Libya, but they escape five of them they did sexual offences (Booth& Taylor, 2014).

The green book

The Green Book is a short book setting out the political philosophy of Libyan leader Muammar Gaddafi. He published the first edition in 1975. he written the book very simple understandable style with many memorable slogans, Gaddafi divided the book into 28 chapters following:

Chapter (1) The Instrument of Government: he asks himself what form of government should be established? Then he answers the government should be direct democracy. But he does not implement democracy, but dictatorship

Chapter (2) Parliaments: what is the basic feature of representative democracy? he answers it's parliament. Once elected the members usurp the authority of their constituents and for their term of service.

Chapter (3) The Party: How we can implement the part in Libya? he said political parties themselves also usurp the people's authority so that the authority will be with the party, if they want to keep themselves in power they have to improve society, he mentions political parties are susceptible to corruption if I know I will put them in prison.

Chapter (4) Class Society: we have to divide Society into political, social, or tribal groups. I will keep the political power with class A 4 Class Society

Chapter (5) Plebiscites: No Plebiscites, because I cannot depend on one's political opinion does not reduce to a yes-or-no vote.

Chapter (6) Popular Conferences and People's Committees: it's very important to our committees the solution to the problem of democracy so that we have to develop the Popular Conferences.

Chapter (7) The Law of Society: He depends on the basis of law is in custom and religion, the authentic source of social regulation, he used religion to keep him in the power, not in written constitutions.

Chapter(8) Who Supervises the Conduct of Society? he mentions the Whole is the legislature for the Whole, and the Whole is the law enforcement for the Whole.

Chapter (9) how can Society Redirect its Course when Deviations from its Laws occur? The solution to this cycle is again the system of Conferences and Committees.

Chapter (10|) The Press: this chapter's a law of the press he concludes the journalists and companies have the right to express themselves in a private capacity, "the press" as a means of expression for society must be issued by the Conferences and Committees. Otherwise, journalists would again usurp power away from others in the realm of ideas he didn't give any rights to the journalists.

Chapter(11) The Economic: he used the unions to the minimum wage to the employees to equality for all workers. What is needed is the abolition of wage-earning in favour of a "partnering".

Chapter (12) Need: the need is a central economic problem in Libya. so that the government should eliminate such exploitation.

Chapter (13) Housing: the rental of housing, is exploitation everyone should have only one house.

Chapter (14) Income: Individual income is essential to an economy. the income should not be realized as wages paid by an owner, but he has to work in the industry.

Chapter (15) Transportation: Transportation should also be available to all the people

Chapter (16) Land: It should be available and equally among all, to produce equality of outcome. No one has the right to save for themselves, except up to their own arithmetic share of a given good among the whole population.

Chapter (17) Domestic Servants: the service-rendering domestic servants are effectively slaves. The economic model already sketched can also be applied to their situation.

Chapter(18) The Social Basis: Individuals, families, tribes, and nations are social units, and their social ties drive the process of history. Just as the sun would dissipate without gravity, nations dissipate without national unity.

Chapter (19) The Family: it's the ethnic nation-states they are natural, objective human social categories, on a continuum. Opposed to these is the artificial modern construct of the state.

Chapter (20) The Tribe: he mentions the next largest human group level is the tribe. The various human social units are decreasingly important to individuals on a personal level, as their size increases.

Chapter(21) The Merits of the Tribe: Tribes are provided social cohesion, able to internally monitor themselves due to their numbers.

Chapter (22) The Nation: nationalism is a central social category

Chapter (23) Woman: Women and men are equal, they have the same physiological needs, and are thinking and feeling beings. If we make sexual dimorphism it will give rise to gender roles that are natural. so that freedom consists of the following nature, the structure of the families with women they having the ability to raise without being forced by society to seek work which is suitable only for men.

Chapter (24) Minorities: In Libya we have two types of minorities: those already having a nation, and those having none, making their own. Either way, their rights must be protected.

Chapter (25) Black People: they are poised to dominate the human population because their culture includes polygamy and shuns birth control

Chapter (26) Education: education in Libya is dictatorial it should be made available in whatever fashion people wish to engage with it.

Chapter (27) Music and Art: we have to speak just only one language to understand Artistic and cultural

Chapter (28) Sport: People should engage in sports directly with Horsemanship and the Stage and theatre but other entertainments are foolish for us (Al-Qaddaf, 1975).

Map of contesting fighting group

ISIS

ISIS seeks to expand its caliphate in Libya. Its immediate objectives are to 1) prevent the reconstitution of a unitary Libyan state to be a democracy 2) control and ultimately to join ISIS, and 3) control Libya's oil infrastructure, to build a state under ISIS.

ISIS started in Iraq and Syria, tactics they used the same tactics in Libya by using conventional military forces to attack, also they photos everything and publish it into the media it's kind of their international media campaigns to fear the world and the coercion of the population through brutality.

Libya it's a provided fertile ground for ISIS to sow its members inside the country. The first indications of support for ISIS appeared in spring 2014 in Derna, by ISIS leader Abu Bakr al Baghdadi recognized the establishment of ISIS on November 13, 2014, he controlled three Libyan provinces(Derna, Tripoli, and Sirte); and Fezzan, headquartered in southwestern Libya.

The leader Abu Nabil al Anbari, was reportedly part of a September 2014 delegation dispatched from Iraq and Syria that then aided in the takeover of Derna. He was killed by a U.S. airstrike on November 13, 2015, in Derna.

The second leader completed the march of the first leader his name (Hasan al Salahayn Salih al Sha'ari), he released from an Iraqi prison in mid-2012, then returned to Libya and establishment new ISIS with a new vision in Derna in late 2014 to 2015.

In August 2015 reports claimed that a cell of 17 fighters arrived in Sirte from Iraq and Syria, and it appears that most senior leadership is now basing in Sirte. At the end of 2015 Local militias and tribal forces in Sabratha began a push to expel ISIS from the area by helping U.S sending airstrike on a nearby ISIS training camp. Then ISIS members defected and other groups formed and join Ansar al-Sharia Libya jurist, Sheikh Abu Abdullah.

Ansar al Sharia

Ansar al-Sharia is a Salafi-jihadi group established during Libya's 2011 revolution that has received support from the al Qaeda network. the leader of that group is Ayman al Zawahiri. The aims of that group seeking to establish a polity governed by shari'a law in Libya. they only want to control Benghazi and Derna, to give support to the global al Qaeda network, with a new strategy centred on religious calls all over the world rather than on violence.

Salafi and jihadists cooperate with each other to re-establishing ties between al Qaeda and Libyan Islamist groups, by establishing Ansar al Sharia's primary branches in Benghazi and Derna, they choose leader Sufian Ben Qhumu, to be in Derna, is an al Qaeda veteran and a former detainee of both Guantanamo Bay and Libya's Abu Salim prison, and Similarly, Mohammed al Zahawi, chosen to be a leader in Benghazi, stayed with Osama bin Laden in Sudan in the 1990s before being imprisoned in Abu Salim for his role in the LIFG.

These groups do not operate under al Qaeda's name, but they receive support from the al Qaeda network. The problem situation in Benghazi, Ansar al-Sharia merged with Benghazi's Islamist militias in 2014 to Revolutionary Shura Council. According to that from 2014 until now, Ansar al Sharia's militia forces are currently fighting to defend their positions in Ajdabiya, Benghazi, and Derna along the eastern Libyan coastline.

ISIS and al Qacda's

ISIS and Qaeda's are now competing for leadership to control the jihad in Libya. when Ansar al Sharia's defected from the Sirte group this gives space for ISIS to rise. On the other hand militants in Benghazi, Derna, and Ajdabiya have also reportedly defected to ISIS. The group aims to release photos of training camp graduates to promotes comparable social media.

Libyan National Army

The Libyan National Army (LNA) is a tribal-secularist coalition assembled by General Khalifa Haftar after the fall of the Gaddafi regime. An ex-General who came back to Libya from the United States just in time (in 2011, just after the beginning of the political turmoils), the dictator made him a commanding officer in the 1980s, but Haftar soon turned against his own leader, calling for a coup and eventually having to be rescued by the CIA. Then lived in the U.S. for 20 years, has past links with the CIA he gained U.S. citizenship before returning to his homeland just before Gadhafi. When Muammar Gaddafi's fell in 2011, he controls eastern Libya, has never disguised his ambitions, Haftar returned from exile in the US, to be the next president, he became commander of Dignity Operation in Benghazi and the military officer who is supported by the Interim Government and the eastern parliament in Libya. He never agreed to recognize Al-Sirraj and his Skhirat-signed UN-brokered government as a legitimate body. The objective with LNA's immediate stated objective is the elimination of Islamist groups in eastern Libya, also a key power player in the ongoing civil war, they cooperate with Tobruk-based House of Representatives against the Tripoli-based and Islamist-leaning General National Congress.

Haftar established that army with tribal militia forces and former army units, such as the al Saiqa special forces and naval forces. He launched Operation Dignity in Benghazi in May 2014 with the stated aim of eliminating all "terrorists" in Libya. The LNA simultaneously claimed to take control of Ajdabiya from the al Qaeda- and ISIS-linked factions of the Ajdabiya Revolutionary Shura Council.

Haftar has long worked hand-in-glove with the UAE and Egypt to brings with it the framework of the intra-Gulf dispute with Qatar, which is known to back many of the western militias, It also Saudi support unlocks a sizeable war chest and an important channel of influence to the Trump administration in the Middle East.

The Great Powers of the Middle East A plan to control the Libyan region initially put control of Benghazi and then the capital of Tripoli. Therefore, Haftar had a limited window to convert his recent advance in the southwest of the country into a meaningful victory he sent forces into strategic locations in the south.

Then he launched an attack on Tripoli on April 4, after his cakewalk through the south of Libya from his power base in the eastern half of the country. The assault on the capital was his strongman effort to bring all of Libya under his control and vanquish the country's "terrorist" gangs. But his goal is to eliminate Al-Sirraj and his Skhirat-signed UN-brokered government.

He claimed to be purging the south of terrorists and mercenaries from sub-Saharan Africa, despite the scores of Chadian and Darfuri guns-for-hires within the LNA's own ranks that address its abiding manpower shortage.

Libyans, who endured decades of Gaddafi's rule followed by the bloodshed and turmoil after his overthrow by rebels with NATO support, now face a new chapter of suffering, the cost of his ambitions is becoming clearer more than 260 have already died, including civilians, and many more are wounded. Around 32,000 people have been displaced.

US policy encourages the fighting against extremism and terrorism; however, this time the US against Haftar, also he did not get the message right as its Secretary of State Mike Pompeo has already spoken against Haftar's operation in Tripoli, Trump's speech saying his forces must cease-fire and return to their status quo positions. But he got his support from Middle East countries.

The LNA's focus remains Benghazi, also they took control of Ajdabiya from the al Qaeda- and ISIS-linked factions of the Ajdabiya Revolutionary Shura Council. On the other hand, the brigades are also present in Derna, The LNA conducts occasional airstrikes on ISIS and other Islamist positions in eastern Libya.

Chapter (1)

✳

The beginning of the revolution 2011

This chapter aims to draw a broad picture of the Libyan war that erupted in 2011, by including all sides of the conflict and the international response to the crisis. The first section narrates a brief story of the events that unfolded in the Libyan revolution from the start of the uprising on February 15, 2011, to the most debated NATO ending with the damage done by NATO to the Libyan peoples" revolution attempt.

The Libyan Civil War in 2011

The uprisings in Libya, which eventually led to regime change, started on 15 February 2011 with the arrest of Fathi Tarbel, he is a human rights activist who wanted more compensation for the families of the 1300 victims killed in the 1996 Abu Sulaim prison massacre, according to that Libyan Civil War started in the North African country of Libya fought between forces loyal to Colonel Muammar Gaddafi and the citizens they are seeking to oust his government (Sengupta, 2012).

It erupted with the Libyan Revolution in 17 February started from Benghazi on Tuesday, 15 February 2011, which led to clashes with security forces that fired on the crowd (Shuaib, 2012).

the media covered the protests with Libyan people began much like those of their neighbors in North Africa and the Middle East--for the protection of their universal rights, they are seeking for greater political freedom and representative government. On the other side, the response of Qadhafi with violence including civilian noncombatants, using every tool at his disposal, from artillery barrages to airstrikes, to the employment of foreign mercenaries.

All of the media channel and newspaper show to the world Libyan protesters clashed with police in an anti-government demonstration inspired by the uprisings that brought down the rulers of Libya's. Opposition activists, organizing through social media according to that Moammar Gadhafi cut of the internet. But Local media reports say protesters threw stones at police, who fired rubber bullets to contain the crowds. Hospital officials said 38 people were injured in the clashes. On 17 February 2011 at least 12 people were killed on Thursday and dozens injured in anti-government protests in Libya's northeastern city of Al-Baida and eastern city of Benghazi. Libyan protesters was angry and protest on "Day of Rage" aganist Qadhafi who rule of Colonel 41-year he had been accused of human rights abuses.

It erupted with the Libyan Revolution started from Benghazi, which led to clashes with security forces that fired on the crowd. On that very same day, people in Benghazi encouraged by some activists attacked police stations and public buildings. Two days later was planned by the Libyans by using social networks such as Facebook and Twitter- same like Egypt, and demonstrations spread all over the country, not just in the east but also in the west though far less supported in the latter (Boyle, 2013).

Why Benghazi? Because the Benghazi people have been against the regime for a thousand years, when Gaddafi came and overthrew King Idris, Gaddafi worked to kill the people, who oppose, especially in times of Ramadan, also Gadhafi had ruled Libya for more than 40 years by banning and brutally opposing any individual or group opposing the ideology of his 1969 revolution, criminalizing the peaceful exercise of expression and association, refusing to permit independent journalists' and lawyers' organizations, and engaging in torture and extrajudicial executions. Then, the protests escalated into a rebellion that spread across the country, after that Gaddafi passed from the government and hide from the people for fear of being killed (Human Rights Watch, 2020).

Gaddafi's support for the tribes that were loyal and close to him, from the East, had provoked the latter to nurture resentment against him over the years. At the same time the bread riots in Tunisia and Egypt, the peoples' anger against the regime in Libya as a result of the suppression of genuine democracy. same as Egypt Gaddafi's wants his son Saif al-Islam to take the power this reformers associated with him had awakened a new sentiment that bubbled into protests(Admin, 2013).

According to Human Rights Watch, on the first day the regime's security forces 38 killed one protester and injured 14 others during a peaceful demonstration. On the second day, the Islamists and criminals took advantage by attacking the high-security prisons on the outskirts of the country where their friends were locked up. After freeing these men, the mob attacked the police stations and the official buildings it was strange in Libya the people can do that, and the inhabitants of the town woke to see the bodies of police officers hanging by the neck from bridges (Çubukçu, 2013)

The governments make efforts to regain control were carried out without using excessive force, the forces of law and order fired over the protesters and shot them. The regime in Libya did not allow journalists to work freely and completely misleading, Al Jazeera was in Tripoli, reporters the government security forces firing on demonstrators are causing bloodshed and chaos. The Pro-Gaddafi thugs have terrorized Egyptian migrant workers and take their money, causing hundreds to flee to Tunisia. The protesters entered Zawiyah, they occupied the centre, taking civilians hostage, during the first three weeks, the police were ordered not to do anything against the insurgents and had to evacuate their own buildings because of the attacks (Waal, 2013).

Human Rights Watch confirmed Libya's death toll from five days of unrest had risen to at least 173. Sources at hospitals in Benghazi said the crackdown there had killed at least 200 people and wounded hundreds of others. Riots were largely centred in the eastern cities of Benghazi, Bayda and Tobruk, but there are reports that unrest was spreading to the west of the country (Arraf, 2017).

Channels are photographed helicopters and warplanes struck parts of the city on 21 February 2011, the planes had only hit ammunition dumps. Witnesses in Tripoli gave multiple accounts of armed African mercenaries opening fire on protesters (Cody, 2011).

The journalists confirmed on February 23 that anti-Gaddafi forces were in control of the entire area and were flying the red, black, and green flag of the Libyan monarch that Gaddafi overthrew in a September 1969 coup d'etat. Antigovernment forces now also claim control of Misurata, some 225 kilometres away from the capital, Tripoli, and the largest city in the western half of the country to fall into the opposition's hands (2011 Libya Civil War Fast Facts, 2020, April 03).

The Libyan Human Rights League estimates at least 6,000 people had died in the two-week-old uprising about half of the deaths were in Tripoli. On Thursday 03 March 2011, insurgents opposed to Libyan leader Gadhafi continued to hold two strategic towns along the road to eastern Libya, then Libyan warplanes struck at the rebel-held oil port of Brega, the journalists' coverage Gadhafi forces tried to advance behind a barrage of field artillery, but failed to gain any ground. Both sides held on to their positions along the outskirts of the towns of Brega and Ajdabiya. Reports conflicted over which side controlled an oil refinery near Brega (Dilloway & Akhtar, 2015).

Forces loyal to Libyan leader Gadhafi launched airstrikes and engaged in ground fighting with rebel forces advancing from the eastern part of the country. The government forces pushed back rebels who previously had gained ground.

The defection of Interior Minister Abdul Fatah Younis, he had deliberately given orders not to do anything so that the uprising could grow stronger. In addition, there were claims by the international media that Gaddafi was firing on his own population and he was carrying out air attacks in Tripoli.

Then, the forces opposing Gaddafi establishing an interim governing body, the National Transitional Council they got the power from United Nations, this is their time to hold on to state rule, according to that the United Nations Security Council passed an initial resolution on 26 February, freezing the assets of Gaddafi and his inner circle and restricting their travel, and referred the matter to the International Criminal Court for investigation. when Gaddafi's forces knew they fear and they want to fight so that they made a plan to rallied pushed eastwards and re-took several coastal cities before reaching Benghazi but they fail, UN resolution authorized member states to establish and enforce a no-fly zone over Libya they used all necessary measures to prevent attacks on civilians (Mohammed, 2013).

At the end of February, the towns of the West of Libya had encountered strong tensions and some attacks- those were less in the East- but these events were to exaggeration and disinformation.

The other parts did that plan to destroy Libya so the international media broadcast claims that the regime air force has bombed Tripoli, they used the wrong message and their agenda by the truth no Libyan bomb fell on the capital, but there were some clashes took place in some areas on the ground the other parts used Al Jazeera for information distortion propagated by the media, it is hard to tell what was really going on in Libya, on that time all of the middle east trust that channel(Erdbrink, & Sly, 2011)

Gaddafi's televised speech to Libyan people on 22 February (Associated Press, 2015)

Get out of your homes, go out to the streets, secure the streets, seize the rats, and do not be afraid of them.

I haven't yet given the order to use bullets. When the order is given to use force, we will be ready.

I and the millions will march in order to cleanse Libya, inch by inch, house by house, home by home, alley by alley, individual by individual, so that the country is purified from the unclean.

That speech was portrayed as if Gaddafi forces were brutally massacring the protestors, and his speech was used as a pretext by the UK, US, and France to intervene in the country. The media coverage, the crimes that were committed by the rebels, and targeting black Africans, they working for Gaddafi.

They referred to the crisis in Libya to the International Criminal Court (ICC) and imposed an "arms embargo" on the country as well as declared the names of the people subject to and "travel ban" and "asset freeze". Following Resolution 1970, the General Assembly suspended Libya's membership from the Human Rights Council on 1 March 2011 (Pattison, 2013).

Then an interim government called the National Transitional Council (NTC) emerged on 27 February 2011 and was quickly recognized by France and Qatar, undermining Gaddafi's legitimacy in the eyes of the international community.

The second plan with the new government was established and recognized by the international community, and topple Qaddafi on 10 March 2011 the African Union for the purpose of mediating between the opposition forces and Gaddafi.

French jets started bombing immediately on 19 March after Resolution 1973 adopted by the UNSC imposed a no-fly zone over Libya. Resolution 1973 allowed the international community to take all necessary measures to protect civilians under the threat of attack without deploying the Arab League supported the imposition of a no-fly zone over Libya in the absence of its eleven members and despite two objections –Syria and Algeria, the African

Union rejected the idea of any foreign military intervention, whatever its form, and called for an African solution to the crisis in Libya. They did roadmap by (1) the immediate cessation of all hostilities, (2) the cooperation of the competent Libyan authorities to facilitate the timely delivery of humanitarian (3) the protection of foreign nationals,(4) the adoption and implementation of the political reforms necessary for the elimination of the causes of the current crisis (Pattison, 2013).

On 6 March 2011 Troops loyal to Libyan leader Gaddafi had retaken the coastal towns of Misrata and Zawiyah from rebels, state television reported on Sunday. the next day Forces loyal to Libyan leader Moammar Gadhafi carried out multiple airstrikes on targets outside a rebel-held eastern town, Libyan warplanes struck positions around the oil port of Ras Lanuf. Gadhafi's forces attacked rebels holding the western towns of Misrata and Zawiya. The Libyan leader remained in control of Tripoli, his main power base in the country's west, as well as his hometown of Sirte, 500 kilometres east of the capital) Cole& McQuinn, 2015).

After a week forces loyal to Libyan leader Muammar Gaddafi began using tanks and artillery to fight rebels, who said they lack weapons to fight the army. Fighting between rebels and pro-Gaddafi forces for control of many eastern parts of the country entered its.

The opposition began losing ground against Gaddafi's forces but on March 10, 2011, the Government of France recognized the Libyan Transitional National Council, based in Benghazi, as the sole legitimate government of Libya and announced its intention to send an ambassador there (Fitzgerald, 2014).

Mustafa Abdul Jalil, Gaddafi's former justice minister, emerged as the leader of Libyan National Transitional Council. The council withheld names of members in other cities like Zawiya, Nalot, Musrata, Zentan, Zawara, Tripoli, Jado.

The Libyan opposition welcomed with jubilation the 17 March 2011 U.N. Security Council decision to authorize a no-fly zone over Libya. The resolution gave permission to U.N. members to take "all necessary measures" to protect civilians.

BBC channel covered a ban on all flights over Libya. Anti-Gadhafi protesters in the rebel stronghold of Benghazi greeted the news with cheers, celebratory gunfire and fireworks. U.N. Security Council resolution established the no-fly zone to protect civilians from attacks by the forces of Libyan leader Colonel Gadhafi (Lacher &Al-Idrissi, 2015).

Libya declared an immediate cease-fire across the country and said it was ready to open channels of dialogue with the opposition. The announcement by Foreign Minister Moussa Koussa followed a fierce attack by Gadhafi's forces against Misrata, the last rebel-held city in the western half of the country (Human Rights Watch, 2013).

The UNSC adopted Resolution 1973 in spite of five abstentions, namely Brazil, China, Germany, India, and Russia. The reasons behind these abstentions revealed how divided the international community was on the question of military intervention India abstained due to the crisis in Libya and the ambiguity of said, who was going to enforce the measures. Brazil, abstained because she believed feared that the measures taken might aggravate the crisis in Libya.

Russia expressed its concerns regarding "how it [Resolution 1973] would be enforced and by whom, and what the limits of engagement would be" the French took the lead in bombing Libya on March 23, 2011, Germany withdrew its forces from the operation "they said ("Who's in charge?). four out of eight NATO members taking part in the same military campaign: France "Operation Harmattan", the UK „Operation Ellamy", Canada "Operation Mobile" and the US "Operation Odyssey Dawn". When NATO took over the command on 31 March 2011, the operation in Libya was called. Operation Unified Protector.

NATO after the third day of the bombing, France, the UK, and the US realized that "the bombing alone would not dislodge the Gaddafi regime", they did a secret plan "Operation Dawn Mermaid" to take Tripoli.

The plan was for the NTC to contact the various underground opposition groups and bribed supporters of the regime to get information on several crucial targets in order to facilitate the entrance of the rebels to the city.

On August 22, the rebel forces entered Tripoli and captured the city without much opposition from the loyalists. At the same time, Obama announced the end of the Gaddafi regime from the

White House on the same day. The Qadhafi regime is showing signs of collapsing. The people of Libya are showing that the universal pursuit of dignity and freedom is far stronger than the iron fist of a dictator (Hehir, 2013).

At that time, Gaddafi speech on radio, saying

"We cannot go back until the last drop of our blood. We will defend the city. I am here with you".

The state was destroyed when bombing campaign by the forces of NATO against military installations and civilian infrastructure of Libya and why don't know what is the plan to move away Gaddafi to control Oil and Gas or what in that time the situation was not clear. Then Gaddafi government announced a ceasefire, but fighting and bombing continued.

After that, rebel forces launched an offensive on the government-held coast of Libya, backed by a wide-reaching NATO bombing campaign, seeking for taking back territory before and ultimately capturing the capital city of Tripoli to eliminate the Gaddafi government.

On 19 April 2011, the United Kingdom announced that it was sending military advisers to assist the rebel forces in Libya. Foreign Secretary William Hague said that the deployment of advisers was within the provisions of UN Security Resolution 1973, which expressly forbade a foreign occupation of Libya. The next day France and Italy also announced their intention to send similar advisory elements to Libya. Italy posted eight combat aircraft for Libyan airstrikes on April 27 2011, with additional aircraft patrolling the no-fly zone (Gartenstein, 2013)

On 12 May 2011 British Foreign Secretary William Hague recognizes Mustafa Abdul Jalil, the leader of the rebel National Transitional Council (NTC), as the "legitimate representative of the Libyan people." PM David Cameron also invited the rebels to establish a permanent office in London. Greece announced plans to send humanitarian aid ships, including a mandible hospital to Benghazi.

Russia officially recognized the NTC as a legitimate negotiator on the future of Libya on May 24, 2011. On May 27, 2011, French President Sarkozy announced plans to visit with the NTC in Benghazi.

On June 1, 2011, NATO and five partner states (four Arab states and Sweden) agreed to extend the military campaign in Libya an additional 90 days from the end of June in an effort to protect civilians from pro-Gadhafi forces. They confirmed more than $1.3 billion in aid was pledged to the rebel forces in Libya at a conference of Western and Arab nations held to focus on plans.

On 16 June 2011 Gaddafi son, Saif al-Islam, said that Libyan authorities were prepared to hold free elections within three months, as well as draft a new constitution, also Gadhafi was willing to give up his power through a free election.

On June 29, 2011, French authorities I responded to the speech of Gaddafi son with had airdropped "large amounts" of weapons, munitions, and food to aid Berber tribal fighters in the Jebel Nafusa region.

Russia and the African Union (AU) was very angry they fear that the weapons could end up in the hands of al-Qaeda or another terrorist group, leading to further destabilization in the region (Middle Gate, 2014).

The Turkish government officially recognized the Transitional National Council as the legitimate representative body of Libya on July 3, 2011. Turkey planned to provide $200 million in aid to the TNC in addition to the $100 million already allocated for the rebels (Agence France-Presse, August 18).

UN World Food Program (WFP) established a regular sea route to deliver relief supplies and aid workers to Misrata from Benghazi; the WFP had distributed over 6,000 tons of food to at least 543,000 people (Eljarh, 2019).

The biggest achievement for the Libyan war and to control the country on 16 September 2011, the National Transitional Council was recognized by the United Nations as the legal representative of Libya; the regimes follow up with Gaddafi and killed him in Sirte. The National Transitional Council "declared the liberation of Libya" and the official end of the war on 23 October 2011 (Fitzgerald, 2014).

With a low-level insurgency by former Gaddafi loyalists continued they want to back again. There have been various disagreements and strife between local militia and tribes, the biggest problem issue with the role of militias which fought in the civil war and their role in Libya. Some have refused to disarm, and cooperation with the NTC because they said this cooperation it's not real and legal they has been strained, leading to demonstrations against militias and government action to disband such groups or integrate them into the Libyan military. These issues led to a second civil war in Libya (International Crisis Group, 2018).

The United Nations Security Council unanimously agreed to refer the ongoing situation to the International Criminal Court, impose an arms embargo on the Libyan Arab Jamahiriya, including the provision of mercenary personnel, also Gadhafi and certain family members, and impose a travel ban on Gadhafi, certain family members and senior advisors (Jebnoun, 2015).

United Nations refugee agency confirmed more than 100,000 people had fled Libya into neighbouring Egypt and Tunisia, to escape a deadly anti-government uprising. U.N. High Commissioner for Refugees Antonio Guterres asked the international community to provide quick and generous assistance to Egypt and Tunisia so that they can cope with what he called a "humanitarian emergency." The U.N. agency says Tunisia reported the entry of 40,000 people from Libya since February 20, and Egypt recorded 55,000 people crossing the Libyan border since February 19 (Sarieldin, 2015).

The war on the side of NATO officially ended on 31 October 2011 and the Secretary-General of NATO Anders Fogh Rasmussen visited Tripoli on the last day of the operation, the speech to Libyan people:

Libya is finally free. From Benghazi to Brega, from Misrata to the Nafusa mountains and Tripoli. Your courage, determination and sacrifice have transformed this country and helped change the region.

At midnight tonight, a successful chapter in NATO's history is coming to an end. But you have already started writing a new chapter in the history of Libya. A new Libya, based on freedom, democracy, human rights, the rule of law and reconciliation.

Chapter (2)

✳

Tribal issues in 2012

This chapter focused on the analysis of Libya post-conflict Colonel Qadhafi's bloody end and the collapse of Libya's police and armed forces left in its wake an armed population with 42 years' worth of pent-up grievances. The elections seeking for the dimerization, started with the NTC [National Transitional Council] achieved broad with international recognition. and the NATO accused of war crimes in Libya they did an evidence war crimes and human rights violations were committed by all the participants. Also, the trial of Saif the son of Gaddafi, ending with two important attaches the first on US Consulate, Benghazi the second fighting in Bani Walid.

End of NATO

The Crisis started in three distinct parts Tripolitania in the west, Cyrenaica in the east, and Fezzan in the south its came together as a united country in 1950. Its divisions are partly geographical. The main towns in the east, west, and south are separated with desert, in Libya; they don't have transport and communications only a highway for connection(Cowell & Erlanger, 2011)

The Libyan tribes were distinguished by keeping the tribal structures tightly in the east, and there were Italian colonists. These tribes faced colonization with violence and control. The invaders took place in the east, where Omar Mukhtar led the most famous national hero in Libya, a guerrilla war. And instil in the Libyans that they are tribes to be reckoned (Good, 2011).

On 14 December 2011, the NTC [National Transitional Council] achieved broad with international recognition. the conflict beaning when NTC was headquartered in the eastern city of Benghazi, a traditional base of anti-regime activity that provided army defectors with a relatively secure area of operations, particularly after NATO's involvement.

According to that the eastern rebellion with opposition and commanders who found friendly territory in which to defect at relatively low risk. They think it could only encourage western cities and towns to rise up again (Bronner & Sanger, 2011).

The rebel army looked increasingly like an eastern, not a truly national force. As for the NTC, it focused on obtaining vital international support to citizens after the war, such as teaching citizens treatment at the expense of the state, but they didn't think how to lead the uprising, this gives chance to the rebels to control Libya (Fisher, 2011).

The rebels formed militias and military brigades that were essentially autonomous, self-armed, and self-trained. Some had a military background. They control Zintan and Misrata than they encourage tribal membership they seldom possess a clear political the situation in Tripoli was different there the presence of multiple militias has led to armed clashes as they overlap and compete for power (Crisis Group, 2011).

Hence the Islamic interference of the country, which gave ambitions to the Brotherhood groups to control the state, (such as the Libyan Islamic Group, the local arm of the Muslim Brotherhood) and militantly jihadi (such as the Libyan Islamic Fighting Group) (Wehrey, 2016).

In the past Gaddafi has been wary of the eastern regions so that he overthrew the Islamic Group in the 1980s; in 1989, security forces rounded up thousands of suspected Islamists whom Gaddafi described as more dangerous than AIDS (Synovitz, & Solash, 2011).

on 19 January 2012 NATO accused of war crimes in Libya', from an independent report published by Middle Eastern human rights groups says there is evidence that war crimes and human rights violations were committed by all the participants (The Independent, 2012).

The situation became more complicated when NATO entered in 2011, on 2 March 2012 noted, NATO conducted a highly precise campaign with a demonstrable determination to avoid civilian casualties. On some limited occasions, the Commission confirmed civilian casualties and found targets that showed no evidence of military utility. Basis of the information provided by NATO and recommends further investigations about the crimes against humanity and war crimes that have been committed by the Government forces of Libya, also the acts which would constitute war crimes.

The acts falling under crimes against humanity include murder, imprisonment, torture, persecution, enforced disappearance, and sexual abuse. The commission also found that torture and other forms of cruel, inhuman, or degrading treatment were committed by both the Government and opposition forces in violation of obligations under international human rights law and humanitarian law (Wehrey & Lacher, 2014).

The trial of Saif:

The International Criminal Court (ICC) has issued an arrest warrant for Saif al-Islam Gaddafi for crimes against humanity committed in Libya starting on February 15, 2011. The ICC investigation was authorized under United Nations Security Council Resolution 1970.

The resolution requires including the surrender of ICC suspects, the did a plan they have hired a law firm in London to represent its interests before the ICC, they want Gaddafi domestically for crimes within the ICC's arrest warrant, from that side Libya would have to show that it is genuinely able and willing to prosecute Gaddafi's case in fair and credible proceedings. In addition, the Libyan proceedings must encompass the same conduct as in the case before the ICC.

They have an issued problem, if Libya argues that surrendering Gaddafi to the ICC would interfere with an ongoing domestic investigation for a different case, and then it may postpone surrendering him for a period of time agreed upon with the court (Human Rights Watch, 2011).

as a referring to article 94 of the ICC treaty, the letter said the NTC will postpone the execution of the ICC's request for the arrest and surrender of Saif al-Islam Gaddafi, Libya has until January 10, 2012, to file submissions on the issues outlined by the ICC judges. A Reuters report on 9 September 2012 the trial of Muammar Gaddafi's son Saif al-Islam will be delayed by five months to include any relevant testimony obtained via the interrogation of Libya's former spy chief who was arrested last week. The Government officials said Saif al-Islam's trial on charges of war crimes. But Abdullah al-Senussi, the former spy chief known as "Gaddafi's black box", has pushed that date back, postponing a trial a lawyer from the International Criminal Court (ICC) has already said is unlikely to be fair(Shuaib, 2012).

"We were ready to try Saif al-Islam this month but after bringing back Senussi to Libya, new information will come to light which will delay the trial for at least five months."

This plan to save him and give him much time on 9 July 2012, the top United Nations envoy in Libya, its first free poll in almost half a century - was an —extraordinary achievement and praised electoral authorities for organizing them efficiently.

Libya people are extremely positive with taking enormous pride in having voted after nearly half a century and in how well they organized this vote for themselves, the Secretary-General's Special Representative and head of the UN Support Mission in Libya (UNSMIL), Ian Martin, said to the UN Headquarters, the fact that the African Union, European Union, and Carter Centre, which fielded election observers, all made positive preliminary statements praising Libya's High National Election Commission, not just for its transparency but for its flexibility given some security threats in eastern parts of the country. This is also part of the plan to destroy Libya (BBC News,2012)

The election by 2.7 million people in the North African nation registered to vote for members of the new National Congress, which will be tasked with drafting a new constitution for Libya. More than 3,000 candidates ran for office, including more than 600 women.'66 the results of the election gains for an alliance of parties seen as broadly secular. The National Forces Alliance, led by ex-interim Prime Minister Mahmoud Jibril, has won 39 out of 80 seats reserved for political parties (DeWaal, 2012). The Muslim Brotherhood's party has gained 17. The 200-member General National Assembly will also include dozens of independent candidates (Eljarh, 2014).

The most striking outcome of the congressional election in July was the relative failure of the Islamists, whose main party, Justice and Construction, allied to the Muslim Brotherhood, got only 17 out of the 80 seats elected by proportional representation on party lists, whereas a coalition of secularists, liberals and milder Islamists won 39. An Islamist party including Abdel Hakim Belhaj that was lavishly financed by Qatar got no seats at all (Murray, 2015).

On 8 August 2012, the NTC formally handed over power to the new GNC, the GNC elected a speaker; they choose Mohamed Mugharieff, the former Libyan ambassador to India until to become the founder of the Libyan National Salvation Front, the foremost opposition group to the Gaddafi regime in exile.

By 15 September 2012, Salafists have also attacked shrines in Tripoli, they practise a mystical form of Islam that many puritans consider idolatrous. One such shrine, honouring al-Shaab al-Dahmani, was in full view of the Radisson Blu Hotel, a favourite venue for visiting foreign bigwigs and prominent Libyans. What astonished them was that the destroyers of the shrine were allowed, they did that, to pillage and bulldoze the site without the ministry of interior or its police apparently lifting a finger to stop them.

Libya has a continuing ability of local militias, especially in places such as Misrata and Zintan that bore the burden of the battle against Gaddafi, to ignore the writ of the central government, also, the tribal and ethnic tensions on the fringes of the country and in remote southern cities such as Sebha and Kufra, they continue to provoke periodic outbreaks of violence to return the country (The Economist, 2012).

On 14 October, the election of a new prime minister Ali Zidan, an independent, won 93 votes he is the best candidate favoured by the Justice and Construction Party - in addition, Ali Aujali elected to be Libya's ambassador to the United States, as foreign minister; Mohammed al-Barghathi, who served in the Libyan air force, as defence minister; and Abdelbari al-Arusi, from the western town Zawiyah, as oil minister (Eljarh, 2014).

Libyan Constitution

August 10, the National Transitional Council (NTC) issued the first Libyan Constitutional Declaration. The new constitution includes 37 articles, and that the system of the transitional government during the transitional period is ruled by articles 17 to 30. The transitional phase in the country will take about 20 months, 8 months under the NTC, and 12 months under a General National Assembly. Also, the members of the NTC signed the constitutional declaration and pledged that they would have no role in the presidential or parliamentary elections to come.

After 30 days we will select the temporary head of government and within 60 days it must submit a constitution for a popular referendum. the counsel said, the constitution becomes law, and if the citizens reject it, the Assembly will be given another 30 days to restore the constitution(Libyan Constitution,2011).

The constitution will clarify many articles:

1. The rights and obligations of citizens in a transparent manner, thus separating and balancing the three branches of legislative, executive, and judicial powers.
2. Form political organizations and civil institutions including the formation of political parties, popular organizations, unions, societies, and other civil and peaceful associations.
3. Maintain a constitutional civil and Free State by upholding intellectual and political pluralism and the peaceful transfer of power, opening the way for genuine political participation, without discrimination.

4. Guarantee every Libyan citizen, of statutory age, the right to vote in free and fair parliamentary and presidential elections, as well as the right to run for office.

5. Guarantee and respect the freedom of expression through media, peaceful protests, demonstrations and sit-ins, and other means of communication, in accordance with the constitution and its laws in a way that protects public security and social peace.

6. A state that draws strength from our strong religious beliefs in peace, truth, justice, and equality.

7. Political democracy and the values of social justice, which include:

The nation's economy to be used for the benefit of the Libyan people by creating effective economic institutions in order to eradicate poverty and unemployment –working towards a healthy society, a green environment, and a prosperous economy.

The development of genuine economic partnerships between a strong and productive public sector, a free private sector, and a supportive and effective civil society, which over stands corruption and waste.

Support the use of science and technology for the betterment of society, through investments in education, research, and development, thus enabling the encouragement of an innovative culture and enhancing the spirit of creativity. Focus on emphasizing individual rights in a way that guarantees social freedoms that were denied to the Libyan people during the rule of dictatorship. In addition to building efficient public and private institutions and funds for social care, integration and solidarity, the state will guarantee the rights and empowerment of women in all legal, political, economic and cultural spheres.

A constitutional civil state with Islamic religious doctrine The state to which we aspire will denounce violence, terrorism, intolerance and cultural isolation; while respecting human rights, rules and principles of citizenship and the rights of minorities and those most vulnerable.

Every individual will enjoy the full rights of citizenship, regardless of colour, gender, ethnicity or social status.

Build a democratic Libya whose international and regional relationships will be based upon:

- The embodiment of democratic values and institutions which respects its neighbours, builds partnerships and recognises the independence and sovereignty of other nations. The state will also seek to enhance regional integration and international cooperation through its participation with members of the international community in achieving international peace and security.

- A state which will uphold the values of international justice, citizenship, the respect of international humanitarian law and human rights declarations, as well as condemning authoritarian and despotic regimes. The interests and rights of foreign nationals and companies will be protected. Immigration, residency and citizenship will be managed by government institutions, respecting the principles and rights of political asylum and public liberties.

- A state which will join the international community in rejecting and denouncing racism, discrimination and terrorism while strongly supporting peace, democracy and freedom.

Attack on US Consulate, Benghazi

The US ambassador and three other Americans are killed when armed men storm the consulate in Benghazi on 11 September 2012, as a result, of a film produced by the US that mocks the Muslim prophet Muhammad as cover for the attack (Coughlin, 2012).

The timeline on the attack:

At 9:40 p.m., September 11, members of Ansar al-Sharia attacked the American diplomatic compound in Benghazi resulting in the deaths of U.S. Ambassador to Libya J. Christopher Stevens and U.S. Foreign Service Information Management Officer Sean Smith.

The members of the Islamic militant group Ansar al-Sharia launched a mortar attack against a CIA annex approximately one-mile (1.6 km) away, killing CIA contractors Tyrone S. Woods and Glen Doherty (Council & Atlanticcouncil, 2017).

Congressional and governmental probes into the attack on Benghazi, the attack was thought to be perpetrated by an angry mob responding to a video made in the United States that mocked Islam and the Prophet Mohammed, but it is later determined to be a terrorist attack.

The investigation shows: On September 11: (Events listed in local Benghazi time).

9:42 p.m. - Armed men begin their assault on the US mission.

9:59 p.m. - A surveillance drone is directed to fly over the US compound, but it is unarmed.

10:32 p.m. - The Office of the Secretary of Defense and the Joint Staff are notified of the attack by the National Military Command Center at the Pentagon. "The information is quickly passed to Secretary Leon Panetta and General Martin Dempsey."

11 p.m. - Panetta and Chairman of the Joint Chiefs of Staff Dempsey meet with President Barack Obama at the White House, where they discuss the unfolding situation and how to respond. The meeting had been previously scheduled.

11:10 p.m. - The surveillance drone arrives over the Benghazi facility.

11:30 p.m. - All surviving US personnel are evacuated from the mission. Stevens and State Department computer expert Sean Smith is killed in the initial assault.

September 12: Midnight to 2 A.M Panetta and other senior leaders discuss possible options for further violence if it were to break out. Panetta gives verbal orders for Marine anti-terrorist teams from Rota, Spain, to prepare to deploy to Tripoli and Benghazi. Panetta also orders special operations force team training in Croatia and an additional special operations force team in the United States to prepare to deploy to a staging base in southern Italy.

1:30 a.m. - A six-man security team from the US Embassy in Tripoli arrives in Benghazi.

2:39 a.m. to 2:53 a.m. - The National Military Command Center gives formal authorization for the deployment of the two special operations force teams from Croatia and the United States.

5:15 a.m. - Attackers launch an assault on a second US facility in Benghazi. Two former US Navy SEALs acting as security contractors are killed. They are identified as Tyrone Woods and Glen Doherty.

6:05 a.m. - A C-17 aircraft in Germany is told to prepare to deploy to Libya to evacuate the mission personnel.

7:40 a.m. - The first wave of Americans is evacuated to Tripoli via airplane.

10 a.m. - A second group, including those killed in the attack, are flown to Tripoli.

2:15 p.m. - The C-17 departs from Germany for the flight to Tripoli.

7:17 p.m. - The C-17 leaves Tripoli with the American mission personnel and the bodies of Stevens, Smith, Woods and Doherty.

7:57 p.m. - The US special operations force team based in Croatia arrives at a staging base in Italy.

8:56 p.m. - One of the Marine anti-terrorist teams from Spain arrives in Tripoli.

9:28 p.m. - The US-based special operations force team arrives at its staging base in Italy
CNN, 2020)

Intelligence officials CIA say that leaders of the AQIM movement have been traveling regularly to the desert town of Ghat in south-western Libya, close to the border with Niger.

Fighting in Bani Walid

United Nations Secretary-General is alarmed by the fighting in and around the Libyan city of Bani Walid, and in particular, the reports indicating growing civilian casualties due to indiscriminate shelling.

Their aim is to establish a foothold in Libya from which to launch attacks against Western targets. On 24 October 2012, the Islamic group did fighting in Bani Walid, according to Human Rights Watch the number of victims from the fighting and indiscriminate it's increasingly at least seven people not associated with any armed group had been 60 killed. On October 19, causing thousands of Bani Walid 22 people were killed in the fighting. Journalists and human rights monitors have not been allowed into the town to coverage that figure (Zenko, 2016)

Bani Walid, about 170 kilometres southwest of Tripoli, is home to Libya's largest tribe, the Warfalla. In 1993, a group of Warfalla was among those who staged a failed attempt to overthrow Gaddafi.

Bani Walid and Misrata have a history of antagonistic relations. The tension over the fighting in Bani Walid has spread to other parts of Libya. In Benghazi on October 21, the protesters ransacked the Libya Al Hurra TV station, claiming the station had broadcast misleading news about Bani Walid justifying the attacks (Human Rights Watch, 2020).

Chapter (3)

✳

National Oil corruption after closure of ports

By Libyan National Army

This chapter analyst Libyan conflict is the result of a complex and controversial series of developments, where local political events have been strongly influenced and driven by exogenous factors. A dual set of conflicting interests can be found in both Qatar and Europe. And then a description of the collapse of the central institutions in Libya and the creation of dozens of militias and Islamist groups that controlled the rural area, which led to the failure of both domestic and foreign aspirations in a crisis that managed to affect the Libyan Civil War, which made the situation very mysterious and difficult to resolve.

The first transition phase

Following the fall of Qadhafi's regime in 2011, Libya became is a parliamentary democracy with a temporary Constitutional Declaration that allows for the exercise of a full range of political, civil, and judicial rights.

The National Transitional Council (NTC) oversaw a free and fair election in July 2012 and handed power to an elected parliament, the General National Congress in August 2012. (GNC) appointed a prime minister in November 2012 to head an interim government.

According to the plan from abroad, these steps led to the formal establishment of the new "State of Libya" on January 9, in the first half of 2013 some form of lustration is normal in a post-conflict situation, in Libya, as in Iraq, the matter went too far The Role of the Exile Community became a means by which (primarily) conservative Islamist groups, whose leaders had not been tainted by association with the Gaddafi the regime, sought to strengthen their political hand against the moderates.

The amid of that year preparations for another election for members of a constitutional drafting assembly, but GNC members were polarized by disputes, to elevate the status of Islamic law in the country's legal system (Sanalla, 2017).

Due to that, the disputes flared over governance, the selection of new interim representatives, and responsibility for ensuring security in the face of a rising wave of criminality and Islamist insurgent violence (Raval, 2017).

In July 2013, Ibrahim Jadhran, the head of the Petroleum Facilities Guard (PFG) from Ajdabia, the young militia leader, from the Magharba tribe, used federalist and anti-Muslim Brotherhood rhetoric to justify the takeover and blockade of(Es Sider, Ras Lanuf and Zueitina), it's the most important three of Libya's vital oil terminals on the Mediterranean. He made a threatening speech to end the blockade, the General National Congress (GNC) had to demand to cede power to Libya's also eastern region of Cyrenaica, especially in regard to selling oil (Ghaddar & Lewis, 2016)

Due to that Mustafa Sanalla, the head of National Oil Corporation (NOC), estimated that the losses incurred due to Jadhran's blockade amounted to some USD 30 million per day. Jadhran take that step to move of popular support and he went to an eastern government of his own and hired Canadian lobbyist Ari Ben-Menashe to advocate for him abroad and get the power from them but with an agreement to sell oil outside the legitimate NOC channels, thereby and establishing a parallel oil and gas corporation based he also wants the US and Russia's endorsement of a federalist structure that would grant Cyrenaica autonomous status (McGregor, 2016).

The government eastern officials had shut the ports of Zueitina and Hariga, stopping legitimate NOC tankers from loading oil at the facilities, so that the conflict started again with oil production, was slashed to 150,000 barrels per day.

This step moved Hafter and Jadhran for a political gambit they want to sell oil outside of the Tripoli-based NOC. But, NOC head Mustafa Sanalla knew that and he sent communiqués to both the UN and foreign embassies, warning him, the illicit sale of oil by a parallel NOC in the east could lead to Libya's further fragmentation. After a few days, l US stepped in, asking Haftar to withdraw and signalling its intention to help keep al-Kabir in his post.

Benghazi conflict in 2013

Began after clashes erupted between protesters and militants from the Libya Shield brigade on 8 June 2013 in Benghazi it's a conflict that is a part of the aftermath of the Libyan civil war. More than 31 people were killed and 100 wounded in clashes in Benghazi between protesters and a militia operating. Most of the dead were civilians, with only 5 soldiers and one militia member reported killed Stephen, 2013).

On 15 June, hundreds of plain-clothed gunmen attacked several security installations and torched parts of the building. So that six Libyan soldiers were killed. All of the dead were members of an elite Libyan Army unit called Saaqa. Clashes were reported near the road leading to the airport, forcing its closure. The head of Benghazi's Counter Crime Agency has suggested that Gaddafi elements were in fact behind the attacks (Stephen, 2013).

On 19 June, a huge explosion totally flattened the police station in the Al-Hadayeq district of Benghazi and then the next month on 2 July, a car bomb exploded at a checkpoint that was being manned by special military forces, injuring four soldiers and three civilians. In the same month, Muslim Brotherhood critic Abdelsalam al-Mosmary was fatally shot after leaving a mosque during Ramadan (Aljazeera, 2013).

On 29 July, the militia attacked the Tripoli headquarters of the al-Watan party, they smashed windows, shot at the door locks to open them, and threw Molotov cocktails inside (Shennib &Bosalum,2013)

About the media, the revolution took a deadlier turn as it became characterized by armed conflict, involving forces loyal to Colonel Muammar Gaddafi and those seeking to oust his government (Ellawati & Amzein, 2013).

The tumultuous events in Libya quickly transformed Libya's media landscape and now Libyan journalists started to report with a large degree of autonomy and gone were the days of media reporting restrictions and the spectre of censorship hanging over them.

The proliferation of newspapers and magazines was the real success of the story in this climate of newly found freedom. This was evidenced through the emergence of a plethora of Libyan satellite TV stations broadcasting from inside and outside to more than 50. The number of print media publications vastly increased as well as the appearance of dozens of specialized publications.

Suddenly, journalists started discussing political issues freely despite newly found freedoms being at constant risk of threat from heavily armed militias as well as the remnants of the state apparatuses such as the army and police that had collapsed in major cities such as Tripoli. Benghazi and Derna. Officials were powerless to maintain security and prosecute those who commit crimes, including murders and assassinations.

The role of Qatar and France in Libya

Qatar convinced to implement a new strategy in the region, based on the establishment and/or support of local moderate Islamic political forces. they, former French President Nikolas Sarkozy was being persuaded by his adviser Bernard-Henri Lévy that there was a window of opportunity in Libya when Gaddafi died, which might be open a rich new market for energy. from that point Qatar and France—with the support from the UK in an attempt to provoke a major popular protest in Libya. In addition, this strategy was based on the assumption that only through a transition led by Islamic movements could the Gulf monarchies resist—and survive—the general trend of transition that was being observed by the Middle Eastern powers (Sahiounie, 2020).

In 2013 the political environment emerged from the collapse of the regime, with a polarization of interests that soon led to a de facto division of the country. then the rise of the Muslim Brotherhood, among the Libyan Islamist militias, the largest, most efficient and best organised was undoubtedly the group known as Ansar al-Sharia, the existing Islamist militias that had chaotically emerged following the clashes of 2011 (Ashour, 2015).

Among many other Islamist forces, alarmed Saudi Arabia and the United Arab Emirates (UAE), which have always considered the Ikhwan (from the Arabic, 'brothers') to be an existential threat to the survival of the Gulf monarchies?

As we know in September 2012, the Benghazi population revolting against the units of Ansar al-Sharia, forcing them to fall back to more remote inland villages. So that, the city of Benghazi, the other, smaller Islamist organisations were gradually forced to dissolve or leave the city, often reorganising themselves into smaller groups. During 2013 the forces of Ansar al-Sharia did not represent any real threat to the security and stability of Tripoli and Benghazi, as they were mostly being sheltered in rural areas (Pedde, 2017)

The political divisions were expanding in the country and the Transitional Council of Barqa (the Arab name for Cyrenaica), a body primarily comprised of Arab tribes, declared the east a separate federal region, after allied tribal militias around the Gulf of Sirte took control of the oilfields.

In the west, indigenous Berbers, who make up about a tenth of the population, formed a council of their own and called on larger Berber communities in the Maghreb and Europe for full support. Port cities started to claim self-government and set up their own border controls (Wehrey, 2014).

Chapter (4)

❋

The second Libyan civil war (2014)

This chapter provides an overview of recent key developments of the Libyan conflict. The first part analyses contributing factors of an evolving shift in the power balance between the conflict parties between Haftar and the Government of National Accord.

The third part in Libya, from May 2014 to the present, (The second Libyan civil war) this period focused on who want the power using tension and violence among loose political-military coalitions, the multifaceted conflict between their members and violent Islamist extremist groups, and enhanced efforts by third parties to promote reconciliation.

Begging of the second Libyan civil war

The second conflict civil war in Libya is characterized by a myriad of armed groups and actors who are divided across different ideological, national and regional, also the armed groups did a tendency to depict the conflict.

In this phase, we will focus on the factors of the regional tensions between the country; tribal and ethnic tensions. In addition, armed groups used violence to keep them in power. Also with growing competition over resources in the country, these conflicting allegiances and identities have further intensified with armed groups vying for a stake in Libya's future

The incompatibility between the Government of National Accord (GNA) in Tripoli, under Prime Minister Sarraj, and the House of Representatives (HoR) in Tobruk, under the influence of Chairman Aguila Saleh Issa and General Haftar both of them needs the power, fighting each other with numerous local supporters.

By 2014 the civil war in Libya had been transformed into a proxy war, which pitted Islamist forces supported by Qatar, Sudan and Turkey, against more secular forces supported by Saudi Arabia, the UAE and Egypt from hidden support by the United States. the civil war started when Egypt and the United Arab Emirates launched airstrikes against Islamic militants in the Libyan capital they are afraid of Turkey.

Since 2012 the Government sought to bring under the authority of the State the armed brigades which emerged during the 2011 armed conflict, to control most detention facilities where torture takes place. Fighting between militia groups increased significantly. because Libya has the regional and tribal identities of the groups involved.

The Government had affiliated brigades to specific ministries, even though in many cases the brigades have retained actual control of the detention centres. In April 2013 Libya also adopted a law criminalizing torture, enforced disappearances and discrimination and in September 2013 a new law on transitional justice required all conflict-related detainees to be released or referred to the public prosecutor within 90 days of the promulgation of the law, the number of fatalities has dropped significantly, to fewer than 300 in 2013 (Imam, Abba, & Wader, 2014).

The strongest man in Libya Khalifa Haftar

All the newspaper writes about:" The military strongman leading the offence against Libya's UN-backed government", "Khalifa Haftar, Libya's strongest warlord, makes a push for Tripoli" and "The Libyan crisis: did he sell who is strongman Khalifa Haftar?"

We must know who this man is, who they say is the strongest man? An ex-General who came back to Libya from the United States just in time (in 2011, just after the beginning of the political turmoils), the dictator made him a commanding officer in the 1980s, but Haftar soon turned against his own leader, calling for a coup and eventually having to be rescued by the CIA. Then lived in the U.S. for 20 years, has past links with the CIA he gained U.S. citizenship before returning to his homeland just before Gadhafi. When Muammar Gaddafi's fell in 2011, he controls eastern Libya, has never disguised his ambitions, Haftar returned from exile in the US, to be the next president, he became commander of Dignity Operation in Benghazi and the military officer who is supported by the Interim Government and the eastern parliament in Libya. He never agreed to recognize Al-Sirraj and his Skhirat-signed UN-brokered government as a legitimate body.

He wants to take the power the same as Sisi in Egypt outshout elections through loyalist to Haftar's they issued statements and held demonstrations in Benghazi and other cities calling for mandating him as the ruler of Libya, this gives him power outside Libya to make him a strong man. The Haftar's loyalist demanding an end to the elections' preparations saying," We only need Haftar as the president here in east Libya, we don't need elections or anything like that.

Who makes him the most powerful man in Libya? Haftar has long worked hand-in-glove with the UAE and Egypt to brings with it the framework of the intra-Gulf dispute with Qatar, which is known to back many of the western militias, It also Saudi support unlocks a sizeable war chest and an important channel of influence to the Trump administration in the Middle East (AlAshry, 2019, 30 May)

The Great Powers of the Middle East A plan to control the Libyan region initially put control of Benghazi and then the capital of Tripoli. Therefore, Haftar had a limited window to convert his recent advance in the southwest of the country into a meaningful victory he sent forces into strategic locations in the south.

The amplification chaos in the second civil war

At the beginning of 2014, Libya was governed by the General National Congress (GNC) in the 2012 elections. The GNC was made of two major political parties, the National Forces Alliance (NFC) and the Justice and Construction Party (JCP). Both of them failed in the parliament to reach political compromises on the larger more important issues that the GNC faced.

On 20 February 2014, members were elected to the Constitution Drafting Assembly (CDA) led by appointed chair Ali Tarhuni. They were charged with writing Libya's permanent constitution the first session in Bayda on 21 April the session about concerned the government structure, distribution of wealth, and the rights of Libya's indigenous communities, namely the Amazigh, the Tuareg and the Tebu. They only need two-thirds of its members for a quorum. But Amazigh community boycotted their two seats because the (CDA) ignored their language and rights (Omagu & Odigbo, 2017).

On the other hand, two members from Derna failed to be elected because their city was under the control of extremist armed groups. The situation of violence deteriorated in mid-2014, when Ahmed Maiteeq, was appointed as the Prime Minister the people saw him as backed by Misrata-based Islamist groups. So, the conflict started with the party's division according to political isolation law, In addition, the continuous unstable security situation impacted the GNC's ability to deliver real progress towards a new constitution. The country involved with chaos and political propaganda towards Brotherhood groups, which led to failed the country also the GNC included members associated with conservative Islamist groups called (the war) (Ladjal, 2016)

Some members involved with corruption cause the conflict of interest with militias and were accused of channelling government funds towards armed groups and allowing others to conduct assassinations and kidnappings (Wehrey, 2016).

After the ouster of Prime Minister Ali Zeidan on 4 May, then Ahmad Mitig has been set, a prominent businessman from Misrata who had the backing of revolutionary blocs, was appointed prime minister. But some parties, including the National Forces Alliance (NFA), challenged the vote. Due to that some members contravening the rules of procedure, and of casting their vote by telephone. The struggle over the political appointment became a legal case that reached the Supreme Court in Tripoli (Mangan & Murtaugh, 2014).

On 16 May 2014, General Khalifa Haftar launched Operation with the purpose of eradicating Islamist militias in Benghazi. After two days later, Zintani militias allied with Haftar raided the GNC and declared the legislative body suspended. On 29 May, caretaker Prime Minister Abdullah al-Thinni announced that he would not relinquish power, citing constitutional violations in Mitig's appointment. He said I will be waiting for the Supreme Court to have ruled on the matter, The reason this there is no legal framework and threats by armed groups, also they have manipulation of the justice system(Tuncer, 2017).

The GNC's took a decision to cancelled Haftar this decision lead Haftar to conduct an abortive coup. This decision was a failure to address the country's economic, political, and security problems. But GNC's said, the decision came after an Islamist/ Berber/Misratan bloc gained control of the county we cannot control it in the future and we have to arrange new elections on

25 June 2014 House of Representatives (HoR) by low turnout of approximately 18% of eligible voters reflected public dis political and armed struggle (Chivvis, & Martini, 2014). The elections resulted in the defeat of political Islamist factions and they also did control the international airport in Tripoli amid the threat of full-fledged civil war. The tension started again with political Islamists parties which weakened their opponents within the General National Congress (GNC). so that the National demonstrations erupted near the end of the GNC's term, with protesters demanding the elimination of party lists in favour of independent candidates. The committee tasked by the GNC to draft the new electoral law (Alfasi, 2016).

On 9 June, the Supreme Court ruled that Mitig's appointment as prime minister was "unconstitutional". The ruling further split the country between supported and rejected. This political standoff left Libya with two prime ministers split east versus west they used clashes as a coup attempt to disrupt Libya's democracy. The coup results on 20 June 2014, Haftar establishment of Benghazi as a Revolutionaries Shura Council (BRSC), with many groups (Islamist militias called Ansar al-Sharia in Libya (ASL) and the 17 February Martyrs Brigade) This coup lead to the emergence of a coalition of Islamist in Misratan militias, set to take control of the capital (Sawani, 2020)

On 13 July 2014, Libya Dawn militias launched Operation in Zintani to control Tripoli International Airport, which had been under the control of the al-Qa'qa. In August 2014, two lawsuits reached the Supreme Court in Tripoli contesting the constitutionality of the HoR elections after the newly elected in Tobruk, they mention the court to nullify paragraph 11 in the seventh amendment to the Interim Constitutional Declaration (ICD), HoR should appoint or hold direct elections of a president by popular vote within 45 days of the HoR's first session (United Nations Support Mission In Libya, 2019).

They argued about the paragraph had been adopted in violation of ICD provisions and GNC rules of procedure. On 4 August the GNC argued that its term had not expired in accordance with the Interim Constitutional Declaration (ICD), and refused to relinquish power to the newly elected HoR. On 6 August, the HoR adopted the eighth amendment to Article 30 of the ICD to delay the elections of a president. While the High National Election Commission (HNEC) was technically and logistically ready to hold presidential elections, on 23 August 2014, Dawn forces control most of the capital and the International Airport (Arturo, 2017).

In September 2014, the House of Representatives (HoR) fired Sadiq al-Kabir, the governor of the Central Bank of Libya (CBL) in Tripoli according to an investigation of al-Kabir's involvement in "financial irregularities. His deputy, Ali Salim al-Hibri, was appointed interim governor in his place ((Wai, 2014).

On 6 November, the Supreme Court upheld the claimants' controversial argument. the Supreme Court's verdict by the Libya Dawn military alliance, with Omar al-Hassi as prime minister. The Supreme Court's verdict raised concerns among the opposition about transparency and the potential intimidation of judges in Tripoli. The HoR in Tobruk subsequently rejected the ruling (Amina, 2018).

The UN Support Mission in Libya (UNSMIL) envoy Bernardino León brokered what would become a lengthy dialogue between rival factions in the desert town of Ghadames between members of the Tobruk-based House of Representatives (HoR) and the Misrata and Tripoli. Afterwards, the two groups of parliamentarians agreed to meet and resolve the outstanding differences over the political process and to call for an immediate national ceasefire and to resume flights at the country's major airports, just weeks after the destruction of Tripoli's international airport by rival Operation Dignity and Libya Dawn military the international community recognized Prime Minister Abdullah al-Thinni and the HoR, based in Bayda and Tobruk, as Libya's legitimate government, rather than Prime Minister Omar al-Hassi of the National Salvation government and the rehabilitated General National Congress (GNC) in Tripoli (Wehrey, 2017).

On 6 November 2014, the Libyan Supreme Court Canceled a constitutional amendment on the basis of which the HoR was established. And they rejected the decision they said it was rendered under pressure from Islamist militias controlling the capital, and continued to hold its sessions. On the other said, the HoR endorsed Operation Dignity to be under the General Chief of Staff of the Libyan Army, Abd-al-Raziq al-Nazuri.

The U.N. Security Council has authorized financial and travel sanctions on individuals and entities responsible for threatening "the peace, stability or security of Libya," for successful completion of political transition, and an arms embargo is in place (Wehrey & Jeffrey, 2019).

Deterioration economic survival with the National Oil Corporation (NOC), the Central Bank of Libya (CBL) and the Libyan Investment Authority (LIA). Armed groups extorted millions of dollars through violence, and their influence over government institutions and policy became the new status. The resulted in no legitimate government, and unified state institutions and security apparatuses, undermined the rule of law, the economy, and state-building. The environment was also conducive to the proliferation of extremist groups such as the Islamic State, which seized its opportunity to profit from the chaos (United Nations Support Mission in Libya, 2018).

The players in Libya in 2014

Khalifa Haftar and the "Libyan National Army"

Haftar has emerged as the most high profile individual fighting Libya's Islamist militias. In May, he and his self-declared Libyan National Army began an assault against Islamist group Ansar al-Sharia. Haftar declared the offensive "Operation Dignity." In the same month, Haftar and his supporters had captured the Islamist-dominated parliament in Tripoli, the General National Congress, and announced it would be dissolved. His group made a bombastic start and broadened their offensive so that it was against all Islamist groups operating in Libya. He also had a good connection CIA, as well as his aggressive stance against even moderate Islamist groups. His relationship with the government in Tobruk is ambiguous (Tharoor & Taylor, 2019).

The Islamists

The Islamist militias that Haftar pretended fighting are a diverse grouping known as the Dawn of Libya, they seized the airport and other parts of Tripoli despite being hit by airstrikes. but the Dawn of Libya grouping recently denied any link to Ansar al-Sharia, the notorious Salafist militia first targeted by Haftar. Ansar al-Sharia has become one of the most notorious Islamist groups operating in Libya after the civil war that ousted Gaddafi, they were involved in the 2012 attack on the U.S. Consulate in Benghazi, second, they also carried out a very public execution in the eastern city of Darna.

The city militias

The city militias got their support from the old regimes against Gaddafi they did the dramatic events of Libya's 2011 rebellion they disparate fighting units formed in cities and among various tribes and banded together in a patchwork alliance that ousted the regime with the aid of a NATO bombing campaign. By 2014 the alliance fell apart, before that they did in Misurata militia even opened fire on hundreds of protesters in Tripoli who had been demonstrating against their presence in the capital, the Misurata fighters have joined with Islamists battling more secular forces, including the Zintan brigades and tribal units once loyal to the Gaddafi state.

Qatar

Qatar played an overt role in aiding the rebellion against Gaddafi in 2011, they were operating inside Libya and that Qatari fighter, since 2011, the Qataris have emerged as one of the key backers of political Islam in the Middle East and North Africa, supporting the Muslim Brotherhood in Egypt to control the country, and they have hands in of Islamist outfits from Tunisia to Syria.

Egypt

Egypt had been involved in two airstrikes on Islamist forces in Libya. Fighter planes from the United Arab Emirates were believed to have used Egyptian bases as a launchpad for the attacks. Sisi's role as a figurehead of the regional anti-Islamist movement can be seen in Haftar, who has taken it upon himself to lead the Libyan battle against political Islam. Haftar using "appropriating the tone and language" of the Egyptian president.

The United Arab Emirates

The United Arab Emirates implement airstrikes, they did air force is well-regarded and helped in the fight against Gaddafi's government during the 2011 civil war. The UAE is a military ally for the United States and a militia commander told them, they launched the airstrikes had used munitions manufactured by the United States. they used the bombs were American-made and Israel.

Saudi Arabia

The kingdom has a good strategy in the 2011 Arab Spring uprisings, as a series of Arab autocrats backed by Riyadh were replaced by chaotic, seeking for democracies that reshaped the geopolitical map of the Middle East they get support from the UAE and Sissi's Egypt, they fund billions of dollars in aid. Saudi ties with the United States, a longstanding ally, because of the disagreements in the region's democracy uprisings. There are even signs of a growing axis between the Saudis, Sissi's Egypt, and the Israeli government of Prime Minister Benjamin Netanyahu -- political manoeuvring which all casts a shadow on the turmoil in Libya.

Chapter (5)

✳

The role of ISIS in Libya (2015)

This chapter focused on the Islamic State extremist militia seizes control of the port of Derna in eastern Libya and the Libyan army and Tripoli-based militia alliance declare partial ceasefire this is to give more chance to control the other country. In addition, Egypt's role appeared strongly with Egyptian jets bomb Islamic State targets in Derna, a day after the group there released a video showing the beheading of 21 Egyptian Christians. This event has many ramifications. In the middle of March, the Libyan Army offensive to retake Derna fails to dislodge the group. ISIS establishes to controls the city of Sirte. At the end of the year, Tripoli court sentences Gaddafi's sons Saif al-Islam and eight other former officials to death for crimes committed during the 2011 uprising against his father. The armed group let Gaddafi's son freed.

The political divisions structured

On the first of 2015, there were multiple divisions structured the political and military landscape in the region—the product of successive wars and changing political alignments in Misrata and Zintan and the Amazigh towns became strongholds of revolutionary forces(Ukessays, 2017).

With the Gaddafi regime's 2011 collapse, the revolutionary forces—and newly formed armed groups that pretended to be 'revolutionaries'—strengthened their military dominance by taking control of state arsenals. Power struggles within the revolutionary coalition compounded rivalries over control of the security sector ((Essam & Arfaoui, 2013). Over time in 2014 confrontation escalated into civil war in western Libya Zintani forces were the only major component of the former revolutionary coalition to side with Khalifa Haftar's self-declared army in eastern Libya (Furness& Trautner, 2020).

The first of January holds talks in Geneva and Ghadames, The legal challenge that resulted in the Supreme Court ruling to invalidate the House of Representatives (HoR) elections in June 2014 had badly effectively with complexity to the crisis this made Libya, without a legally recognized government and widened the gap between competing tribes and nationalist factions that had already been embroiled in conflict.

A new round of talks brokered by the UN Support Mission in Libya (UNSMIL) convened in Geneva and, the General National Congress (GNC) set conditions for participation. They asked that the Supreme Court ruling be respected and that the GNC this conference to end the country's political and security crisis, UNSMIL broadened its approach by setting up a simultaneous dialogue that included representatives of municipalities and armed groups, women, and youth, as well as political parties, tribal leaders and civil society.it is the biggest achievement in Libya to end the war (Hossam, 2016).

But the conference produced nothing accordingly, on 12 February, the GNC and UNSMIL took the second round in Ghadames. But HoR and GNC representatives refused to meet in the same room. so that, Bernardino León the UN's envoy held simultaneous caucuses but no one accepts it they were accused of prolonging the process to hold on to power, which also damaged the legitimacy of dialogue. at the end of the negotiations no solution and continued to undermine Libya's security and living conditions(Mahdi, 2017).

In the middle of March 2015, Prime Minister Omar al-Hassi his poor performance and he divisions government, also the GNC viewed al-Hassi's statements about the dire state of Libya's finances as an attempt to cause a public outcry and were disappointed that the international community refused to recognize and aid the cash-strapped and isolated Tripoli-based government(Mohsan, 2017).

Furthermore, the fight for assets and power between forces allied to rival governments across Libya's west, east and south. They also made journalists and activists silenced because the journalists want to publish the war (Radsch, 2015).

For example New York, November 17--The Committee to Protect Journalists is concerned Mohamed Neil, a Libyan photojournalist missing since October 29. Neili, who works for the Chinese state-run Xinhua news agency, disappeared after leaving his house in southern Tripoli, according to media outlets and a local press freedom centre (Libya Observer, 2018), and demanding a ransom of 500,000 Libyan dinars (US$367,840), then four days later, the family received a second phone call, in which the ransom was reduced to 300,000 dinars.

Another example, Journalists condemns the murder of a Libyan television journalist in the eastern city of Benghazi. Muftah al-Qatrani, 33, was shot dead in his office at Al-Anwar, he had been covering the fighting between Islamist militias and pro-government groups (CPJ, 2015).

After that, on 11 July 2015, eighteen out of the 22 participants of the UN-facilitated Libyan Political Dialogue signed a preliminary framework agreement in Skhirat, Morocco, this Dialogue includes four representatives from each parliament – the internationally recognised House of Representatives (HoR) in Tobruk and its predecessor, the General National Congress (GNC) in Tripoli, that Dialogue a way out of a conflict that has divided Libya into two rival sets of parliaments, governments and military coalitions since July 2014 (Lacher, 2019).

In the beginning, the GNC delegation stayed away from the final talks and refused to sign the agreement because Skhirat agreement envisions the creation of a consensus-based national unity government ("Government of National Accord") this government would have wide powers to govern from its seat in Tripoli, they would manage the foreign and security policy and oversight of state finances and institutions. In the end, GNC's refusal to sign on to the deal. Skhirat conference an achievement to gives Libyans hope that a year-long conflict (Crisis Group, 2016)

In December 2015, UN envoy Martin Kobler attempted to convince members of the House of Representatives (HoR), the General National Congress (GNC), and Haftar of the Libyan National Army (LNA) to sign off on the Libyan Political Agreement (LPA). They did the structure of the Presidential Council (PC) with one prime minister and two deputies to a nine-member team of the prime minister, four deputies, and four state ministers (Lacher, 2019)

On the other hand with the support of the United Nations, the governments of Egypt, the UAE, Saudi Arabia, and Qatar all publicly recognized the Government of National Accord as "the sole legitimate government of Libya, with Prime Minister Fayez Serraj as the leader of the Presidency Council (Jstor, 2015).

The members from Barqa, Fezzan, Misrata, Zintan and Tripoli, political institutions such as the HoR and the GNC, ideological groups, and the Libyan National Army (LNA). The next day, before the signing of the LPA in Skhirat, Kobler visited Haftar's to convince Haftar to support the LPA and nominate a candidate to the PC. Haftar signalled his lack of support for the expanded PC because some of its members were allegedly associated with armed groups that the LNA was battling in Benghazi. According to that, Haftar agreed to nominate one of four deputies to the PC. Then on 17 December 2015, the LPA signed. This agreement marked the beginning of a new transition phase in the conflict between Libya's competing governments and divided institutions and left unresolved many legal disputes challenging the legality and constitutionality of the GNA and LPA(Ohchr, 2017).

Since 2015, Egypt and the UAE (as well as others) have attempted to orchestrate talks between Field Marshal Haftar and his GNA counterpart, Fayez Serraj, reportedly at the official invitation of the United Nations Special Representatives of the Secretary-General (SRSG) (Thomas, 2019). The results of ending 2015 damage and disorder from the war has been considerable, here are frequent electric outages, little business activity, and a loss in revenues from oil by 90%.according to the conflict Over 4,000 people have died from the fighting and some sources claim nearly a third of the country's population has fled to Tunisia and Egypt as refugees (Bender, 2015).

ISIS controlled Libya

Evolution of the Islamic State in Libya In the immediate aftermath of Libya's 2011 revolution and even before Libya's full-blown second civil war broke out in 2014, a multitude of jihadi organizations started to emerge. Some, like the Libyan Islamic Fighting Group, and the Islamic State were mash-ups of local jihadi groups and ideologues and fighters they are related to the Islamic State in Iraq and Syria (Bender, 2015).

They started in Iraq and Syria's then shift to Libya came shortly after its leader, Abu Bakr al-Baghdadi, announced the formation of the group. In 2013, al-Baghdadi sent an emissary to evaluate the possibility of exploiting the accommodating jihadi environment in Derna (OHCHR, 2015).

Al-Baghdadi signalled the importance of Derna by sending senior Islamic State leadership to manage the country. In 2015 we can call it's a good environment for ISIS to control Libya after they losses in Iraq and Syria, the situation was perfect is fertile and attractive to IS's organizational strategy because many reasons: security vacuum that has fluctuated and been impacted by local developments, as well as foreign interests and interventions.

Why ISIS chosen Sirte?

While re-examining the rise of in 2015, IS saw the city of Sirte a perfect place they find that the key alliances the group formed with some elements of the disgruntled tribes, along with its brutal tactics, were crucial to IS's success(BBC, 2015).

Sirte, it is located south of the Gulf of Sirte, between Tripoli and Benghazi. It is famously known for its battles, ethnic groups, and loyalty to Muammar Gaddafi. Also due to its development, it was the capital of Libya as Tripoli's successor after the Fall of Tripoli from 1 September 2011 to 20 October 2011. The settlement was established in the early 20th century by the Italians, at the site of a 19th-century fortress built by the Ottomans. It grew into a city after World War II (Trauthig, 2019).

As the birthplace of Muammar Gaddafi, Sirte was favored by the Gaddafi government. The city was the final major stronghold of Gaddafi loyalists in the Libyan Civil War and Gaddafi was killed there by rebel forces on 20 October 2011. During the battle, Sirte was left almost completely in ruins, with many buildings totally destroyed or damaged (Dejevsky, 2015).

The Islamic State leadership in Mosul was attempting to develop its Libyan territory as a "fallback" option. The Islamic State is expanding quickly in Libya it will make a matter of grave concern. The group first from ISIS appeared in Libya, it was allegedly composed of fewer than 800 fighters In December 2014, from February 2015 put the number between 1,000 and 3,000. The United Nations maintained in November 2015 that the Islamic State in Libya had 2,000 to 3,000 fighters. They are gradually increased year by year at the first of 2016; they had grown to between 5,000 and 6,000 fighters (Ispi, 2017).

The number of Islamic State fighters in Iraq and Syria, which is around 18,000 fighters. Thus, the average assessment of the number of Islamic State fighters in Libya is roughly 30 per cent of the average fighters in Iraq and Syria. Also, we have to ask where the Islamic State in Libya's fighters? They come from Iraq, Syria, North African and sub-Saharan Tunisia, Algeria, Chad, Egypt, Morocco, Niger, Nigeria, Senegal, and Sudan (Engel, 2015).

The fighters were members of Boko Haram or Islamic State sympathizers from elsewhere in sub-Saharan Africa. Not only are there more foreign fighters from the Middle East also Europeans fighting alongside the Islamic State in Libya, but there were also as many as 4,000 Western Europeans. In addition, there were roughly 3,000 from countries of the former Soviet Union and a further 1,200 from South and Southeast Asia. Lastly, there were almost 10,000 fighters from throughout the Arab world (Pusztai, 2015).

In that year Libya became a Ward of the Islamic State according to the inability to control territory and govern populations, Islamic State has limited independent financial viability they diverse revenue streams have been widely reported. They did much violence in the world for example they got financial support from Qatar and they have robbed banks of a reported total of US$1 billion. they controlled Oil and Gas in Libya to engages the oil sales, they allegedly earned as much as US$500 million (Ispi, 2015).

Islamic State Attacks in Libya:

They have used imprecise weaponry in densely-populated residential areas in what often amounted to indiscriminate attacks, leading to civilians fatalities and damage to civilian infrastructure. According to airstrikes by Operation Dignity, Libya Dawn. The Egyptian Government announced airstrikes against targets in Libya on 16 February 2015 in retaliation for the beheadings of 20 Egyptian nationals by a Libyan armed group pledging allegiance to ISIL (El-Shenawi, 2015).

Libyan Air Force units aligned to Operation Dignity also announced airstrikes on the same day. Instance the Egyptian air-force led to civilian casualties and/or damage to the civilian infrastructure they destroyed homes and other civilian property(OHCHR, 2015).

On 20 February 2015 another operation in Qubbah with bomb attacked 42 people and children were killed, this attacked allegedly in retaliation for the airstrikes on Derna, on 16 February by a Libyan armed group pledging allegiance to ISIL.

What is the result of the Egyptian air strike?

In Benghazi, civilians were caught up in fighting between Operation Dignity, over 90 civilian fatalities as a result of shelling or in the crossfire, since the beginning of 2015 to the end of July had exceeded 750, In May, at least 11 children and a civilian adult were killed in Benghazi. Relatives reported the death of three children aged between two and 12 when their house in the Bel'un neighbourhood of Benghazi (Pack, Smith & Mezran, 2019).

May 13, a shell hit a house in the al-Salam neighbourhood during a wedding celebration, resulting in the death of nine civilians, including eight children aged between two, and 15. Four further children, a man, and a woman sustained shrapnel injuries. At least 15 Benghazi residents died in another week of heavy fighting between 7 and 14 July (Reliefweb, 2015). On7 July. Victims included four brothers who died in the reported mortar shelling of their homes. On 14 July, a further five elderly men sustained fatal shrapnel wounds. On 15 October, the neighbourhoods of Kish, Tabalino, and Sirti in Benghazi were shelled leading to the death of two civilians (a man and a woman) (BBC News, 2015).

October 23, al -Kish Square in Benghazi, where hundreds of persons were participating in a demonstration against the Libyan Political Agreement, was shelled by unknown perpetrators, at least 45 persons injured as a result of shrapnel wounds (BBC News, 2015).

Armed confrontations broke out in the Tripoli neighbourhoods of Fashlum and Tajura on 17 April 2015 between armed groups supporting Libya Dawn and Operation Dignity. As a result of it many people died, the number of families suspected of supporting Operation Dignity fled Tripoli for Zintan, alAziziya and eastern Libya (BBC News, 2020). Prime Minister Abdallah al-Thinni's government established a factfinding committee on 2 June, to investigate the violence in Tajura. The committee found that 20 people had died and 500 were displaced from Tajura as a result of the violence (Apap, 2017).

During this period, Sirte witnessed armed clashes between a Libyan armed group with airstrikes. the majority of casualties were fighters, a number of civilians were also killed or injured, Libyan the fighting erupted in Sirte's 3rd district after a local imam, Khaled Ben Rajab al-Ferjani, was shot dead on 10 August. He was known for his vocal opposition to a Libyan group pledging allegiance to ISIL (Gazzini, 2020). By 13 August, ISIS killed 16 men from the 3rd district and they practised violence against civilians to intimidate citizens by four bodies hung from poles in three separate locations (News. UN, 2015).

At the end of 2015, the overall situation remains highly volatile due to continued fighting across different parts of the country. All parties in the country that had conflict appear to be committing violations of international humanitarian law, such as murder and torture of civilians and the taking of hostages; and destroying or seizing the property of an adversary (Zelin, 2014).

Chapter (6)

✳

Sirte: ISIS Seizes Territory in Libya in (2016)

At the beginning of January 2016, ISIS launched a campaign on the oil fields east of its stronghold in Sirte and the new UN-backed Government of National Accord arrives in Tripoli by boat after opposing forces block airspace. Also on the middle of 2016 UN staff returns to Tripoli after the absence of nearly two years. In addition, the Libyan National Army of Khalifa Haftar seizes key oil export terminals in the east and seizes it to carry out its terrorist operations.

ISIS launched a campaign on the oil fields

At the beginning of January 2016 ISIS launched a campaign on the oil fields east of its stronghold in Sirte in pursuit of this objective. ISIS's ground forces took complete control of a village to the east of Sirte, and used it to stage sustained attacks on oil export terminals at Ras Lanuf and al Sidra, as well as on inland oil infrastructure (Dobbs, 2012).

ISIS called this campaign as a successfully campaign because Libyan affiliate's capability designed and executed a complex campaign and established support zones for future attacks on oil fields, making it the group's largest and most successful ground operation outside of Iraq and Syria to date (Coyne, Estelle, & Gambhir, 2016).

The group conducted a campaign against Libya's oil resources and security that aims to both perpetuate instability in the country and set conditions for ISIS to capture Libya's oil wealth. The aims of ISIS seeking to gain access to oil revenue in Libya, have done it before in Iraq and Syria where revenue from black market oil trade is a significant source of funding for the group's military and governance efforts (Nayed, 2017).

The group executed attacks across multiple populated areas during the oil fields campaign, including a suicide truck bomb at a police training camp in Zliten that killed at least 60 and wounded at least 200 (Assad, 2019).

This bombing targeted territory held by the Misrata-based militias that previously fought against ISIS's takeover of Sirte and were intended to prevent attacks on Sirte as ISIS executed the oil campaign. ISIS attacked oil infrastructure near Zueitina, far to the east of the al Sidra frontline, signaling coordination between militants based in both central and eastern Libya. ISIS has yet to take control of operational oil infrastructure in Libya (UN Security Council, 2019).

In February 2016 ISIS has executed a sophisticated, multi-front campaign against Libya's oil facilities. President Obama reported ruled out significant military intervention against the group. The administration opted to continue intermittent strikes against ISIS leaders in Libya instead (Zaptia, 2018).

The group had more than 5,000 fighters and is reinforced by leadership sent from Iraq and Syria. Libyan ground forces are also unlikely to expel ISIS from its areas of control. ISIS's safe haven in Libya will allow it to survive even if it is defeated in Iraq and Syria. ISIS will use its Libyan base to exacerbate regional disorder and likely to attack Europe(International Crisis Group, 2018).

The political situation

The Libyan Political Agreement (LPA) established three governing since 2011first,(the House of Representa tives (HoR) in Tobruk)second (the High Council of State in Tripoli) third the Presidential Council (PC). The Presidential Council arrives in Tripoli on 30 March 2016, after three months in exile in Tunis, and failed in various attempts to land at Tripoli's Mitiga Airport, the Presidential Council (PC) of the Government of National Accord (GNA) arrived at Tripoli's Abu Sita naval base in a convoy of ships (Stephen & Wintour, 2018).

Prime Minister Khalifa National Salvation government had rejected the Libyan Political Agreement (LPA) and refused to recognise the GNA. They also announcement vowed to arrest members of the PC and the GNA cabinet. On the other side, the National Salvation government still controlled government offices in Tripoli with pay Tripoli-based armed groups, especially at Mitiga airport and around the naval base, to secure their operations.

From 4to 6 Jan the attack on Sidra terminal in Sirte basin, resulting in eleven guards and dozens of militants reported killed; and attacks on nearby Ras Lanuf oil port 7 Jan. Militants 8-9 Jan attacked power plant in Benghazi. At least 50 killed by truck bomb targeting police academy in Zliten 7 Jan; IS claimed responsibility. Deadly fighting reignited between Tebu and Tuareg armed groups in Obari 10 Jan despite local peace deal (Zaptia, 2018).

On 25 January 2016, the HoR convened in Tobruk to vote on the LPA. They dropped one of the additional provisions, Article 8, with controversial clause stated that all senior military, civil and security posts should immediately be transferred to the PC upon the signing of the LPA. But Haftar realized that the provision would sideline Tripoli-based General National Congress 27 Jan said it opposed any change to LPA. The critical situation started when HoR pitted itself against the newly formed State Council over its interpretation of the agreement's text, and the extent of power-sharing within it (Wintour, 2018).

Moreover, HoR voted to reject the GNA cabinet's 32 ministries, requesting a smaller number to replace its bloated composition. An agreement among the nine members of the PC had produced the large number of ministries to satisfy various constituencies and to give President Fayez al-Serraj power to appoint a number of portfolios(Ibrahim, 2018).

Militias allied with the UN-backed Government of National Accord (GNA) from the western Libyan city of Misrata and the eastern oil crescent region have advanced rapidly into ISIS's control zone since May 12. Haftar did a stratic he has not mobilized the army to Sirte, but it is using counter-ISIS operations as cover to project influence over key oil sites in the region. On the same time, the Misratans did pressuring ISIS's remaining bastions in the Sirte city center and may even claim control of the city.

Then ISIS become at least 2,000, are fighting to slow the Misratan advance, relying on vehicle-borne improvised explosive device (VBIED) attacks and sniper fire. By June 2016, over 425,000 IDPs were identified, primarily from the east of the country. The current push to dislodge IS from strategic areas is expected to result in further mass displacement(Lewis, 2018).

On May 29 Misratans reach the western outskirts of Sirte city and seized the easternmost ISIS-held town, Ben Jawad. Both the PFG and the LNA used the counter-ISIS mobilizations as justification for contesting or consolidating control of key oil sites in eastern Libya(Zaptia, 2018). On June 7 Misratan militias withdrew but then advanced into Sirte city centre from the west and south. In addition in Benghazi is affected by displacement. More than a third of the original population of the city, or almost 190,000 people, was found to be displaced in June 2016. Most (60%) remain in the city. As a result, the city currently hosts the largest share of all IDPs in Libya. However, with conflict having deescalated in many parts of the city, increasing returns are recorded (Assad, 2018).

The LPA's Government of National Accord (GNA) had run out in 2015 when they started with a geographically and ideologically balanced nine-person Presidency Council (PC) as well as two legislative bodies, the State Council in Tripoli and the HoR in Tobruk (Lederer, 2018).

In 2016 Presidency Council (PC) established a process by which the HoR was supposed to consult with the State Council, and endorse a cabinet selected, whose ministers would reflect appropriate horse-trading among Libyan constituencies, the requirement of a functioning HoR proved to be the Achilles' heel that ensured the GNA would never be effective.

The HoR's speaker, Aguila Saleh Issa, rejected the idea "she mention anyone outside of his control should exercise power from Tripoli" which was effective to give the chance to others. When they turned off the electricity in the building and locked the doors to prevent a vote (Lewis, 2018).

The head of the PC, Fayez al-Sarraj, acted as prime minister; other members, including two representing the easterners and one from the Tuaregs, resigned. A few PC members carved out concrete portfolios, especially Ahmed Maiteeg from Misrata, who focused on practical issues such as securing the coastal highway. Prime Minister Sarraj elevated his status domestically through frequent meetings with foreign counterparts (Libya Herald, 2017).

Prime Minister Sarraj made the brave decision in March 2016 to take up residence in Tripoli in the face of threats issued by the self-proclaimed head of the previous government in the capital displaced by the GNA. He got supported by the Italian government, as well as Maiteeg, who had friendly forces available to help. He then built up sufficient support to enable the government, however shaky, to remain there and provide some basic stability to the country because Tripoli is the capital (Porsia, 2017).

The U.S. and allies worked closely with the Sarraj government and military forces from Misrata and Tripolitania to oust ISIS from Sirte in 2016, at the cost of hundreds of Misratan lives. At the same time, the UAE, Egypt, and France provided various forms of support to General Hifter's LNA forces in the east (Jonathan, 2019).

Since the government led al-Serraj took office in April 2016, Haftar has increasingly represented an obstacle to a reunification of the country under the LPA and contributed. The repeated rejection by the Tobruk Parliament of Serraj's proposed Government of National Accord (GNA) gave rise to a new phase of further divergence.

Haftar's replaced elected mayors of Cyrenaica towns with the faithful military to take full control of the region. According to that he gain a political role and legitimacy, (we don't know from where) this role requires presenting himself as the leader in fighting Islamic terrorism and the emergence of radical groups in Libya but he cooperates with him (he fight ISIS and cooperate with them under the table). His narrative leveraged the fight against (ISIS) to join the international campaign against Islamic State and radicals in the region (Zaptia, 2018).

On June 18, The Benghazi Defense Brigades (BDB) conducted its first attack against the LNA in Ajdabiya, this attack prompted the House of Representatives, the eastern rival of the GNA, to declare martial law over eastern Libya, a direct challenge to the GNA's authority. from 21 to 30 June, The LNA attacked the PFG in Ajdabiya under the guise of counterterrorism operations, and seize militant strongholds in western Benghazi (Pollock & Wehrey, 2018).

In July Islamist militants attacked the LNA, the BDB mobilized northward from Ajdabiya toward Benghazi, they did break a temporary two-week ceasefire with the LNA and expressed support for the BDB. ON the other side Misratan forces failed to progress in their campaign against ISIS in Sirte. Three French soldiers died in an LNA helicopter crash in response to this French President Francois Hollande confirmed the deployment of French Special Forces in support of the LNA in Benghazi (World Bank, 2017).

The French support for the LNA sparked anti-Western and anti-GNA protests throughout Libya. On the other hand, BDB claimed responsibility for shooting down the helicopter. From that support, LNA continued its campaign against the BDB despite resistance and succeeded in slowing the BDB's advance toward Benghazi.

The first of August U.S. conducted its first airstrikes targeting the Islamic State of Iraq and al-Sham (ISIS) in Sirte, Libya, according to the request of the Government of National Accord (GNA), US-supported because they hold objectives in Libya also the GNA does not have its own military forces (Lee, 2018).

In December 2016, Haftar called on the LNA to advance to Tripoli. Heavy fighting continues in Benghazi between the LNA and Islamist groups. In addition, GNA allied militias announced that they had retaken Sirte from IS. As tensions between Misratan militias and the LNA grow, the conflict also has intensified in southern Libya due to ethnic and historical tribal disputes between Awlad Sulieman and Qadhadfa, between Awlad Sulieman and Tuareg and between Tuareg and Tebu.

MIRAL SABRY ALASHRY

Financial corruption

In May 2016, it was the worst issue of financial corruption sources from the eastern CBL revealed that al-Hibri's signature was on new Libyan banknotes that had been printed in Russia and were circulating throughout eastern Libya. The US embassy declared the Russian-made notes to be counterfeit and said they could "undermine trust in Libya's currency and the CBL's ability to manage monetary policy". In addition, eastern CBL stressed that there would be no dissimilarities between the country's banknotes (Phillips, 2018).

In September 2016, General Haftar and the LNA launched operation "Sudden Lightning" taking Libya's Oil Crescent and ports at Ras Lanuf, Sidra, Zueitina and Brega from the GNA-aligned Petroleum Facilities Guard. Fighting continued with claims that attacks were carried out under the leadership of al-Mahdi al-Barghathi, the defence minister of the GNA. The operation reveals deeper fragmentation in the coalition backing the Presidency Council which is likely to make it more difficult to reach a negotiated solution to the Libyan conflict.

As of September 2016, there were over 313,000 IDPs and 463,000 returnees. Over 85% of IDPs were displaced since mid-2014. These persons enjoy no civil rights protections whatsoever, as reported by UNHCR on 16 January 2015, has estimated that around 90,000 people have been pushed out of their homes (Herbert, 2017).

In November 2018, The case was announced by the representative of the eastern CBL he had received some 9 billion dinars worth of banknotes printed in Russia. The Libyan citizens from Misrata and Tripoli did not accept this currency, which differs from the UK-printed banknotes issued by bearing the respective governors' signatures. On the other hand, the CBL itself accepted the Russian-manufactured banknotes as legitimate. In effect, it tolerated complex schemes used by eastern Libyan authorities to convert Russian-manufactured banknotes into US dollars through Tripoli's black market.

Another case The Information and Finance Unit in the Central Bank of Libya and the Audit Bureau has delivered a number of financial corruption files to the Attorney General Office. The files include money laundry cases, bank bonds, and credits used to smuggle hundreds of millions in foreign currency by using counterfeit Customs papers. General Attorney Office has finished investigating all the data of the cases and issued arrest warrants for the persons involved, some of whom had previously forged Documentary credits and imported empty containers, 50 of which were examined by the General Attorney Office in Tripoli port, 200 in Misrata, and others in Al-Khumus port (Micallef & Reitano, 2018).

Commenting on the news of Hannibal Gaddafi, who is jailed in Lebanon, Al-Sawr said that there are some talks underway with the Lebanese authorities that aim at extraditing him, underlining that the General Attorney Office had already provided the Lebanese authorities with a file of Hannibal's crimes of murder and corruption. On the other hand, Al-Sawr disclosed that the General Attorney Office has got over 300 cases for persons that are accused of terrorist-linked activities(Assad, 2016).

In 2016 the dynamics that have supported the war economy's rise remain. There is still the danger that economic predation continues to such an extent that Libya's finances and institutions are eroded further, with no actor in the war economy incentivized (or likely) to bring damaging activities to a halt. Between 2013 and 2016, Libya's foreign exchange reserves fell from $109 billion to around $70 billion, according to the World Bank. the migrant's number had reached around 163,000, the International, organization for Migration (IOM) estimates at between 700,000 and 1 million (Amnesty International, 2017).

Chapter (7)

✳

International Focus on Libya (2017)

This chapter focuses on the escalation of the Libyan crisis in 2017. The role of international parties in Libya, like Russia, participates in Libya as part of a larger plan. Libya is part of Russia's efforts to keep Egyptian President Sisi away from the United States and the Gulf states. It is an important stage of global geopolitics as well as counter-terrorism operations.

This credit also focuses on the role of both the Egyptian and the Emirati interference in Libya and Turkey's stakeholders with the national reconciliation government to control the Middle East.

How the superpowers control Libya

American security remains at risk, Trump administration reconsiders America's strategy of the conflict became again after the Islamic State lost control in Sirte. Also, the US new strategy cannot contain Libya's problems in Libya. America's interests there transcend al Qaeda, ISIS, and other Salafi-jihadi groups. Trump knows that the Libyan conflict has serious implications for the U.S. and its allies in Europe. The war itself exacerbates the migrant crisis that is destabilizing Europe.

The Libyan crisis escalated in 2017. In January, IOM reported that 363,348 migrants arrived in Europe by sea in 2016, of which 181,436 arrived in Italy having mainly (estimated 90%) departed from Libya. according to that, IOM has developed its Strategic Plan for 2017/2018 to both demonstrate the principles and outline the objectives towards achieving good migration governance. This comprehensive document lays the strategic direction for programmatic development that addresses current and anticipated needs in the coming years in Libya (The International Organization for Migration, 2019).

On the other side, Russia is also engaging in Libya as part of a larger plan. Libya is part of Russia's efforts to woo Egyptian President Sisi away from the U.S. and the Gulf states. It is an important theatre of global geopolitics as well as of counter-terror operations (Fitzgerald & Toaldo, 2018).

Russian experts said, U.S. strategy will fail in Libya, as they did it before in Yemen, Iraq, and Syria. The U.S. must develop a new strategy in Libya that prioritizes resolving the civil war. They should also support changes to the UN-backed unity government that promote inclusivity and reward stakeholders who are willing to compromise (Al Jazeera, 2018).

Since 2011 U.S. used the strategy of containing ISIS in Libya that cannot work in a conflict involving regional systems and global players. American interests in Libya go beyond preventing ISIS and al Qaeda from holding cities (Harchaoui, 2019).

ISIS seized Sirte and declared its rule there in May 2015, but the U.S. helped cobble together enough local forces to expel it from the coastal city in 2016. But ISIS began to reconstitute its fighting forces rapidly after that defeat U.S in January 2017 degraded the group but should remind us that all is not well. Libya remains an important theatre of war against ISIS.

LNA commander Field Marshal Khalifa Haftar got his full support from the regional political process championed by Egypt, Algeria, and Tunisia; he got a political deal with the others. GNA, it is the only Libyan body that the U.S. will engage in, lacks credibility. Even its staunchest supporters acknowledge the need for reform (Opec News, 2017).

Haftar objective, not to engage with many moderate Islamist actors, including Misratan powerbrokers, who form a key political bloc in western Libya, he wants to control Misratan militias and Islamist forces in Tripoli, he directs his energy and his forces. He thus ignores the threats that the U.S. cares most about while pursuing the straightforward military defeat of all Islamists (Casciani, 2017).

Hafter's think that he got the power from the U.S no it's a trap for the U.S., not good partners. U.S. has invested minimal resources in resolving Libya's civil war, which is the root cause of ISIS and al Qaeda's expansion in Libya. We have instead pursued a limited counter-ISIS strategy within Libya, alongside security assistance (International Crisis Group, 2018).

A containment strategy is also doomed to fail because UAE, Egypt, and others are lined up on one side of the Libyan civil war, opposite Turkey, Qatar, and Sudan. All of them want to seek for own geopolitical ends adds entropy to the system that drives continued conflict.

Another strong entry at the stage is Russia to revision challenge the influence of the U.S. and its allies, by using Haftar they support LNA with new arms deals and the rumoured training of LNA troops. it is the same as what they did successfully in Syria. they sent a message to the world that "Russia is the key mediator and counterterrorism partner in order to secure strategic victories" and we want reestablishment of a military footprint on the southern Mediterranean". But the message is hidden is an investment in Libya's oil sector.

Hence, Russia has become a major player in the Arab region deepening ties with Egypt, on the other side Egypt should support LNA's. secondly, LNA also bolsters ties to the UAE and Saudi Arabia under Russia's support, the third major player to Russia reducing the war between Iran and Russia(Brahimi, 2017).

The United States took another strategy against Russia by planning to step up military support for the Saudi-led intervention in Yemen, to get Iran threatening. on the other hand, Iran already supplies advanced weaponry that allows the al Houthi-Saleh faction to counter coalition capabilities and threaten freedom of movement in the Red Sea.

As the conflict increases within the region, the conflict also increases in Libya, in the mid of 2017 hardline Islamist militias in Misrata city are attempting to overthrow a moderate council that supports the UN-backed Government of National Accord (GNA).

The Libyan National Army seeks to fight in advancing on air bases and oil sites in central and western Libya to rebuild its manpower and military capabilities in the country. In addition, Al Qaeda and ISIS seek to attack commercial airliners with explosive devices concealed in portable electronic devices. Due to that U.S enacted new aviation security restrictions preventing passengers from carrying portable electronics, such as laptops. The U.S. restrictions apply to inbound flights from 10 Muslim-majority countries.

A coalition of militias led by the Benghazi Defense Brigades (BDB), seized the al Sidra and Ras Lanuf oil terminals from the Libyan National Army (LNA) on March 3. The BDB has indicated that it may cede control of the terminals to Libya's National Oil Company and forces aligned with the UN-backed Government of National Accord (GNA). The LNA, responded with a barrage of airstrikes on March 12 and may be massing a force to retake the ports (Samer, 2019).

Haftar has been consolidating his position in Libya, in May 2017 the LNA recently declared victory in Benghazi it is the second-largest city in Libya, and ousted rival Islamist militias from key military bases in central and southwestern Libya. This ability to navigate Libyan tribal dynamics enabled him to take control of most of Libya's oil infrastructure. The second aims to control Derna city for complete control of all of eastern Libya.

The third control of Sirte, on the central Libyan coast and Tripoli, Militias aligned with the UN-backed Government of National Accord (GNA) recently ousted rivals from Tripoli they want to enter the capital city. Haftar's campaign wants to eradicate political Islam this is what he want to promoted and terrified by neighbouring countries because the neighbouring countries suffer from Islamic terrorism, from here it gets the most support, which has the full backing of the Egyptians and Emiratis, all of his messages he will kill all of the Islamic groups

A Libyan militia released Saif al Islam al Gaddafi, on June 9 this reflects the Gaddafi regime will return to power again from the other side reflects the increasing anther conflict that Haftar will bring back the old regime (International Foundation for Electoral Systems, 2018)

Saif al Islam's release is a reconciliation of interests between the Arab forces because Haftar is backed by Egypt and the UAE, favoured by Saudi Arabia, Jordan, and Russia, and possibly championed by some in the U.S.

according to that all of the media channels called him the strong man cause he did forces secured a major strategic victory in early June when, thanks to Egyptian and Emirati air support, they drove rival forces from several towns and bases in central Libya, Haftar wants to be like Egyptian President Abdel Fatah al Sisi, both of them want establishing military rule they are against Salafi-jihadi groups.

On 29 July 2017, the CDA committee members, voted in favour of their completed draft. Saleh's statement about the reconsideration of the constitution-drafting process and possible dissolution of the CDA was a strong enough motivation for CDA members to vote for the draft constitution, thus securing the two-thirds majority required to put it up for referendum. according to that, the legal challenges continued to cast doubt on the legitimacy of the drafting process, and the document is produced. On 12 October 2017, Bayda's court of appeals ruled on a case brought by several CDA members who claimed procedural irregularities took place when the draft was voted on. The court cancelled the vote that took place on 29 July (Wester, 2020)

In August 2017, Fahmi Salim Ben Khalifa was arrested by a Salafi-leaning group in Zuwara called the Muqanein and handed over to the Special Deterrence Force in Tripoli. He comes from the coastal town of Zuwara, has been renowned for his involvement in smuggling fuel and illicit goods across the sea and the Tunisian border since Gaddafi (Libya Business News, 2015).

Before 2011 he was sentenced to 15 years in prison but he escaped and returned back during the uprising of 2011 with a new face he supports the revolutionaries from Zuwara, donating large sums of money to pay for the treatment of wounded fighters to be a righteous man but his real face involved with sending ships loaded with the fuel off the Libyan coast, then unloaded onto other vessels and sent to the coast of Malta, where they became "certified" imports from Saudi Arabia and sold to Italian oil companies, he sold USD 4 billion worth of Libyan fuel in Italy through this scheme.

In Libya, these smuggled deals have not been witnessed before, with the cooperation and planning of the Italian sub-state during this year, the amount of wealth stolen from Libya in the form of smuggled gasoline and diesel and exported to Italy has never exceeded USD 150 million per annum, the World Bank estimates that flows from Libya into Tunisia are valued at approximately USD 148 million.

In October 2017, Haftar issued a decree that broadened the mandate of the Military Authority for Investment and Public Works (MAIPW), an administrative committee was formed to oversee with Mohammed Fakhri, the former interior minister of the al-Bayda government, appointed as board chairman, to essentially giving the LNA a "legal mandate" to manage any service and manufacturing project in the areas under its control.

Al-Fakhri explained that the LNA was keen to take over agricultural projects. In October 2017, Haftar ordered the closure of Tobruk's port, citing endemic corruption and illicit smuggling at the port due to a lack of security. on the other hand, Haftar is the only person who did that so that, he switched the ships were re-routed to Benghazi, where the LNA had taken over port security and customs. Due to that, a leaked phone call, Werfalli used his position stealing large sums of money he wanted by the International Criminal Court (ICC) for war crimes after that he left the country. Then, allegedly in a deal struck between the MAIPW and Turkey loaded with 5,000 tons of scrap metal, this reflects that Haftar wants an economic sphere, to use to finance the protraction of the conflict. Hence the control over the state's resources and the deprivation of citizens of these resources. Libya became poor and had no resources (Alshadeedi, & Ezzeldine. 2019).

In October 2017, Italy and Anas Dabbashi did a deal that was never acknowledged by Italy or the GNA, the 48th Battalion, headed by, and sanctioned by the Government of National Accord (GNA) — to stem migration flows to Europe when the fighting erupted between rival armed groups in Sabratha, and thousands of families to flee the coastal city. the cooperation scheme weakened other armed groups in Sabratha which did not financially benefit from being involved in those activities.

Italian politicians were under pressure to curb migration ahead of the elections in Italy. In July

2017, because Sabratha was widely regarded as a hub for human trafficking in Libya. The Italian government had arranged for several militias to receive official salaries from GNA ministries. fight over by ended with Dabbashi's forces being ousted from Sabratha and led to at least five deaths and over 40 people injured.

CNN report in November 2017, Libyans in acts of slavery sparked international outrage and put Libya in the spotlight as a brutal transit country for migrants, and the interception of migrants at sea and confinement of migrants in detention centres (Boserup & Collombier, 2018).

In October 2017, Haftar issued a decree that broadened the mandate of the Military Authority for Investment and Public Works (MAIPW), an administrative committee was formed to oversee with Mohammed Fakhri, the former interior minister of the al-Bayda government, appointed as board chairman, to essentially giving the LNA a "legal mandate" to manage any service and manufacturing project in the areas under its control (Wehrey & Lacher, 2019).

al-Fakhri explained that the LNA was keen to take over agricultural projects. In October 2017, Haftar ordered the closure of Tobruk's port, citing endemic corruption and illicit smuggling at the port due to a lack of security. on the other hand, Haftar is the only person who did that so that, he switched the ships were re-routed to Benghazi, where the LNA had taken over port security and customs.

December 17, 2017, marked the second anniversary of the signing of the UN-brokered Libyan Political Agreement (LPA), which established the Government of National Accord (GNA) unity government.

GNA sought to preserve its own power, On the same month Gunmen, assassinated Mohammed Eshtawi he was an early supporter of the GNA and had faced challenges from hardline Misratan Islamist factions, no group has claimed responsibility for his killing (Eaton, 2020).

Haftar rejected the Libyan Political Agreement (LPA) and associated institutions. Haftar stated that the LNA will now answer only to the will of the Libyan people. He took steps to increase his control over election centres and electoral commission offices in the east.

In addition, the Nawasi brigade criticized Haftar's rejection of the LPA as a coup against the democratic process on the same day Haftar, rejected the UN framework on December 17 and signalled his intent to take control of the country. Then gunmen assassinated the mayor of Misrata city Mohammed Eshtawi, setting the stage for Libya to return to open conflict that will further destabilize the region and strengthen Salafi-jihadi groups (Wehrey & Lacher, 2019).

Moreover, this day marked the second anniversary of the signing of the UN-brokered Libyan Political Agreement. Opponents of the GNA argue that its mandate expired on this date, but GNA supporters argue that it cannot expire because of the leadership of the Libyan House of Representatives, which sought to preserve its own power.

Both Eshtawi's death and Haftar's turn away from political resolution worsen the polarization of the Libyan political sphere and escalate the conflict and weakens moderate factions who are willing to make compromises but the risk of armed escalation remains high, the divisions and insufficient command and control within the LNA and the Misratan bloc allow individual groups to destabilize tinderbox areas like Tripoli, southwestern Libya, and the oil crescent region (United Nations Support Mission In Libya, 2018).

In July 2017 the leaked a phone call, Werfalli used his position to steal large sums of money he wanted from the International Criminal Court (ICC) for war crimes after that he left the country (Human Rights Watch, 2018).

In September 2017, allegedly in a deal struck between the MAIPW and Turkey with loaded with 5,000 tons of scrap metal, this reflects that Haftar wants economic sphere, to use to finance the protraction of the conflict. Hence the control over the state's resources and the deprivation of citizens of these resources. Libya became poor and had no resources.

In October 2017, Italy and Anas Dabbashi did a deal that was never acknowledged by Italy or the GNA, the 48th Battalion, headed by, and sanctioned by the Government of National Accord (GNA) — to stem migration flows to Europe when the fighting erupted between rival armed groups in Sabratha, and thousands of families to flee the coastal city. the cooperation scheme weakened other armed groups in Sabratha which did not financially benefit from being involved in those activities.

Italian politicians were under pressure to curb migration ahead of the elections in Italy. In July 2017, because Sabratha was widely regarded as a hub for human trafficking in Libya.

The Italian government had arranged for several militias to receive official salaries from GNA ministries. fight over by ended with Dabbashi's forces being ousted from Sabratha and led to at least five deaths and over 40 people injured (International Crisis Group, 2018)

CNN report in November 2017, Libyans in acts of slavery sparked international outrage and put Libya in the spotlight as a brutal transit country for migrants, and they interception of migrants at sea and confinement of migrants in detention centres.

December 17, 2017, marked the second anniversary of the signing of the UN-brokered Libyan Political Agreement (LPA), which established the Government of National Accord (GNA) unity government.

GNA sought to preserve its own power, On the same month Gunmen, assassinated Mohammed Eshtawi he was an early supporter of the GNA and had faced challenges from hardline Misratan Islamist factions, No group has claimed responsibility for his killing ((Abdalla &Garber. 2018).

Haftar rejected the Libyan Political Agreement (LPA) and associated institutions. Haftar stated that the LNA will now answer only to the will of the Libyan people. He took steps to increase his control over election centres and electoral commission offices in the east.

The Nawasi brigade criticized Haftar's rejection of the LPA as a coup against the democratic process on the same day Haftar, rejected the UN framework on December 17 and signalled his intent to take control of the country. Then gunmen assassinated the mayor of Misrata city Mohammed Eshtawi, setting the stage for Libya to return to open conflict that will further destabilize the region and strengthen Salafi-jihadi groups.

Moreover, this day marked the second anniversary of the signing of the UN-brokered Libyan Political Agreement. Opponents of the GNA argue that its mandate expired on this date, but GNA supporters argue that it cannot expire because of the leadership of the Libyan House of Representatives, which sought to preserve its own power.

Both Eshtawi's death and Haftar's turn away from political resolution worsen the polarization of the Libyan political sphere and escalate the conflict and weakens moderate factions who are willing to make compromises but the risk of armed escalation remains high, the divisions and insufficient command and control within the LNA and the Misratan bloc allow individual groups to destabilize tinderbox areas like Tripoli, southwestern Libya, and the oil crescent region, the Constitutional Drafting(World Bank, 2019).

The Constitutional Drafting Assembly (CDA), which was tasked with drawing up a permanent constitution for Libya, was mired in internal divisions. Some members are fear because their rights would be threatened by Libya's majority population living in Tripolitania, they have problem issues in the Constitution related to cultural, heritage, and identity rights.

The UN intervened in March 2016 and moved the meetings from Libya to Salalah, in Oman to complete the Constitution. However, the Salalah meetings led to further tensions within the CDA, with some members refusing to endorse the draft constitution.

Bayda's court of appeals accepted the legal challenge to the Salalah draft. In mid-2017, Agilah Saleh, the president of the House of Representatives (HoR), announced that the CDA's mandate had expired, He was not declared. But the HoR declared that they would consider dissolving the current CDA team and appoint a new committee for the task (Hamada, Sökmen and Zaki, 2020).

Chapter (8)

✳

Libyan Conflict and Diplomatic Efforts (2018)

This chapter focuses on supporting the great forces of the two governments as well Khalifa Haftar claims that his forces are fully in control of Derna, the last Islamist stronghold in the east and the only city in the region, at the end outside his control.

The Libyan conflict and the diplomatic efforts

Libya became a failed country with a humanitarian crisis and a serious threat to US national security and adversaries, including ISIS, Al Qaeda, and Russia, are exploiting the collapse and establishing themselves in Libya at America's expense.

Due to that, the United States has outsourced the Libyan political crisis to a United Nations mission with a new strategy but they failed also defeat ISIS with military action through airstrikes and support for local forces but the instability situation give feedback that the military victory is impossible and give opportunities to ISIS and Al Qaeda, to operate in Libya. And the other scenario there is a battleground in a regional proxy war and a theatre for Russia's expansion into the Mediterranean (Arabic, 2018)

The strategy of ISIS is disrupting oil production and expanding its reach southward they using Libya to receive foreign fighters from Europe to continue the unprecedented mobilization of sub-Saharan jihadists, and as a base from which to plan and coordinate attacks against the West.

The Libyan conflict is not just a counterterrorism problem; it is also a geopolitical one. Russia is building ties with power brokers across the Libyan political spectrum and amassing influence in the Libyan oil sector, as well as leveraging its engagement in Libya to foster military cooperation with Egypt. Also, Russia is taking advantage of the American retreat from the regain to expand its military and economy, also using its power in Libya to pressure European states sensitive to the flow of energy and migrants (Africa News Portal, 2018).

In the year 2018 Haftar suffered a stroke. Family members and LNA officials have denied the reports and attempted to divert media attention to the LNA's military efforts. The media said Haftar has passed through the most dangerous stage of his illness, and if he is still ill he will remove from the political scene and could derail fragile progress toward national political reconciliation. Haftar's incapacitation would produce a leadership vacuum and could cause the LNA to fracture. On April 11, 2018, Members of the Awaqir tribe, which has increasingly tense relations with LNA leadership, attacked the LNA headquarters at al Rajmah.

The LNA's weakening invites rivals who have suffered losses to the LNA to attempt to recapture key sites, like the oil terminals in the lucrative oil crescent region or key military positions in the southwest. ISIS may also leverage the leader's absence and the chaos to accelerate attacks intended to degrade security and disrupt oil exports in north-central Libya (Barakat, 2018).

In addition, the power vacuum or internecine struggle in the east would allow Salafi-jihadi militants to return to eastern cities and towns. The LNA is accused of humanitarian abuses they using like the waqir tribe and select Salafi militias in Benghazi.

By 2018, almost 1.1 million Libyans needed urgent humanitarian assistance according to the UN, Libya's oil production averaging 1 million barrels a day in 2018 but they face a crisis. U.N. Special Representative Ghassan Salame during years of turmoil punctuated by armed conflict, a lucrative shadow economy has emerged in the oil-rich nation, based on foreign currency exchange scams, smuggling, and extortion. his objective to been working to convince the international community that any political deal to unify rival factions based in Tripoli and eastern Libya would only be "cosmetic" if the shadow economy was not tackled. Libya needs to address the black market and address the predation of public money (Lewis, 2018).

Libyan National Army (LNA) and militia coalition that controls most of eastern Libya, has begun a counter-offensive to recapture the sites. The fighting in the "oil crescent" region, home to about 80 per cent of Libya's oil production, has damaged critical infrastructure and halted exports.

The LNA captured the sites. Jadhran and his tribal supporters have framed their operation as an effort to return to their home city of Ajdabiya and the al Qaeda network in Libya that seeks to counter Benghazi. The participation of fighters from the Tebu reflects their growing concern with the rival Arab tribes that the LNA uses to project power to the south (Alghad, 2018).

The objective of the LNA's since April 2018 has been seizing Derna city this reflects the influence of Egypt and an effort to distract from the LNA's weakness elsewhere, also the LNA has already shifted units from Derna and Benghazi to counterattack in the oil crescent.

Moreover, the LNA recapture al Sidra and Ras Lanuf rapidly, relying on its airpower, and Egyptian support and they want to push farther westward and southward to protect itself from repeat attacks, this advance will open new fronts for armed conflict, in Sebha to the southwest to make tribal conflict(Asaad, 2018). They are using Emirati air support was key to the LNA's defence also Emirati forces direct a large-scale operation in Yemen.

The LNA's drawing of forces away from Benghazi and Derna will lift pressure from the Salafi-jihadi networks that are latent in both cities. ISIS, which has sought repeatedly to breach LNA checkpoints in the oil crescent region, will seize the opportunity to conduct its own attacks on oil sites or penetrate Libya's northern coast for attacks on population centres. The seizure of

Ras Lanuf and al Sidra reveals a key flaw in the international effort to resolve the Libya crisis. May 2018 Paris declaration control the militias that seized the oil ports also the strategy reliant on elite agreements and elections will not succeed in an environment in which armed groups can seize power at will(Aimade and McMahon, 2018).

In June the United Nations has imposed sanctions on the leaders of human trafficking networks in Libya, including those associated with the country's EU-funded coastguard. The sanctions include a global travel ban and an assets freeze of six of the most prolific smugglers who took advantage of the insecurity in Libya to move hundreds of thousands of migrants by sea to Europe (Ghobara, 2018). Among those named by the UN were Abd al Rahman al-Milad, regional Libyan coastguard leader whose unit was funded by the EU, and Mus'ab Abu-Qarin, said to have organized journeys overseas for 45,000 people in 2015 alone (Ensor, 2018).

In May 2018, after subjecting Derna to a punishing blockade for over a year, Khalifa Haftar announced the beginning of a Libyan National Army (LNA) military offensive aimed at capturing the only town in eastern Libya that remained out of the control of his forces. The offensive included aerial bombardment of targets within Derna but also the deployment of tribal militiamen from its hinterland. Haftar's backers in Cairo were particularly keen to see his forces take control of Derna, given its proximity to Egypt's border with Libya and the fact that Egyptian militants had hidden there. In June, Haftar announced the "liberation" of Derna but clashes have continued, and the town remains restive today, with scores dead and thousands displaced (Arafat, 2018)

In June 2018, an alliance formed by Ibrahim Jadhran and remnants of the Benghazi Defense Brigade (BDB) captured the oil ports of Ras Lanuf and Al Sidra from Haftar's Libyan National Army (LNA), causing not only their closure but also a production loss of 240,000 barrels per day (Ali, 2018).

Next month, the LNA mobilized to recapture the oil terminals, and he frustrated the Central Bank of Libya (CBL), accusing it of financing militias, then the eastern officials had shut the ports of Zueitina and Hariga, stopping legitimate NOC tankers from loading oil at the facilities. Oil production, which stood at slightly more than a million barrels per day, was slashed to 150,000 barrels per day.

Armed Kani Brigade from Tarhuna attacked Garabulli, some 50 km's from Tripoli, adding more tension and conflict and the battle ended in a truce, with a death toll of 117 people, many of them civilians, and nearly 600 wounded. The ceasefire conditions included the institutionalization of security and tangible steps to introduce economic reforms (Asaeid, 2018).

In November 2018 the UN's the House of Representatives objection to the Interim Constitutional Declaration the UN envoy Ghassan Salamé, realized that the House of Representatives (HoR) and the State Council were holding the political process hostage. They had repeatedly failed to amend the Libyan Political Agreement (LPA) in 2017 but they accept a mechanism to choose a new unity government (Alghad, 2018)

They took a long time, and they are freezing the Constitution, On 5 September 2018 Salamé, suggest moving to the next phase of his plan (a National Conference in Libya), where participating citizens would agree on a new way forward. this conference will take a place In January 2019, to establish a new legal framework that would pave the way for elections to appoint a new unity government by June 2019 (Hassan, 2018).

On 29 November 2018, the HoR enacted a constitutional amendment Interim Constitutional Declaration (ICD), and lead to a referendum on the CDA's draft constitution. The HoR's initiative, pushed through by President Saleh, is meant to work against Salamé's efforts to bypass the HoR and the State Council to hold the National Conference (Sputnikhttps, 2018).

In November 2018, the US, the UK, and France secured the UN Security Council's approval to sanction Salah Badi, the Samoud Brigade commander from Misrata, because he played a key role in the clashes and led multiple anti-GNA attacks in 2016 and 2017 when he sought to restore the internationally unrecognized National Salvation Government of former Prime Minister Khalifa Ghwell, and then he did an attacked with neighbourhoods in Tripoli in September 2018.

France argued at the UN Security Council that sanctions were an adequate punishment for the deadly fighting in Tripoli, whether they will succeed in maintaining peace or deterring Badi or others from acting as spoilers. There is also a risk that institutions implementing selective sanctions could lose credibility with Libyans, especially if the criteria are not applicable to all armed actors involved in the conflict (Yassin, 2018).

Gaddafi's fall left much of Libya controlled by militias and ISIS, due to that the state's breakdown opened the floodgates to hundreds of thousands of migrants, perilously attempting to reach the Mediterranean for the dangerous crossing to Europe.

Al Qaeda used that war for taxing, illegal activities like human trafficking and smuggling, also al Qaeda spawn terrorist threats and spreading instability across northern Africa. And Russia, which is building influence in Libya, has an opportunity to exploit the migrant crisis (Aimn, 2018).

There is a weak point in Europe from this war in the Middle East by Russia and Turkey, they did it in Syria, working through proxies to regulate the flow of migrants into Europe, also threatening the U.S (Juha, 2018).

Congress and successive administrations have shied away from all involvement in Libya beyond a limited counterterrorism policy. Donald J. Trump mentions the crisis is seen as a regional problem to be resolved by Europeans who are most affected by the influx of undocumented migrants (El-Tayeb, 2018).

The current U.S. policy toward Libya also assumes that the current UN-led political reconciliation process will establish a central governing authority. France and Italy recognize correctly that managing the irregular migration crisis is key to resolving the Libya conflict, but their interventions often work at cross-purposes. In addition, the presence of an estimated 670,000 migrants in Libya—almost 12.5% of the total Libyan population—has been fueling social tensions and making conflict resolution even more complex (Ali, 2018).

Chapter (9)

✳

Libyan Crisis Never End 2019

This chapter analyzed how Haftar announces Operation Flood of Dignity to "liberate" Tripoli, he fights in the south and west of the capital. And escalated the situation in Libya LNA forces advanced west of Tripoli and claimed to capture Sorman, Sabratha, and Gharyan, and how the militias seized Souq al Khamis and Wadi al Rabi'a road south of Tripoli, but they suffered a setback in Zawiya, west of Tripoli, where a militia imprisoned 145 LNA troops and confiscated 60 LNA vehicles. In addition, LNA announced that they have captured the 4th Brigade Headquarters in the town of Azizya after fierce fighting with the GNA. The UNHCR attempted to evacuate detained refugees from the Qasir bin Gashir detention centre after it became stuck in the crossfire between the two sides they were transferred to Sekah Road detention centre, but around 120 people were left behind and were still in the Qasir bin Gashir

Moreover, how US Shifts Course On Libya, Al-Sarraj Launch A Peace Initiative, Attack on Libya Detention Center, how Middle East Countries Cooperate to Support Stability in Libya, Germany Organizes Libya Conference to Shore up Arms Embargo and at the end of the year Libyan Refugees in Crisis, Russian intervention in Libya, America intercepts, Greece Expel Libyan Ambassador, UN Security Council Warns Libya to Stop, After Arms Embargo and Mercenaries Arrivaled to Raise Fears.

The conflict escalated between the two governments

The civil war in Libya is a key driver of the Salafi-jihadi presence after the 2011 conflict in Benghazi allowed the al Qaeda-linked Ansar al-Sharia to infiltrate fighting and forge partnerships against common enemies.

Strife in 2013 and 2014 allowed the Islamic State to exploit seams between warring factions and seize the coastal city of Sirte. Libya's civil war largely froze—with some notable exceptions—between 2015 and 2017 Salafi-jihadi groups are seizing the opportunity to recoup their losses (Mohammed, 2019).

A BRSC supporter posted that the BRSC will fight against Haftar's Libyan National Army (LNA) in Tripoli. A member of the Ajdabiya Revolutionaries Shura Council, which is connected to both Ansar al-Sharia and the BRSC, is already fighting in Tripoli. The civil war caught fire at the start of 2019.

U.S. counterterrorism policy in Libya relies on the UN-backed Government of National Accord (GNA) to resolve the civil war and political crisis, the GNA will weaken further and fighting will continue.

The fighting began with an LNA offensive on Tripoli that was intended to establish LNA commander Haftar as Libya's, pre-empting a UN conference planned for mid-April. Haftar fighting continues, following the playbook of military threat paired with negotiations that it has deployed successfully in the oil crescent and the southwest. On the other hand, they faced fierce resistance and maintain long supply lines with insufficient forces or accept a humiliating retreat (Abbas, 2019).

The LNA built a new strategy that formed an operations room to "liberate" longtime rival Misrata, a great step that will encourage Misratan forces to stay in the fight. Misrata-aligned forces in Sirte have also gone on alert, signalling a potential expansion of the conflict into central Libya (Eremnews, 2019).

Libya's combustion threatens U.S. interests and allies while providing opportunities to enemies and adversaries. Russia has spotted the opportunity of UN weakness and European division in Libya they made a deal that will advance Moscow's interests (Almayadeen, 2019).

On the first of April Haftar announces Operation Flood of Dignity to "liberate" Tripoli, he fights in the south and west of the capital. And escalated the situation in Libya LNA forces advanced west of Tripoli and claimed to capture Sorman, Sabratha, and Gharyan (Ahlmasrnews, 2019).

On the next day, Tripoli militias reversed the LNA's momentum. The militias seized Souq al Khamis and Wadi al Rabi'a road south of Tripoli, but they suffered a setback in Zawiya, west of Tripoli, where a militia imprisoned 145 LNA troops and confiscated 60 LNA vehicles (Elbalad, 2019).

On 10 April LNA announced that they have captured the 4th Brigade Headquarters in the town of Azizya after fierce fighting with the GNA. The UNHCR attempted to evacuate detained refugees from the Qasir bin Gashir detention centre after it became stuck in the crossfire between the two sides they were transferred to Sekah Road detention centre, but around 120 people were left behind and were still in the Qasir bin Gashir (Almasryalyoum, 2019).

LNA spokesperson, Brig Gen. Ahmed al-Mismari, said the LNA has secured the al-Yarmouk camp and are advancing toward the Dabali military camp. LNA has arrested pro-GNA "African mercenaries" at Tripoli Int'l Airport.

On 11 April GNA claimed several airstrikes on LNA targets in Suq al-Khamis, Tarhuna city, and Ayn Zara region, the GNA has recaptured Wadie Alrabie, Bridge 27, Bridge of Souq Al-Ahad and Tripoli International Airport, in addition, the GNA claimed that it negotiated the surrender of soldiers belonging to the LNA 8th brigade in Ayn Zara (Almasryalyoum, 2019 April 11).

On 12 April the LNA conducted an airstrike against the GNA in Abdel Samad Camp, south of Zuwarah. and they killed dozens of GNA fighters, also they made air force conducted air raids against GNA targets in Wadi Al Rabie, south of Tripoli, as well as an arms cache in the North-East Tripoli neighbourhood of Tajura. The media reported there are explosions were reported at GNA-held Mitiga International Airport as a result of GNA anti-aircraft guns firing before the fighting Omar al-Bashir sending two planes loaded with 28 fighters, as well as a large number of weapons and ammunition, from Khartoum to GNA-held Mitiga International Airport on 28 March. On 12 April that the United Arab Emirates sent military equipment to the LNA at Benina International Airport in Benghazi.

The UNHCR called for the release and evacuation of detained refugees held in wartorn areas. The UNHCR confirmed that 728 people were still trapped in the contested Qasir Bin Gashir detention centre, stating that it attempted to evacuate them to the Zintan detention, the detainees refused to go, insisting that they are evacuated out of Libya (Al-Khair, 2019).

On 13 April Aguila Saleh mention, we need a partial lifting of the international arms embargo imposed on Libya, to allow countries to legally arm the Libyan National Army. On the other hand, the stated that the Tobruk-based government intends to hold elections after capturing Tripoli.

On 14 April the LNA report a statement, the terrorist group's ISIS were fighting alongside the GNA in Tripoli. On the other side, the GNA Presidential Council denied the claims. Discussions to re-calm the situation with President of Egypt, El-Sisi, met with LNA Haftar in Cairo to discuss the situation from that meeting all of the newspaper report that El-Sisi, support Haftar.

The LNA air force activity was reported, Mi-35 helicopters and Su-22 bombers targeting numerous GNA positions in Azizya, Al Sawani, the 4th Brigade HQ, Ayn Zara, Wadi Al Rabie and Tajura, and they recaptured Yarmouk camp, as well as several other military camps in the area and is positioning itself toward capturing the Green Plateau of Tripoli (Mahmoud, 2019)

The LNA sent military reinforcements to Ra's Lanuf and Es Sider oil ports, in anticipation of a counter-attack by the GNA. The GNA shot it down LNA warplane crashed in southern Tripoli, by a missile, fired by GNA forces from a suburb of Tripoli Hafters, report the GNA militia commander of planning to bring over 350 mercenaries to the capital to fight the LNA, he also stated that there were still 728 detained refugees residing in the camp. They accused the GNA of subjecting them to "years of much torture and suffering", reiterating their desire to leave the country entirely (DW, 2019).

On 15 April the escalation of the dispute between LNA and GNA forces in Ayn Zara suburb. The LNA military sent large reinforcements they arrived in LNA-controlled Gharyan. As a result of shelling on a building, 3 million books were destroyed as a result of shelling on a building belonging to the Libyan ministry of education(BBC,2019)

GNA forces were constantly advancing on all axes, managing to "defeat the aggressor force" and that they were able to "inflict on the aggressor militias huge casualty." He also accused the LNA of various war crimes. GNA head, Fayez al-Sarraj, vowed to have all LNA leaders and commanders involved in the offensive prosecuted. Bombardments of Tripoli with Grad rockets and missiles continued late-night shelling on April 15. Four people were reported dead.

The Tripoli-based internationally recognized government reported that a 5-year-old boy was killed, and his three siblings seriously injured, in shelling of the Tariq al-Soor neighbourhood; separately, a 66-year-old woman was killed, and two children were wounded, in the Abu Salim neighbourhood in southern Tripoli.

On April 17 UN spokesperson condemned the attacks; Tripoli witnessed the heaviest fighting since the outbreak of the clashes with indiscriminate rocket fire on a high-density neighbourhood in the Libyan capital, through 24 hours more than 4,500 displaced. Moreover, two GNA soldiers were killed by an LNA airstrike in Tripoli's Ayn Zara suburb.

On 18 April GNA units attempted to advance towards the Saadiya area, the LNA air force conducted multiple airstrikes on GNA targets in the area, executed LNA jets also conducted several air raids against GNA targets in Libya's Wadi al Rabie suburb(Kamal, 2019)

On 20 April LNA drone aircraft, allegedly supplied by the United Arab Emirates, they have struck the GNA military camp in Sabaa. On 30 April Recep Tayyip Erdoğan voiced his support for the GNA, also GNA forces captured the settlement of El-Sbeaa (Espiaa), south of Tripoli(Mashali, 2019)

On the first of May, an aircraft was shot down in al-Hira and the pilot was detained and he is from Portugal but the Portuguese Ministry of Defence mentions the pilot was not a Portuguese soldier. On 11 May Haftar advanced in Tripoli's southern districts, most notably the al-Aziziya area. The LNA also carried out airstrikes on several militia positions towards Sirte.

By 13 May, the GNA announced that Haftar's forces occupied both the Tripoli Airport and Gharyan, also occupied the areas in Tripoli Airport Road, Qasir Benghashir, and near Gharyan as well as in Sooq Al-Khamis. By 14 May, the LNA announced that their ground defences shot down a military aircraft of the GNA in the Jufra District, in central Libya (Deutsche Welle, 2019).

Russian military intervention in the embattled North African country, thousands of Russian mercenaries from the infamous mercenary Wagner Group have joined the conflict, signalling the Kremlin's intent to shape the result of Libya's long-running civil war. GNA, receiving barely lukewarm support from the U.S. and Europe, has accepted Turkish military aid. The war has been largely stalemated for months but is causing mounting civilian casualties and destabilizing other parts of the country, including areas where ISIS is active. Moscow is attempting to help Haftar's forces break the stalemate in Tripoli by deploying private military contractors (Ramy, 2019).

The Kremlin's interests in Libya include acquiring military based on the Mediterranean, inking economic deals to mitigate sanctions effects, and securing influence over hydrocarbon exports and migration flows that serve as another leverage point on Europe.

During the first of the year, Haftar has failed to even enter Tripoli after eight months of fighting with significant foreign support. Haftar's campaign to control Benghazi, and the eastern Libyan economy is a house of cards sustained by Russian-printed banknotes.

They used Kremlin counterterrorism as justification for establishing military positions. What should the U.S. do? in that situation to ending the various threats from Libya terrorism, mass migration and addressing the humanitarian crisis requires ending the war.

Europe, of course, has a greater interest in Libya, on migration, terrorism, and oil. But a deep divide between France and Italy on the Libya file will prevent any effective response (Heba, 2019)

The U.S. can take the first step by sharing the information about Haftar he holds U.S. citizenship and his continued protection of a commander accused of war crimes. also U.S has information about UAE about they support U.S can help Libya strengthen the GNA's economic institutions and keep the oil(Ali, 2019).

On 13 June, LNA forces successfully shot at a GNA warplane which was firing at their forces in Al-Dafiniya, west of Tripoli. On 26 June the GNA announced that it had captured the town of Gharyan from the LNA (Almasryalyoum, 2019). Dozens of LNA soldiers were killed in fighting in the town, the GNA's airforce attacked convoys of LNA troops as they withdrew from the area (Elbasset, 2019).

On 2 July GNA forces in Tajoura migrant centre airstrike by the LNA hit the Tajoura Detention they killed at least 53 of them and injured 130 others (Masrawy, 2019)

On 6 July the Popular Front for the Liberation of Libya had joined the LNA in its offensive (Enabbaladi, 2019). On 17 July Seham Sergiwa a parliamentary member for Benghazi was detained by the LNA a very strange situation overlapping forces Sudanese they sent 1000 Sudanese Rapid Support Forces (RSF) (Akhbarelyom, 2019)

On 29 July 2019, Ghassan Salamé, head of the United Nations Support Mission in Libya (UNSMIL), proposed a Libyan peace plan to the United Nations Security Council (UNSC), includes a truce between the Government of National Accord (GNA) and Libyan National Army (LNA) and their associated militias an international meeting of countries implicated in the conflict, to stop the fighting, implement the legally existing arms embargo, and promote the following of international human rights law, and a Libyan meeting similar to the originally planned Libyan National Conference (Li Xia, 2019)

Most Wanted Terrorist' Deadly Militant Hisham Ashmawi Extradited To Egypt from Libya one of the most-wanted Egyptian militants who were captured in neighbouring Libya last year has been transferred to Egypt. Egyptian media broadcast footage of Ashmawy arriving in Egypt on a military aircraft early, the Libyan armed forces handed over the terrorist Hisham Ashmawy to the Egyptian general intelligence". he did scores of terror attacks in Egypt.

A former officer with Egypt's Special Forces, Ashmawy left the army in 2012 and later joined Ansar Beit al-Maqdis which is based in the Sinai Peninsula. Hesham Ali Ashmawy Mos'ad Ibrahim, born in 1978 he is an Egyptian Islamist militant and former Egyptian Army officer in 1996 and eventually became an officer in the Thunderbolt unit. the Egyptian Army mention Hesham showed increasing signs of radicalization over the years, his accusations of spreading extremist thought and of incitement against the Egyptian Armed Forces led to his eventual dismissal from the military in 2011.

Then, he embraced al-Qaeda and went on to join Ansar Bait al-Maqdis in 2012, but eventually defected from the group in 2015, Hesham suspected by the government of orchestrating and being involved in a number of terrorist attacks on security targets and state institutions, because he did not like Sisi regime, which took power from the Muslim Brotherhood in Egypt.

After that, he has done many terrorist operations in the 2014 Farafra ambush, and in February 2015, he killed 29 Egyptian troops and injured 60 others. The Assassination of Prosecutor General Hisham Barakat. He is especially wanted in Egypt because of his involvement in 17 terrorist operations which killed dozens of army and police officers. The most important of these was the targeting of the 101st battalion in al-Arish.

The declaration of allegiance to the Islamic State of Iraq and the Levant. He formed instead his own network, al-Mourabitoun, which based itself in Libya and remained loyal to al-Qaeda. Ashmawy is believed to have gone to Libya in 2013, before Maqdis pledged allegiance to the Islamic State group in November 2014, becoming one of Egypt's most wanted terrorists. He is operating alongside Emad al-Din Abdel Hamid, another army officer-turned-jihadist chief.

Ashmawy was captured by Haftar's forces in October 2018 in the city of Derna, east of Libya after that Egypt's President Abdel Fattah al-Sisi had previously asked for the jihadist leader to be handed over.

On 8 October 2018, Ahmed al-Mismari, spokesman of the Libyan National Army (LNA), announced the capturing of Ashmawy during a surprise operation by a unit of the 106th Mujahfal Brigade in the mountainous al-Maghar district of Derna.

Then, Nasser Ahmed al-Najdi, commander of the LNA's Battalion 169, told Asharq Al-Awsat that the operation was the result of intelligence sharing between Egypt's government and the LNA under the command of General Khalifa Haftar. After that, Egypt's President had asked for the jihadist leader to be handed over.

In addition, months after a tunnel network was uncovered in Derna during a battle between LNA forces and the Shura Council of Mujahideen for control of the city. Ashmawy was using that network to move around between cities in the region.

The Libyan authorities said in their statement that Ashmawy would be extradited to Egypt following investigations. Haftar did this because he wanted Egypt to support him to control Tripoli this means the Libyan National Army (LNA) is backed by Egypt and the United Arab Emirates (AlAshry, 2019 June 1)

US Shifts Course On Libya

Trump officials have snubbed strongman Khalifa Haftar as the US shifts course on Libya. Less than two months after Trump appeared to show support for Haftar in a surprise phone call, the US is now rethinking its policy towards the country's civil war, according to multiple sources in the US and the region.

For now, US officials insist that Trump's phone call to Haftar was a personal favour to the Egyptian president, Abdul Fatah al-Sisi, who was visiting Washington a few days earlier and did not signify a shift in US policy, because of al-Sisi support Haftar. Haftar's offensive stalled on the outskirts of Tripoli, and the lead on Libya policy has been handed back to the state department. Secretary of state Mike Pompeo has been consulting Libya experts in the past two weeks and is considering a range of options, including a US-enforced ceasefire.

A call to encouraged on15 April, Haftar want to get a visit by the field marshal to Libyan National Army (LNA) hired lobbyists in Washington Marshal is a dual Libyan-US national, or one of his top aides, to reinforce the impression that he had US backing in his offensive against the UN-backed government in Tripoli. Jonathan Winer a former US envoy on Libya said "State and defense were not aware of the Trump call, let alone supported it."

Ahmed Maiteeg, the deputy prime minister of the Tripoli government, mention to NBC News on Thursday that," Trump-Haftar call was confusing, "we see the US government as our main ally".

There are two roads in Libya, the first one Qatar and Turkey, has lined up behind Sarraj but Egypt, the UAE, and Saudi Arabia have all taken a stake in Haftar.

Haftar thinks on that time that the US will support him, he thought to have been a potential game-changer in diplomatic moves that are so far yet to take shape. On the other hand, France has voiced support for Haftar's military efforts against jihadist groups in Libya, but they didn't support him in the Tripoli offensive, in addition, Haftar's fighting with all force to control Tripoli.

The House foreign affairs committee has called for the justice department and FBI to investigate war crimes allegedly committed by Haftar and the LNA. But Haftar's said he should kill ISIS and extricate the country from foreign military entanglements.

According to that, he made on Thursday conducted an airstrike for a second night on the military section of the only functioning airport of the Libyan capital. Civilian air traffic from Tripoli's Mitiga airport has continued despite the war, they attacked the military part of the airport, targeting a "Turkish plane,"

Sarraj situations

The crisis escalated between Haftar and Sarraj, Haftar's forces remain a potent threat to Fayez al-Sarraj every one wants the power which each lay claim to rule the country, they attempt to strike a ceasefire between both sides, have so far failed, and regional powers backing Haftar and Sarraj appear more intransigent than ever. Sarraj, who heads the Tripoli-based Government of National Accord, will start a series of meetings with the leaders of Italy, Germany, France, and possibly Britain. Sarraj's government will meet President Emmanuel Macron comes after the GNA repeatedly accused Paris of politically backing the assault which Haftar's self-styled Libyan National Army (LNA) launched on Tripoli on 4 April (AlAshry, 2019 June 11)

Al-Sarraj Launch A Peace Initiative

Fayez al-Sarraj, Chairman of the Presidential Council of Libya and prime minister of the Government of National Accord (GNA) of Libya, launched a peace initiative aimed at stabilizing the civil war-stricken country is a welcome move. He suggested setting up a national peace forum with help from the UN, to be followed by simultaneous presidential and parliamentary elections.

He thinks this will bring him peace to Libya, on the same time Khalifa Haftar fighting in Tripoli he killed nearly 700 by the fighting, nightly bombing raids, and prolonged electricity outages, Libya has been in danger of slipping down the international agenda, leading to backers of both sides pouring arms into the country and possibly entrenching the civil war.

The conflict in Libya started in 2011 the country descended into chaos after protests against

Muammar Qadhafi also the NATO invasion helped oust Qadhafi, but neither the foreign powers nor their local allies managed to fill the vacuum left by the regime that had been in power for four decades.

The second conflict between Hafta and al-Sarraj based in Tobruk he gets his support from the Libyan National Army, he has captured huge swathes of territory, while the Tripoli government, which has international recognition, is defended by a host of militias, including Islamist groups. Haftar claims he is fighting terror groups and wants to unify Libya under his leadership, while al-Sarraj says his government is legitimate.

The current crisis was triggered when Haftar moved his troops to Tripoli to oust the government of al-Sarraj, he wants to take the power Without thinking about the civilian population. Hundreds of people have already been killed, but both sides have refused to agree to a ceasefire despite international calls.

Haftar's gets his support from Egypt, Saudi Arabia, and the UAE, while Turkey and Qatar back the Tripoli government. This means the division of the Middle East a group of countries united to control the Middle East to ensure their stay in power.

Al-Sarraj's offer could be a new beginning only if a ceasefire is reached, and we have to respect him he wants the power but without killing anyone. the war will not change the regime country, changing a regime using force could be easy as the example like what happened in Iraq 2003, we have to think rebuilding a new state is not easy, it can't be done with the aid of military power (AlAshry, 2019 June 29).

Attack on Libya Detention Center

Attacked on Libya Detention Center with the bombing of a Libyan migrant detention centre that left more than 44 dead and more than 130 severely injured, the United Nations describing the attack as "a war crime and odious bloody carnage".

The centre that was bombed by two airstrikes in the east of Tripoli was housing and left the detention centre a charred ruin. The LNA warned that it was stepping up air raids on the capital in response to recent military reverses, the result of the bombing left more than 610 people dead.

Libya's UN-recognised Government of National Accord (GNA) and the Italian interior minister, Matteo Salvini, blamed Khalifa Haftar for the bombing they said that since April 4, 2019 hundreds of people have died.

The UN secretary-general, António Guterres, called for an independent investigation into the "outrageous" bombing. UN spokesman Stéphane Dujarric said the secretary-general condemned "this horrendous incident in the strongest terms".

They claimed that Haftar was responsible for that bombing because the detention centre is close to a military supply depot for militia working to protect the GNA.

But Gen Khaled el-Mahjoub, a spokesman for the LNA, denied targeting the detention centre, saying "We didn't give orders to target the shelter," he also mentions that we had warned that as part of "exhausting all traditional means" to capture Tripoli, LNA would conduct "strong and decisive airstrikes" against select targets.

UN refugee agency had previously called for people to be removed from the detention centre in Tajoura, they mention we are expressing fears that they were likely to be victims of air raids being mounted by Haftar's air force.

Ghassan Salamé UN special envoy for Libya said, "This attack clearly could constitute a war crime, as it killed by surprise innocent people whose dire conditions forced them to be in that shelter," and we will put pressure on Haftar's backers, notably the United Arab Emirates and Egypt, to withdraw their support, or at least demand an end to the nightly air raids (Al Ashry, 2019).

Middle East Countries Cooperate to Support Stability in Libya

War has been raging on in Libya for more than six months in 2019 with General Khalifa Haftar's forces to take over the Libyan capital Tripoli has now turned into a battle of attrition. Over than 992 people have been killed, more than 3,000 injured and some 90,000 displaced from their homes. Thousands of residential buildings have been damaged or destroyed due to indiscriminate shelling.

We can see there has been no clear winner. Factions aligned with the Government of National Accord (GNA) have managed to stop the advance of Haftar's forces and killed his hopes for a quick victory in Tripoli.

Through this moment neither the GNA nor Haftar are willing to back down nor agree to a ceasefire. All of them want the power the UN Security Council has also been unable to reach a consensus on any resolution that would end the fighting and restart the negations process. On account of the international community remains divided on Libya, with regional and world powers backing each of the two sides and further fuelling the conflict.

The UN has put a lot of effort into trying to bring the ongoing civil war in Libya to a peaceful resolution. In addition, UN representatives still insisted that a political solution must be pursued.

Haftar's forces launched their offensive in April until now, he also adamant in his stance and says that he is not ready to commit to any ceasefire or political process, whether backed by the UN or any other political actor.

He seems bound on continuing his assault on Tripoli, it appears that a political solution to the conflict is very much unlikely. The only way the fighting can come to an end is if one of the sides achieves a conclusive military victory.

Various regional and international players are intervening in Libya with the hope of securing a victory for the side they favour.

But on what side, the first side, Libya would be doomed to a one-man military rule it will be like Egypt. Also, Haftar will take the capital, and then he would effectively have control over Libya's important strategic assets oil, the political centre, and its key institutions. On the second side, the country would still have a chance to pursue a political solution. If all the Middle East governments cooperated to overcome Haftar's positions politically and militarily from the west and south, this would significantly weaken him (AlAshry, 2019 August 21).

MIRAL SABRY ALASHRY

Germany Organizes Libya Conference to Shore up Arms Embargo

Germany's Foreign Minister, Heiko Maas, confirmed Germany will set up an UN-backed conference aiming at stopping arms trafficking to Libya and reimpose the arms embargo. The international conference on the future of Libya attempt to force many regional actors to stop funding and arming the country's warring sides.

The UN has admitted its strengthened arms embargo on the country has been totally ignored by a range of countries. Also, the UN envoy for Libya, Ghassan Salame, said "It remains abundantly clear that without the commitment of key external actors engaged in Libya, the conflict will continue." Without mentioning them by name, Salame was mainly pointing to Turkey and the United Arab Emirates.

In addition, he has mentioned the view of the international role of the many regional actors, the war will continue indefinably, possibly turning the country into a new Syria. Heiko Maas hinted at the problems ahead in terms of the aims and guest list for the conference. Maas said, there is still a lot of work before we can have such a conference. But we have started working on a process because "Germany wants to launch a consultation process with all relevant actors."

In the past there were two previous conferences, one in Palermo and another in Paris, which failed to bring about any breakthrough before Haftar the military commander in the east of Libya, tried to capture the capital, Tripoli, this is the seat of the UN-recognized government.

Salamé address to the UN security council called for a three-stage process in the future conference firstly local ceasefires, secondly, a national conference finally, a national meeting inside Libya.

Maas stressed has been touring European and Middle East capitals in support of his conference plan. Salamé told the Security Council: "It remains abundantly clear that without the commitment of key external actors engaged in Libya, the conflict will continue."

The UN panel of experts was investigating over 40 cases of arms embargo breaches of varying magnitude, "There have been no interdiction or searches conducted at sea, despite such activities being authorized by UN resolutions.

The aims of the conference were to send a strong message on the need for respect of the arms embargo, to commit to non-interference in Libyan affairs and to address the main causes of conflict as formulated by the Libyans themselves and to emphasize its clear and active support for whatever political formula the Libyans agree to (AlAshry, 2019 September 19).

The US Kills IS Leader Abu Bakr Al-Baghdadi

Donald Trump has announced the Islamic State leader, al-Baghdadi, has been killed in a raid by US special forces on his Syrian safe house, he detonated his suicide vest after fleeing into a tunnel, chased by US military dogs. The operation was conducted on the night in the province of Idlib it takes two-hour, it's one of the few areas of the country still outside Syrian regime control. Trump said, Baghdadi detonated a suicide vest and killed himself and three of his children, "He died like a dog, he died like a coward the world is now a much safer place," This made ISIS forces retreat in Libya (AlAshry, 2019 October 28).

Libyan Refugees in Crisis

Hundreds of thousands of Libyan are suffering from war, they are living in unsafe conditions with little or no access to health care, essential medicines, food, safe drinking water, shelter, or education. An estimated 1.3 million people are in need of humanitarian assistance in Libya.

The country presents a complex displacement scenario with 217,002 people displaced inside the country (IDPs) and 278,559 people who have returned home (returnees). Every day there are launching precision missiles that killed at least 53 refugees housed in a Libyan refugee detention centre near Tripoli, one of the worst single atrocities of the Libyan civil war.

In November 2019, the former British ambassador to Libya, Peter Millett, to call on the UN security council to discuss at the ambassadorial level how outside powers are prolonging the conflict in Libya and extending the suffering of the Libyan people. Libya also hosts 43,113 refugees and asylum-seekers who are registered with UNHCR. Refugees are travelling alongside migrants through dangerous routes towards Europe. Up to 90 per cent of people crossing the Mediterranean Sea to Europe depart from Libya so that it's a very difficult situation. According to the number of refugees if this war continues much longer Libya will have become a failed state, and the responsibility will lie with the outside powers."

Hence the responsibility lies with Turkey was the third country pouring arms into Libya in support of the UN-backed Government of the National Accord which has been under attack in Tripoli from Libyan warlord Khalifa Haftar's forces, the Libyan National Army. Libya is subject to a UN arms embargo.

The last incident due to the coordinates of the detention centre had been given to Haftar's forces so the strike against the detention centre was either the product of a dreadful accident or a terrible crime. The army used a foreign jet launched the guided weapon on behalf of the Libyan National Army, there is an unknown number of Mirage 2000-9 fighter jets were operating from two airbases inside Libya at the time of the strike." The two airbases are named Al Khadim and Al Jufra. Furthermore, Haftar's air force does not have the equipment or ordinance types to support the operation of such aircraft.

Only the UAE and Egypt have the Mirage 2000-9 jets in the region all of them support the region of Libya. Also, the Militia supporting the UN-recognized Government of National Accord based in Tripoli had an arms supply dump near to the detention centre.

We can see all of the forces are fighting Libya from inside and outside the country thousands of citizens die every day and the European Commission and UNHCR do not help them, Libyan refugees need to advocate for alternatives to detention, including care arrangements for children and family tracing. They also need centres to provide humanitarian assistance and advocate for enhanced access to screening, identification, and registration (AlAshry, 2019 November 8).

More than 400 people, who came to the Tripoli gathering and departure facility in October from Abu Salim detention centre in the south of the country, without food for weeks.

The UN has been accused of trying to starve out refugees who are sheltering for protection inside a centre run by the UN refugee agency in Tripoli. According to a recent assessment by the International Organization for Migration said, in the camp, there are 100 minors, they are "currently starving" apart from some food that other refugees manage to sneak out of another part of the centre. The refugees said they received food assistance a couple of weeks ago.

Most of the refugees tried to reach Europe by crossing the Mediterranean but were returned to Libya by the EU-backed Libyan coastguard. As stated by the UNHCR is planning to withdraw food from 600 other refugees and migrants in the centre – who include survivors of bombings, torture. this is will gain more violence.

After the war in 2011, an estimated 1.3 million people need humanitarian assistance in Libya. They are living in unsafe conditions with little or no access to health care, essential medicines, food, safe drinking water, shelter, or education.

The Guardian got documentation circulated among UN staff on Tuesday, the agency said it would "phase out" food catering from 31 December. The document said the information should not be made public before mid-December, when 230 more refugees have been evacuated to other countries, in order to prevent disruption. After that, the facility will no longer be used as a transit centre, the document said until the remaining refugees and migrants "vacate voluntarily".

Also, the UNHCR said that it would continue to finance cleaning in the centre after the withdrawal of food, partly to "prevent the reputational risk of having deficient/broken toilets and showers". In addition, they will make a healthcare clinic on the site that would continue to operate.

UNHCR will make food withdrawal include 400 survivors they are booked on 3 July Tajoura detention centre bombing, in which at least 53 refugees and migrants were killed after an airstrike hit the hall in which they were being held.

On the other hand, if they are forced to leave and fend for themselves in Tripoli "it will be a very dangerous scenario". Refugees are frightened of forced recruitment by militias, being caught up in the ongoing civil war, or being kidnapped anew by traffickers. also, they will die from the war that kills thousands of citizens every day.

Though there are other possible scenarios these include that Libya's department for combating illegal migration (DCIM) "moves in and forcibly removes all the migrants/asylum-seekers to detention centres", or that it turns the facility into a detention centre run by its own guards.

The aims of the UN-run it offers immediate protection and safety for vulnerable refugees in need of urgent evacuation and is an alternative to detention for hundreds of refugees currently trapped in Libya so that it's time to save refugees in Libya (AlAshry, 2019 November 29).

Russian intervention in Libya, America intercepts

Russia's role in helping President Assad secure victory in Syria's civil war has emboldened Moscow to expand its operations into Libya, on the other side the U.S knows about their aims as they warned in an interview.

Because Russia is tipping the scales in Libya in favour of the military leader, Khalifa Haftar, this appears to have prompted the US to issue a strong warning to the general to pull back.

Interior Minister Fathi Bashagha said, the Russians succeeded in Syria, so they think they will be successful in Libya, I think it's time for the U.S. to exert more diplomatic muscle to end the civil war in the oil-rich North African nation. also, Moscow will exploit the situation and expand its presence in the Mediterranean beyond the sole naval base it operates in the Syrian port of Tartus.

In addition, the US has been accused of taking little interest in the eight months of fighting on the outskirts of Tripoli that began when Haftar's Libyan National Army mounted an assault on Tripoli, Hafter killed a thousand civilians this provoking a fierce counter-offensive by militia forces supporting the Government of National Accord (GNA).

There are some countries that support the strong man Haftar for example Qatar and Turkey and they are backing forces loyal to the GNA while Egypt, the United Arab Emirates, and — at least at times — the Trump administration have supported anti-jihadi rebel leader Khalifa Haftar.

There are US special forces in Libya, but they are dedicated to fighting Islamic State not to help civilians that need them to be involved rather than siding with the government.

A US official said, "The Government of National Accord's delegation expressed grave concerns regarding the security situation and its effect on the civilian population. Thousands of civilians, children, and women have been killed and many in the refugee camp look to Europe to open the door for them."

Libyans have suffered from torture, rape, and murder inside Tripoli's refugee detention camps and they want to prove their deployment of Wagner to Libya. More than 300,000 people have been displaced.

Furthermore, the United States calls on the Libyan National Army to end its offensive on Tripoli, this will facilitate further US-Libya cooperation to prevent undue foreign interference, reinforce legitimate state authority, and address the issues underlying the conflict.

US government agencies underscored support for Libya's sovereignty and territorial integrity in the face of Russia's attempts to exploit the conflict against the will of the Libyan people. This support may be the result of undeclared and directed interests in the past US has appeared neutral by calling for a ceasefire rather than urging one side to withdraw.

It remains to be seen if this new political support is not countermanded in a tweet by the president, Donald Trump, and whether the statement leads to practical US pressure either on Haftar or his sponsoring allies to pull back.

So that, the GNA appears to have persuaded the US that Russia wants to install an authoritarian government in Libya that will brush aside plans prepared by the UN special envoy, as Russia wants to control the Middle East (AlAshry, 2019 November 19).

Greece Expel Libyan Ambassador

Greece has called for the expulsion of the Libyan ambassador in an escalation of a dispute over a controversial deal signed between Libya's UN-supported government and Turkey on maritime boundaries in the Mediterranean.

According to, Nikos Dendias, Greek foreign minister "in the morning we called the ambassador, Mohamed Younis AB Menfi, to be informed of the decision, we given him 72 hours to leave the country." Turkey's foreign minister condemned the move as outrageous. The direct talks between the Turkish President, Recep Tayyip Erdoğan, and the Greek Prime Minister, Kyriakos Mitsotakis, on the margins of the NATO summit, failed to resolve the row over the sudden Turkish-Libyan claim to an exclusive economic zone.

Under the terms of a deal reached between Libya and Turkey on November 27, Turkey gets access to a zone across the Mediterranean, ignoring the objections of Greece, Cyprus, and Egypt.

On the other hand, Mitsotakis said, the claim had no legal basis and insisted it would collapse. The Greek parliament statement noted,"They are oblivious to history and geography as they do not take Greek islands into account," adding that Ankara's move had pushed the NATO country into "unprecedented diplomatic isolation".

The Libyan foreign minister said Greece's diplomatic move was unacceptable. The row is part of a long-running dispute between Turkey and Greece over drilling rights in the Mediterranean, as well as a byproduct of the need of the Libyan UN-recognised government in Tripoli to remain close to Turkey as one of the few outside actors backing its effort to hold on to the capital.

There are a host of issues between Greece and Turkey over ranging from mineral rights in the Aegean Sea to the future of a reunified Cyprus. Also, the tensions are running high because of Turkish drilling off Cyprus, and the EU has prepared sanctions against Turkey in response.

Moreover, Cyprus will take Turkey to the international court of justice in the Hague, and has enlisted the support of the EU. But Greece has said it will not tolerate any drilling southeast of Crete and has warned it will send its naval forces to prevent such a move if necessary. These issues result in bad relations between countries.

Turkey claims the UN convention on the law of the sea allows a country to stretch its territorial waters by 12 nautical miles out to sea, this gives a right to fishing, mining, and drilling, the area can extend for an additional 200 miles. Further, if the maritime distance between the two countries is less than 424 miles, a bilateral deal, such as the one it has struck with Libya, is needed to determine a mutually agreed-upon dividing line for their respective exclusive economic zones. The controversy comes from here in the interest of these escalating political developments.

The deal between Turkish and Libyan is largely designed as a legal defence against Cypriot and Greek claims to the waters. Nowadays Libya is diplomatically dependent on Turkey, but on the other hand, the Tripoli government is taking a risk if it alienates key partners in the EU.

According to that deal, Turkey supported the Tripoli government with arms, as the United Arab Emirates and Egypt have been providing direct military support to the warlord Field Marshal Khalifa Haftar, who is mounting an increasingly effective effort to dislodge the GNA (AlAshry, 2019 December 9).

UN Security Council Warns Libya to Stop, After Arms Embargo

The United Nations Security Council called all countries to implement an arms embargo on Libya and to stay out of the conflict after U.N. sanctions monitors accused Jordan, the United Arab Emirates, and Turkey of repeated violations.

These three countries routinely and sometimes blatantly supplied weapons with little effort to disguise the source. It is also likely to link the UAE to a bombing of a detention centre that has been described as a war crime.

UN already accused of overseeing a new age of impunity, the findings are a further test of the organization's ability to enforce its own resolutions. In addition, the U.N. experts monitoring the implementation of sanctions on Libya reported last month said, " Jordan, the United Arab Emirates and Turkey have repeatedly violated an arms embargo on Libya also the foreign attack aircraft is responsible for a deadly strike on a migrant detention centre.

The U.N. missions of Jordan and Turkey did not immediately respond to a Reuters request for comment at the time on the accusations. According to that indictment, the United Arab Emirates said it was "firmly committed to complying with its obligations under the Libya sanctions regime and all relevant Security Council resolutions."

Ghassan Salame, the UN special envoy for Libya, said in Libya the arms embargo had been violated at least 45 times since 4 April 2019 when Haftar wants to occupy Tripoli by foreign powers in Libya – diplomatically and militarily – was now the biggest obstacle to peace in the country, and divisions in the UN security council meant the UN had been unable even to call for a ceasefire. Moreover, Haftar had sanctioned 800 drone strikes, and the Tripoli-based government more than 270.

On the other hand, the country responsible for a particularly egregious air assault on the Tajoura refugee detention centre on 2 July 2019 that led to 54 deaths, but it will make it clear the attack used weapons available only to a foreign power.

Salame mentioned we hoped to address the issue of external intervention by convening a final round of pre-meetings that would lead to a Libyan peace conference in Berlin it will organize it on 2020, attended by the security council members plus Turkey, Italy, the UAE, Egypt, and others.

The aims of the conference will be to extract a commitment from all the external actors not to interfere further and to set up a permanent international body to monitor and enforce the agreements reached in Berlin. after that, the UN weapons experts' report is produced annually and is subject to delays as member states wrangle about the contents.

In Libya they have two sides, the first one with UAE, Jordan, and Egypt has been arming troops deployed by Haftar, the eastern Libyan military leader before the UN launched a carefully constructed peace conference. The second side, with Turkey that has been supplying weapons to Libya's UN-recognised government of national accord.

The war had been stuck in a stalemate in Tripoli suburbs, the recent intervention of hundreds of Russian mercenaries had tipped the balance heavily towards Haftar. Russian intervention meant the war would spread to the centre of Tripoli, this will be leading to a bloodbath.

In addition, the Libyan foreign minister, Mohamed Syala, said there was a real risk that Tripoli would fall to the Russian-led forces, adding, "The problem is Russia declares one thing and then on the field does something else. Certainly, for Russia, Libya has strategic importance and seeks to have a foothold in the country." In addition, the UN experts' report was completed before the Russian intervention but does highlight the role of mercenaries from Sudan and elsewhere (AlAshry, 2019 December 12, 2019).

MIRAL SABRY ALASHRY

Mercenaries Arrivaled to Raise Fears

A new wave of mercenaries from Sudan is fighting in Libya this month, deepening concerns that the conflict in the North African state has descended into an intractable international war that could destabilize much of the region.

The groups were fighting with the Libyan National Army (LNA) led by General Khalifa Haftar against the internationally recognized government in Tripoli. There are more than 3,000 Sudanese mercenaries now fighting in Libya, significantly more than most previous estimates.

UN said the interference of fighters from Sudan in Libya was a direct threat to the security of the war-torn country. A UN panel of experts said in a 376-page report to the security council that the presence of the Sudanese has become more marked in 2019 and may lead to further instability. Hafter said that his forces were preparing for a "decisive battle" to take full control of the city. he started this war in April aimed at capturing Tripoli but the offensive stalled, leaving both sides dug in and shelling one another along the city's southern reaches with increasingly sophisticated weapons.

Some of the biggest Sudanese groups based in Libya once fought in Darfur, the restive western region of Sudan, in a series of insurgencies against militia and troops sent by the repressive regime in Khartoum. In addition, Jordan, Turkey and the United Arab Emirates routinely and sometimes blatantly supplied weapons, with little effort to disguise the source" in violation of a UN arms embargo. But "neither side has the military capability to effectively decide the outcome to their advantage.

The Sudanese mercenary commanders said the new wave of recruits included many who had fought against the rule of Omar al-Bashir, who was deposed in April when Sudan's military withdrew their support after months of popular protests.

The aims of the Sudanese mercenary commanders said the new wave of recruits included many who had fought against the rule of Omar al-Bashir, who was deposed in April when Sudan's military withdrew their support after months of popular protests, so their aims to fight with Hafter.

On the other hand, most of them had been recruited in Darfur in recent months while others had travelled from there to Libya to enlist, they also want to return to Sudan to fight against the current transitional government, installed after al-Bashir's fall. One of them said, "I know that we are mercenaries and we are not fighting with honour and dignity. but this is temporary, we will go back home after we are done with our mission here," also "no timetable" for leaving Libya but that any stay was temporary.

Mercenaries are there to have a secure base and to get weapons and other military logistics then they will go back to Sudan. According to that, the new influx of recruits could be a significant destabilising factor in the long term. They are coming in to earn money. It could be one year, two years or more but eventually, the conflict will cool off. At some point, they will start to return home to Sudan. But where is the future to Libya still, they will have a war there are also claims that a large contingent of Sudanese fighters from the feared paramilitary Rapid Support Forces (RSF) was deployed to Libya at the request of Hafter?

A thousand Sudanese troops from the RSF, which has been accused of major atrocities earlier this year and in Darfur, were deployed to Libya on 25 July 2019 by Mohamed Hamdan Dagalo, a warlord turned senior official also known as Hemedti. The Sudanese mercenaries are also involved in smuggling and other activities. Moreover, LNA supports them to smuggle migrants hoping to travel to Europe across the frontier between Sudan and Libya, and the hostile desert. Sudanese troops played a crucial role in "liberating" the oilfields seized by Hafter's forces. The claim is corroborated by previous reports from the UN panel of experts who said Sudanese mercenaries helped the LNA secure the country's strategic "oil crescent" (AlAshry.2019 December 27).

Chapter (10)

✳

Intervention (2020)

This chapter describes Turkey Support Libyan government, Putin, Erdogan Urge Libyan parties to start a ceasefire, the first step of pace with the Berlin Conference after that the government deploys warships to enforce Libya arms. In the middle of the year, UN envoy Ghassan Salame quit, after that Libya Records first Covid-19 Case has spread at the same time the Covid-19 spread in the world, and few infections have occurred in Libya, UAE Gives Libyan Army An Israeli Air Defense System, UN Libya mission 'Alarmed' by rising In violence, European Union sent statement calls for a humanitarian truce in Libya, Haftar ends Skhirat political agreement, Moreover, Russian foreign interventions and the war between Turkey and Egypt.

Turkey Support Libyan Government

In the first year of 2020, Turkey's entry to Libya, the historical conflict between Libya and the Ottoman Empire through the coastal areas of Libya during the mid-16th century, and had made a great impact on the society of Libya, and known as Tripolitania under the Ottomans. In the 18th century, Ahmed Karamanli founded the semi-independence Karamanli dynasty, which ruled Libya and still acknowledged Ottoman control.

Libya was one of the most prosperous parts of the empire with strong Libyan characters, in the late 18th century, and the Barbary Wars launched by the United States only ensured the complete collapse of Karamanli authority. In the end, until the Italian conquest, Ottoman rule in Libya was secured, but it was neglected from the mainland due to its lack of development.

When the war started in 2011 was among the first to immediately cut ties with Libya, demanding Gaddafi to quit the Government and Turkey would offer him in exile. At that time Gaddafi refused to do so and Turkey threw its support to anti-Gaddafi forces, notably National Transitional Council in July 2011.

Then Turkey took the chance since the collapse of Gaddafi's regime and Gaddafi's death,

Turkey has, together with Qatar, played an instrumental role in promoting Islamist Government in Libya, but was soon interrupted by the rise of anti-Islamist Khalifa Haftar.

They returned again in December 2019 Turkey has underlined its willingness to send troops to Libya to defend the country's UN-recognised government against General Khalifa Haftar, the eastern Libyan military warlord who is thought to be planning a decisive assault on the government of national accord in Tripoli.

They support Libya with a bill that allows troops to be deployed to Libya in support of the Tripoli-based government in the country's worsening civil war according to that Turkey's parliament has approved by a large majority, the vote taken during a special sitting, comes amid fears that the threat of Turkish intervention, in addition to that by other regional competitors, could intensify violence in Libya. MPs voted 325-184 in favour of the deployment.

This is intended to putting pressure on rival eastern forces in Libya led by Gen Khalifa Haftar who have been challenging Fayez al-Sarraj's internationally recognized Government of National Accord.

On the other side, the emergence of a new potential front for confrontation in a region where Turkey is flexing its diplomatic and military muscle against rivals including Egypt and the United Arab Emirates supports Khalifa Haftar because they see that the war in the Middle East was caused by Turkey.

In addition, the vote it was disclosed that the US president, Donald Trump, had also discussed the situation in Libya with Erdoğan, in a phone call in which the two "stressed the importance of diplomacy in resolving regional issues". Also, Erdoğan is expected to discuss Libya with the Russian president, Vladimir Putin, next week. In order that the Turkish decision was quickly criticized by Egypt, one of the key backers of Haftar's forces, which said in a statement it "strongly condemned" the plan.

During that time Turkish support for the GNA government led by Fayez al Serraj has until now been limited to drones and armaments, and it would be a major escalation to send ground troops to defend Tripoli. On the other side, Turkey's foreign minister, Mevlüt Çavuşoğlu, said no formal request for troops has yet been made by the GNA, but added: "sending troops is the easiest way".

All the time Haftar claims to be removing Islamist terrorists from Tripoli. His opponents describe him as a war criminal that will snuff out any chance of democracy in Libya. Therefore, Haftar's assault was launched in April, but until now has been bogged down in the suburbs of the capital, the conflict has been made more complex by the arrival of 200 Russian mercenaries backing Haftar, an intervention that Serraj is highlighting to drum up support for his government in Washington.

After that more than 28 people have been killed in an attack on a military academy in the Libyan capital of Tripoli, the government's health minister said. Also, there has been an increase in airstrikes and shelling around Tripoli in recent weeks, with fears that fighting could escalate further after Turkey's parliament voted to allow a troop deployment in support of the GNA.

On Saturday the forces allied with the GNA described the attack on the military camp at Al-Hadhba as "an aerial bombing" launched by their eastern rivals. Hamid bin Omar, health minister for the GNA, said the number of dead and wounded was still rising. Tripoli ambulance service spokesman Osama Ali said some body parts could not be immediately counted by forensic experts. Emergency teams withdrew after coming under fire while trying to access the area (AlAshry, 2020 January 6).

Putin, Erdogan Urge Libyan Parties to Start Ceasefire

On April 4, Khalifa Haftar ordered his Libyan National Army to advance to the capital, Tripoli, where the internationally recognized government is based. The LNA says its aim is to restore security and fight armed gangs and "ISIS". According to that LNA made advances elsewhere in Libya, a situation likely to have spurred Haftar on to seek military control of the whole country.

On the other side, Prime Minister Fayez al-Serraj of the UN-backed Government of National Accord (GNA) has vowed to defend Tripoli, accusing Haftar – who is popular in the city of Benghazi for his role in driving out Islamists – of launching a coup.

Since April, the forces of Hafter have pursued a withering offensive on the environs of the capital, Tripoli, locked in a battle of attrition with militias loyal to the U.N.-recognized Government of National Accord.

More than a half-year of drone strikes, artillery bombardments, while the fighting has led to hundreds of deaths, displaced more than 140,000 civilians.

The conflict started when Turkish President Erdogan signed an agreement with Serraj's government over maritime borders in the eastern Mediterranean, where Ankara is seeking a greater share of the region's underwater resources.

On the other hand, the foreign ministers of France, Greece, Egypt, and Cyprus, though, declared Erdogan's pact with the GNA "null and void" because it adjudicates over the territory where the latter three countries have competing claims and also hope to seek exploration rights.

The strategic mess in Libya smacks when foreign powers jostled for influence in resource-rich lands consumed by political turmoil.

The Europeans, meanwhile, have tried to force reconciliation, to minimal effect. German Foreign Minister Heiko Maas said, Libya cannot become a second Syria and so we need rapidly to enter a political process, an agreement on an effective cease-fire and an arms embargo." But within Europe, there appear to be disagreements over the way forward, with France seen to be more supportive of Hafter.

In addition, Erdogan met with Russian President Vladimir Putin and jointly announced a cease-fire. Europe's engagement with Libya has lost ground to the efforts of both the Russians and the Turks.

Moreover, the Europeans and Americans let this conflict drag on from April 2019 until it reached a stalemate, which allowed the Russians to step in, with a few hundred mercenaries on the ground, and make a difference.

It's hardly certain, that any of Libya's factions will recognize the Russian-Turkish cease-fire. Hafter draws more direct support from Egypt and the UAE. While still in power, both the

Emiratis and Qataris, there are in violation of a U.N. arms embargo. His scolding clearly did not have the necessary effect.

Turkish President Recep Tayyip Erdogan and his Russian counterpart Vladimir Putin have called for a ceasefire to end the conflict in Libya. After talks in Istanbul, Erdogan and Putin said the ceasefire should come into force. The call came amid a warning by German Foreign Minister Heiko the situation will become the same as a Syrian-style and we do not want refugees again.

Turkey sent troops to the North African state to bolster the embattled UN-backed government. On the other hand, Turkey accuses Russia of having about 2,500 mercenaries in Libya to support the UN-backed administration's main rival, Haftar. Russia denies the allegation.

Italian Prime Minister Giuseppe Conte met Gen Haftar in the Italian city of Rome. also, he should meet Prime Minister Fayez al-Serraj. Government sources told the Reuters news agency that it appeared Mr al-Serraj called off the meeting after being incorrectly told that the Italians wanted him to meet Gen Haftar during the trip to solve the crisis. Maas mentioned, "We want to avoid Libya becoming the scene of proxy wars,". "Libya cannot become a second Syria so that we need rapidly to enter a political process, an agreement on an effective ceasefire and an arms embargo". Hundreds of refugees are under siege and have no support also hundreds of refugees and asylum seekers evacuated from Libyan detention centers to a transit camp in Rwanda are to be resettled this year in Norway

Rwanda's foreign minister Vincent Biruta said, Norway and Sweden had so far agreed to resettle people from the camp, Biruta added. Norway agreed to resettle 600 people, while Sweden had so far accepted seven.

According to the latest figures, Rwanda signed a deal with the UN and African Union in September aimed at resettling people who had been detained in Libya while trying to reach Europe. More than 4,000 people are believed to still be living in Libyan detention centres (AlAshry, 2020 January 12).

Berlin Conference

The German government has invited the warring parties in the North African country and their foreign supporters to the chancellery in Berlin. They hope to end the war, they are seeking to achieve stability for the whole region.

The German governments did that through the long-term goal is "a sovereign Libya" and an "inner-Libyan reconciliation process," under the invitation to the conference in Berlin, but Libya nowadays is still a long way from that.

Libya has a conflict with an internationally recognized government in Tripoli led by Fayez Sarraj, but it controls only a small part of Libya.

Meanwhile, rebel General Haftar and his militias are increasingly putting the government under military pressure. Haftar controls most of the country, including much of its oil fields.

The situation is complicated every day by the intervention of foreign powers Turkey to support the government in Tripoli they sent soldiers to Libya. On the other side, Egypt, Saudi Arabia, the United Arab Emirates, and Russia are backing Haftar, and are more or less openly providing him with military assistance.

While, the German government put forward the idea of holding a conference in Berlin to obtain a "real" commitment to respect the arms embargo and they push Haftar and Sarraj to accept the international community's needs "no military solution, only a political one".

On the other hand, Libya also got support from European Union they divided it into "France said we will support Haftar, while Italy, the former colonial power, is said to be close to Sarraj, and this situation is very strange.

According to that German government invited the highest representatives to the chancellery in Berlin: the two rivals, Sarraj and Haftar, the heads of state and government of all the main countries, directly and indirectly, involved, as well as representatives of the European Union, the African Union and the Arab League. Because the meeting is being overseen by the United Nations, UN Secretary-General Antonio Guterres.

Rainer Breul, the spokesperson for the German Foreign Office, said the focus is not yet on peace negotiations, our goal is for international actors to agree on framework conditions to reduce their influence on the ground.

The significance of the Berlin conference, however, extends further than Libya, the key to the further stabilization of North and West Africa. If we succeed in leading Libya into a peaceful future, it would be a milestone for the entire region.

There are many western countries that want to control Libya. If we look at each one, we will find their personal interests in the following: Turkey responded to the pleas of the Government of National Accord (GNA) from Serraj to intervene militarily they got their support from Erdoğan's because the US Withdrawn from ' the Middle East it could give chance to another country to join and get a part from Libya.

According to that Europeans countries have woken up they want to return the role again, because of the loss of prestige and relevance, mostly Italy, after months of neglecting this issue, realized its own sudden irrelevance and jumped again from long time they have good Economic relations with Libya Especially in the export of gas, oil and port fields. On the other hand, the Middle East countries like Egyptians and the Emirati leaders' supporters Haftar, because they are an enemy of Turkey.

When America withdrew, Russia intervened to regain its position in the Middle East so that they chose Libya. Putin and Erdoğan now understand that the two of them could in effect play a determinant role in mediating between the Libyan factions and thus reaching an almost exclusive position of power in the North African country.

Overall, the fact that Moscow and Ankara took this initiative underscores what has been evident for months they did ceasefire agreement but Haftar refuses to sign it. The agreement contained seven points following by: "determine a line of battle contact to ensure a sustainable ceasefire", appoint five representatives each to a military ceasefire monitoring commission, and appoint representatives to future economic, military and political negotiations under UN aegis. These last two points already form the backbone of a roadmap.

Due to that agreement, Haftar refused to sign because the ceasefire terms were too vague, and could have been interpreted as requiring him to withdraw his forces from Tripoli and the environs at a moment when he feels the balance of power is in his favour. In the wake of the failed Moscow meeting maybe the Berlin conference could be a trap.

The governments realized the failure of the Moscow conference, but this conference represents the political transformation in the Middle East if all goes according to plan, representatives of the U.S., EU, UK, France, Russia, China, Italy, Germany, Turkey, Egypt, the UAE, Algeria and Congo-Brazzaville, as well as the UN, Arab League, and African Union, will sign a 55-point declaration. Key items include support for a ceasefire, a commitment not to violate the UN arms embargo on Libya, and a pledge to support a UN "operational" plan for political, security and economic consultations aimed at unifying the country.

Moreover, the leaders want to credible steps" toward dismantling armed groups and militias following the demand Haftar made to this effect in Moscow.

After all, the Europeans found the solution it will be at the Berlin conference. The meeting would provide the perfect stage for this ultimate act of betrayal, they will show at the end of the conference the acceptance by Haftar's entire future role and the legitimization of his attack against Tripoli.

The leaders will fall into the trap through a project in the pipeline to empower a new civilian government of "national unity" led by a new prime minister by-election that would be organized as soon as possible (AlAshry, January 20, 2020).

The First Step of Berlin Conference

The Berlin conference on the Libyan crisis was held on January 19th to protect Libya this conference is one in a series of international meetings on Libya, which have taken place in Paris, Palermo, Abu Dhabi, and Moscow. This conference has been the most important, due to several considerations.

Four international organizations and twelve countries participated in the conference, including the five permanent members of the Security Council. Nine of them were represented by heads of state and government. Also, it's the first time that President Putin's participation was a key factor that encouraged other leaders to attend.

Berlin conference into an "international summit" on Libya. This helped facilitate a consensus among the different parties and the convergence of conflicting positions, even within European countries like France and Italy.

The conference in Berlin of 11 countries was aimed at bringing an end to the fighting between the UN-recognized government in Tripoli led by the prime minister, Fayez al-Sarraj, and the Libyan National Army in the country's east led by Gen Khalifa Haftar. The conference plays a role in transforming relations between Russia and Turkey, Russia's will remain central in pushing the settlement in Libya.

Through the conference, the world leaders seeking an enduring +ceasefire in Libya have agreed at a summit to impose sanctions on those breaking an arms embargo and are considering whether to send a multinational force to Libya as before.

In addition, the second main goal was to get foreign powers wielding influence in the region to stop interfering in the war – be it through weapons, troops, or financing. Moreover, the conference has stopped the escalation of the crisis and prevented it from turning into a full-scale war. Turkey's move to send troops to support Fayez Serraj, the head of the Government of National Accord, would have prompted Egypt to pursue the same course of action to support the Libyan National Army (LNA) and Marshal Khalifa Haftar.

European initiatives that stopped the Russian ceasefire on January 12th succeeded in defusing this crisis, and the conference supported this approach. The German foreign minister, Heiko Maas, said: "We have to make sure Libya doesn't become a second Syria." There are serious concerns that signatories to the summit's declarations will do little to abide by the agreements.

The third important outcome was in confirming the necessity of establishing a truce between the warring parties in Libya especially a message to Turkish President Recep Tayyip Erdogan that both European and international parties would not allow him to threaten their interests. What he did in northern Syria cannot be repeated in Libya.

The fourth result Libya needs credible, verifiable, sequenced, and reciprocal steps, including credible steps towards the dismantling of armed groups and militias by all parties as per art. 34 of the LPA and referred to in UNSC resolutions 2420 and 2486, leading to a comprehensive and lasting cessation of all hostilities including air operations over the territory of Libya. In addition, we must take into consideration the call for the institution of confidence-building measures, such as the exchange of prisoners and mortal remains.

The fifth result to implementation of UNSCR 2368 and other relevant resolutions concerning ISIS and designated individuals, groups, and entities, in particular the provisions related to the travel, also enhanced cooperation to counter the foreign terrorist fighter threat in accordance with UNSC Resolution 2322. Member States to commit to supporting the provision of the United Nations Support Mission to Libya (UNSMIL) in line with UNSC Resolution 2486 (2019) with the necessary personnel and equipment to effectively support the ceasefire.

The sixth result we encourage the full, effective and meaningful participation of women and youth in all activities relating to Libya's democratic transition, conflict resolution and peacebuilding, we urge all Libyan parties to further engage in and support mediation and reconciliation efforts between Fezzan local communities so as to reconstruct the social fabric in an area long neglected, they underline the important role of neighbouring countries in the Libyan stabilization process.

Finally, the final statement of the conference is to be presented to the UN Security Council for approval and a binding resolution. This includes a monitoring mechanism for following up on the implementation of the promised commitments, which will start in early February 2020 (AlAshry, January 22, 2020)

In February, the UN's Libya envoy reported "progress" in talks between military representatives of the country's warring parties on coming up with a lasting ceasefire that could include a UN monitoring role. "Progress has been made on many important issues.

According to that Ghassan Salame, high-ranking military officers from both sides in the

Libyan civil war told reporters in Geneva, there were still "two or three points of divergence" to build a lasting ceasefire.

But Khalifa Haftar the general who leads the self-styled Libyan National Army, based in the country's east had refused to attend. On the other side, the talks had been proposed by world leaders at a summit in Berlin more than a fortnight ago.

In addition, Ghassan Salame, said rival military leaders are negotiating the remaining sticking points in a cease-fire deal. These include the return of internally displaced people, the disarmament of armed groups, and ways to monitor the truce, also the cease-fire agreement is made of a number of issues, and there have been points of convergence on many points. And there are points of divergence.

He mentions the latest round of fighting in oil-rich Libya erupted last April it was difficult when eastern-based forces under the command of Khalifa Haftar laid siege to Tripoli in a bid to wrest power from the U.N backed government led by Prime Minister Fayez Sarraj.

Libya has suffered from the embargo had been violated incessantly", and once again appealed to the countries involved in providing arms and mercenary soldiers to desist. "More than 20m pieces of weaponry are already in the country and that is enough. The country does not need that equipment. The aims of the conference to turn a nominal truce into a lasting and sustainable ceasefire, covering the removal of heavy weaponry.

Moreover, there are no plans for the EU to enforce the ceasefire, merely to check its observance and report any breaches. A proposal from the EU to provide ceasefire monitors will be put on the table at some point, but it will be for the Libyan negotiators to decide if they welcomed this help.

Both leaders sent delegations of military officials to represent them at the Geneva talks. The cease-fire talks come amid intensified diplomacy among world powers seeking to end the conflict that has ravaged Libya for nine years as it destroyed the Libyan society.

Both of the leaders depend on external forces to support them in terms of money, weapons, and strength the first leader Haftar's forces, which control much of Libya's east and south, got his military support military from the United Arab Emirates and Egypt, as well as France and Russia. The second leader got support from Turkey, Italy and Qatar to prop up the embattled Tripoli-based government, Turkey has sent as many as 2,000 Turkmen fighters from Syria to counter the LNA.

Haftar's forces to end their blockade of the Libyan oil industry, saying their actions have meant Libyan oil production has collapsed to 70,000 barrels a day, down from 1.3m barrels a day before the fighting began. He said it would require international action to lift the blockade, but warned that 90% of Libyan government revenue dependent on oil and gas exports.

On the other hand, Haftar has partly imposed the blockade to weaken the GNA but also to protest at the way in which the Tripoli-based Central Bank distributes the oil revenues supplied by the Libyan National Oil Corporation. We find that the beneficiary Turkey and the United Arab Emirates – a sense that the political opprobrium of arming their sponsor is outweighing the benefit of developing long-term influence over such an oil-rich state. Also, Europe, taking a more prominent role in recent weeks been marginalized from resolving the dispute with Turkey and Russia. The UN security council is still working on a resolution demanding the ceasefire is respected, but the international divisions are again making agreement difficult (AlAshry, 2020, February 07)

Deploy Warships to Enforce Libya Arms

The EU has agreed to deploy warships to stop the flow of weapons into Libya. Josep Borrell, the EU's chief diplomat, announced that 27 foreign ministers had agreed to launch a new operation with naval ships, planes, and satellites in order to enforce the UN arms embargo on Libya.

Borrell promised the ships would be withdrawn if they became "a pull factor" that encouraged people to attempt the risky crossing from Libya to Europe. On the other hand, this commitment helped lift opposition to the mission from Italy and Austria, whose governments had blocked an earlier compromise.

In addition, weapons and foreign mercenaries have been pouring into the war-torn north African country, it will be exposing Europe's weakness in its own neighborhood. The arms embargo in Libya has become a joke and the country's financial position is deteriorating rapidly, the world leaders took cease-fire measures in Berlin last month to draw up a Libyan peace plan, both sides in the civil war have ignored international appeals and turned back to their external sponsor nations for further arms and mercenary support. According to that, the UN Security Council passed a resolution calling for enforcement of the arms embargo and a ceasefire.

Ships under the new mission – called Operation EU Active Surveillance – will patrol about 60 miles (100km) off the coast of Libya, an area of the Mediterranean that is the main route for weapons into the country. Also, naval assets can be deployed in the areas most relevant to the implementation of the arms embargo, in the eastern part of the area of operation or at least 100km off the Libyan coast, where chances to conduct rescue operations are lower.

In the past, the EU ministers agreed to create the naval operation in 2015 to combat people-smuggling and prevent loss of life at sea they called Operation Sophia. Last March 2019 the operation's Sophia's sea patrols, after Italy's then government, a populist coalition between a far-right party and anti-establishment party, threatened to veto the entire operation.

That operation got its name after a child born to a Somali mother rescued at sea along with 453 other people on a German naval ship that was part of an EU operation. According to that the EU's then foreign policy chief, Federica Mogherini, the name was "to honour the lives of the people we are saving". The operation was extended to include helping uphold the UN arms embargo on Libya.

Borrell mentioned that it was absurd for Austria, a landlocked country without a navy, to block the revival of Operation Sophia. He had also vigorously rejected arguments that the new naval operation would create a pull effect, also the legitimate concerns of some member states regarding the potential impact on migration flows, it's so-called "pull effects". He promised these would be monitored, but in case of the observation of pull factors on migration we will maritime assets will be withdrawn from the relevant areas.

The conflict in Libya with the volume of unexploded ordnance in Tripoli had increased and this is a risk for the civilians which they living in areas affected by the fighting, also the investigators had visited the site of an airstrike by Haftar's forces and found remnants of cluster bombs, which spray small explosive charges that can fail to detonate, creating continuing danger for civilians. There were more than 900 civilian deaths and casualties in Libya in 2019, according to the advocacy group Action on Armed Violence.

Stephen Goose, arms division director at HRW said, "Cluster munitions should never be used by anyone under any circumstances." Harchaoui, a research fellow with the Netherlands-based Clingendael Institute said, "There's a free-for-all, almost like a green light that is essentially being sent by the member states of the security council".

He mentioned, "All types of ugly ordnance, including cluster ordnance, are shipped into Libya, and no member state of the security council is willing to broach the issue of imposing any kind of mechanism that would be unpleasant or costly to the states that are violating the arms embargo."

Furthermore, Harchaoui said he feared fighting in Libya would worsen despite the calls for a ceasefire. The dangers posed to civilians by unexploded munitions were highlighted. The Department of Defense claimed the mines would be "nonpersistent" and expire after a short period, but anti-mine activists warned civilians would be endangered if these mechanisms failed (AlAshry, 2020, February 24).

UN Envoy Ghassan Salame Quit

At an unexpected time the UN envoy for Libya, Ghassan Salame stepped down due to health reasons. His resignation comes amid an escalation in fighting in the country, and just days after he announced the near breakdown of a shaky cease-fire between the country's two rival governments. This explained that he failed in the reconciliation efforts and the cease-fire, he used words that he is very tired and my health reasons I can no longer continue with this level of stress, and therefore I have asked the (UN) secretary-general to relieve me of my duties.

But where is the reality, did he failed to unite Libyans and restrain foreign interference, or he wasn't able to persuade major powers to use their leverage to end the civil war between Khalifa Haftar, the leader of so-called Libyan National Army forces in the country's east, and the UN-recognized government of Fayez al-Sarraj, based in the capital, Tripoli.

Salamé was afraid because he thought that the powerful nations had not stuck to commitments made at a peace conference in Berlin in January, to use their influence to end interventions by external powers. His decision to quit is likely to be followed by a further rise in political violence, and the continuation of an oil depot blockade that has led Libya's oil production to grind to a halt. This leads to a failure in the next stage, after the United Nations arms embargo, recently endorsed again by the UN security council, has been flagrantly violated, with no attempt to hold the major culprits, Turkey and the United Arab Emirates, in any way accountable. On the other hand, the UN reports repeatedly identified the sources of breaches of the arms embargo but then held back from naming the relevant country.

The conflict started with Salamé, when he in post for two years, he was frustrated by the willingness of European powers including France to covertly back Haftar along with Russia. His goal had been to end the violence and troubles that have wracked oil-rich Libya since 2011 when an international military coalition helped rebels overthrow longtime autocrat Moammar Gadhafi. He joined the council endorsed a 55-point road map to end the war in Libya that 12 key leaders agreed to at a conference in Berlin on Jan. 19 and Salama said the U.N. should remain committed to supporting a Libyan-led and Libyan-owned peace process "and trying to stop outside interference." "It's a pity," said Russia's deputy U.N. ambassador Dmitry Polyansky. "He's a well-placed person with great experiences but we need to learn the details." China's U.N. Ambassador Zhang Jun, the current Security Council president, said: "We do appreciate the efforts he has made in promoting a peace process, a political process, and in bringing an end to the conflict there. But we also know there are many difficulties he has to explain to us."

In the end, Salame did not fail in his mission, but the escalating crisis forced him to choose to resign, and just days after he announced the near breakdown of a shaky truce between the country's two rival governments. One administration controls most of Libya's east and south, while a U.N.-backed but weak administration holds a shrinking area of the west, including the capital Tripoli. A patchwork of armed groups and foreign countries support either side, the situation in Libya is very difficult and cannot resolve the negotiations. The Tripoli administration is backed by Turkey, and to a lesser degree, Qatar and Italy. Hifter on the other side receives backing from the United Arab Emirates and Egypt, as well as France and Russia, the situation here is not in a state of peace, but rather foreign forces and states that want to control the region.

Salame, cannot achieve any tangible progress as long as foreign states remain so brazenly disingenuous vis-à-vis the UN as an institution, last week in Geneva he had exposed a rift within the delegations representing the Tripoli government and the eastern-based government, which is allied with ex-general Khalifa Hifter, also he revealed that delegates to the political negotiations "from both sides" had walked away from the table.

According to that, Salame found this mission became difficult to achieve success for the coming period, also it is difficult to achieve success in Libya unless if the foreign forces moved away from Libya, and removing their hand from the Libyan state (AlAshry, 2020, March 05).

Libya Records First Covid-19 Case

Libya recorded its first case of the coronavirus on Tuesday, the UN-backed government announced, and stoking concern that an outbreak could overwhelm the war-torn countries already weakened health care system.

The first case was a 73-year-old man who crossed into Libya from neighboring Tunisia on March 5, 2020. The Libyan patient had recently travelled to Saudi Arabia, according to the National Center for Disease Control, and is receiving medical treatment for his fever and cough in isolation at a Tripoli hospital.

As the novel coronavirus pandemic sweeps across the Middle East, countries have sought to slow the increase of cases by limiting the movements of hundreds of millions of people. There are over 31,000 cases of the novel coronavirus across the Mid-East, the vast majority in the hard-hit nation of Iran.

Coronavirus could stop the fighting in Libya. Although Libya has only recorded just one case, the World Health Organization representative in Tripoli has warned of the great risks faced if the virus spreads in a country fragmented by conflict.

According to what the world is witnessing, the internationally recognized Libyan government based in Tripoli, and led by Faiez Serraj, announced a series of measures aimed at mitigating the spread of the coronavirus (Covid-19), including a state of emergency and half a billion dinars to fight the virus. They also closed all Libyan land, air, and sea borders for three weeks from 16 March 2020.

In addition, all educational institutions are closed for two weeks, with the possibility of extension, and all sports and cultural activities and gatherings to be halted as well as weddings and occasions halls are to be closed.

The government has allowed cafes and restaurants with "a high standard of hygiene" to be open until 4 pm, while all other establishments and shisha establishments are to be closed. Mosques are also to be closed for prayers. The state internet company has been urged to provide reduced internet packages to enable increased internet use from homes. In response to the coronavirus pandemic, both the Tripoli and Benghazi administrations have pledged money for local health initiatives.

A joint statement from Algeria, Britain, France, Germany, Italy, the Netherlands, the United States, the European Union, Tunisia, and the United Arab Emirates said a truce would help efforts to tackle the virus. As such, this virus could help the two governments to be more cooperative in a spirit of national cohesion and urged to take all the necessary measures to support the health and well-being of all Libyans.

Moreover, this virus will provide a truce that could also enable combatants to return home to provide care for relatives who may be at higher risk.

Meanwhile, the government in eastern Libya had also put into action a state of emergency plan to mitigate the virus. They set up their own virus testing lab to avoid the time-wasting process of sending samples to Tripoli and announced that the suspected seven cases across the country, who were placed into quarantine last week, had all tested negative. These were; two cases in Benghazi, two in Misrata, one in Zliten, one in Zawia, and one suspected case in the Amal oilfield.

As the capital remains under attack with a more silent and deadly form of assault, the governments and businesses quickly turned to email and texting to allay the fears of citizens and customers with messages about coronavirus

The pandemic is causing panic and distress as it travels throughout the globe, ignoring all borders, from cyber attackers taking full advantage of peoples' concerns and desire to arm themselves with information about the spread of COVID 19. Cyber attackers have used an application called 'Corona Live 1.1.' that lulls the user into a false sense of security reassuring them that no special access is required, however, as the individual continues with the application, access to device location, media files and photos are subtly requested. This application is part of a SpyMax example, which is a trojanized version of the 'Corona live' app used by Johns Hopkins

University 'Coronavirus tracker' which covers the entire range of infection rates, number of deaths and geographical spread of the pandemic.

Once the unsuspecting user is reeled in, the application allows access to the perpetrator, of remote activation of the personal camera, microphone, and all private files on the user's device.

One of the operators seems to be a Libyan Telecom and Technology company and internet provider, whose IP address shows they are possibly part of a group used for DSL connections.

It is feared the application not only gives personal data, but could be used in committing extortion through accessing personal data for ransom as usual in Libya, or to gather intelligence and information on political players, which is potentially very dangerous and corrosive to the Libyan nation in the present situation (AlAshry, 2020, March 26).

UAE Gives Libyan Army an Israeli Air Defense System

The United Arab Emirates (UAE) has allegedly supplied the Libyan National Army (LNA) has paid for a sophisticated Israeli air defence system to send it to Haftar to undermine the capabilities of the Libyan Air Force's drones. In addition, the UAE is ramping up support Haftar to try and help his Tripoli offensive survive and to maintain his forces' positions on the outskirts of the capital.

In April 2019 the Libyan National Army, have Russian air defence systems; they have been relatively effective in thwarting enemy airstrikes on their positions. At that time Hafter got his support from Russia but nowadays he has shifted to be with UAE.

According to that, UAE has signed a contract with Israel to provide Haftar with an air defence system made by an Israeli defence firm.

The system has been transferred to Egypt in order to send it to pro-Haftar areas after training some of Haftar forces' military officers on how to use it," the New Arab newspaper reported.

The Libyan Air Force under the command of the Government of National Accord has been bossing the skies in western Libya, destroying many of Haftar's military assets, especially a jamming system given to Haftar's forces by the UAE, besides killing several leaders and foreign fighters in south Tripoli and in Tarhouna. On the other side, UAE has not made any statements about this alleged purchase and no photos of the air defence system have been released from Libya.

It is clear that Haftar wants to rule Libya by force, he wants to control Tripoli and then grip power in the entire country by bloodshed/ Moreover, Libyan fighters and Tripoli residents have been enduring the clashes and indiscriminate attacks in the face of Haftar's forces, his aims wants to regain the family rule, which many Libyans revolted against in 2011 and are still fighting up until today.

This civil war is very weird more than 85% of the armed groups are foreigners, the funding comes from abroad, but for what reasons we don't know.

The commander of the joint operations room of the western region Osama Juwaili said on speaking TV Channel, the Libyan Army forces are avoiding entering clashes with Haftar's forces in certain western region cities that are supporting Haftar, such as Sorman and Sabratha but they might have to if there is no alternative as what happened in Tarhouna.

Also, he lashed at the Arab League and the international community, saying "their masks had fallen since April 04, 2019, saying Haftar attacked Tripoli when the UN Secretary-General was in the capital, but he only expressed his sorrow over the incident (AlAshry, 2020, April 13).

UN Libya Mission 'Alarmed' By Rise In Violence,

The UN mission in Libya condemned the indiscriminate shelling carried out by Haftar's militias against civilians in Tripoli that have killed three civilians and injured several others.

UN said it was alarmed by the escalation of violence in Libya, particularly by the intensification of fighting, resulting in civilian casualties. Also, we have a critical situation in the world with Covid-19 according to that the backed government in Libya has imposed a 24-hour curfew for 10 days to prevent the spread of coronavirus but not to killed civilians. It expressed concern that this would risk new waves of displacement. Haftar's forces fighting near the Libyan capital aim to topple Prime Minister Fayez al-Sarraj so that they can take the seat of the country's internationally recognized government.

Libyan government forces managed to make major gains against the armed rebels, capturing seven cities and towns located northwest of the capital. The rebels retaliated by firing rockets at residential areas in Tripoli.

The UN noted that it is following with grave concern allegations regarding violations committed in western coastal towns recently seized by the Government of National Accord (GNA) forces, and also the violations by general Haftar, including acts of retribution, looting, robberies, and torching of public and private properties. UN mention, these allegations, if verified, would constitute grave violations of international human rights and humanitarian law so that we have to follow the two governments. In addition, acts of revenge will further escalate the conflict and lead to a cycle of revenge that threatens the social fabric in Libya. With the rebels' indiscriminate bombardment of Tripoli with rockets, many of which have landed on civilian neighbourhoods, resulting in casualties, we have to take a humanitarian truce aimed at facilitating efforts to combat the coronavirus outbreak in the war-torn country. Hundreds of people have been killed and more than 200,000 have been displaced since Haftar launched his campaign to capture Tripoli (AlAshry, 2020, April 16).

European Union sent statement calls for a humanitarian truce in Libya

Josep Borrell, High Representative of the European Union, sent a joint statement and Italian, German and French Foreign Ministers has called for a humanitarian truce in Libya in Ramadan. The statement indicated that the signatories want to unite their voices to those of the UN Secretary-General Guterres and his Acting Special Representative for Libya, Stephanie Williams, in their call for a humanitarian truce in Libya. In the same week, the United States and Russia said they could not support a United Nations Security Council resolution calling for a ceasefire in Libya, also diplomats said, as mortar bombs crashed down on a suburb of the Libyan capital, Tripoli.

MIRAL SABRY ALASHRY

On the other hand, Russia objects to the British-drafted resolution blaming eastern Libyan commander Haftar for the latest flare-up in violence when his Libyan National Army (LNA) advanced to the outskirts of Tripoli. Trump administration and Russia are blocking efforts to win binding UN Security Council backing for a global ceasefire. António Guterres, the UN secretary-general, called for an immediate end to fighting involving governments and armed groups in all conflict areas almost one month ago. "The fury of the virus illustrates the folly of war".

Guterres said we need a universal truce from dozens of countries, including leading US allies such as Britain, France and Germany, on the other hand, Emmanuel Macron, the French president, has proposed a draft security council resolution that attempts to overcome US and Russian objections by, in effect, making it impossible to enforce.

US objections arise from White House, Pentagon and State Department concerns that an all-encompassing measure could hinder their ability to prosecute military operations against terrorist groups, for example, the Government of National Accord (GNA) resumed Sunday military operations(second stage) that aim to retake Tarhouna city from Khalifa Haftar's forces, by using Air Force warplanes carried out two airstrikes on locations and military vehicles for Haftar's forces in Al-Masahba area in Tarhouna. The clashes continued in an outlying area of the town for up to six hours, the Government of National Accord (GNA) did that because marking a possible turning point in their attempt to fend off a year-long offensive by Haftar's Army.

The Air Force warplanes had dropped down leaflets writing but two languages (Arabic and Russian)the objective of the leaflets to giving an ultimatum to fighters and mercenaries of Haftar's forces to surrender their to avoid the city bloodshed and destruction. They wrote those who surrender will be safe and urged the residents of Tarhouna to stay away from clashes' zones and to remain at home. Tarhoona, is a Libyan town 65 kilometres (40 mi) to the southeast of Tripoli, in the Murqub District. The geographical boundaries, from the "Valley of the famm Molgha" west to "Burkaat Oueny" eastward. Then from the "Suq al Juma (Al-msab`ha)" north, "Al-mzawgha and Marghna" south, the population about was calculated to be 13,264 in 2011.

Russia's president, Vladimir Putin, is believed to have similar reservations regarding the impact on Russian military operations in Libya unacknowledged support for proxy groups and non-state militias.

The U.S is also concerned that a blanket ceasefire could inhibit Israel's ability to engage in military operations throughout the Middle East especially in the country that faces a warlike Libya Syria. More than 50 governments have also backed Guterres's initiative, including several Nato allies, which the US and Russia declined to sign, they expressed concern that the UN security council had yet to take action. Air Force warplanes carried out over 20 strikes targeting Haftar forces' positions in the city, destroying many vehicles and killing as well as wounding several fighters, by the military source close to Volcano of Rage Operation.

The air defences had shot down a Wing Loong drone as it was striking civilian targets in the vicinity of Abu Grein town. On the other side, the UAE support Haftar's forces the drone was provided loaded with missiles but shot down before returning to where it took off from.

UAE had sent more than 100 shipments of arms to Libya by air since mid-January, despite a UN arms embargo against the war-torn country. However, the airstrikes near Sirte marked the first time that the UAE is operating drones to support the rebels. Due to that, several fighters from Haftar's forces had been killed and injured in attacks on their positions on the coastal road of Al-Wishkah. LNA forces control eastern and southern Libya and have been positioned around the outskirts of Tripoli for a year.

According to that US continues to prevaricate, while negotiations continue. Kelly Craft, US ambassador to the UN, expressed support for a global truce earlier this week (AlAshry, 2020, May 04).

Haftar Ends Skhirat Political Agreement

Eastern Libyan forces laying siege to the Tripoli have agreed on a humanitarian pause in fighting during Ramadan, in response to international appeals for a humanitarian truce so authorities could focus on dealing with the coronavirus pandemic.

But, Libya's internationally recognized government recognized the forces will keep fighting, after a unilateral ceasefire declaration by its eastern-based opponents in Tripoli, also they did not trust the Libyan National Army (LNA) of renegade general Haftar.

On the other side, Haftar and his LNA was adopting a ceasefire for Islam's holy month of Ramadan in response to requests by the international community and "friendly countries".

Due to the greed of the Libyan army in Ramadan this is a good opportunity to dominate, he abruptly declared a popular mandate to take control of the whole country, and he was told by his backers that he had overstepped the mark and needed to bow to international pressure for a lull in fighting if he was to recover lost diplomatic ground.

This was a very strange message to the Libyan and international community, perhaps one of his modern strategy maybe he will progress or fail.

The political declaration was denounced by the US embassy in Libya and by the Russian foreign minister, Sergei Lavrov, as well as indirectly criticized by France, one of Haftar's strongest covert backers but some counties in the Middle East support him.

This declaration means Haftar no longer recognised the authority of the elected House of Representatives (HoR) in the eastern city of Tobruk, which he had been broadly allied with for many years.

Ageela Saleh the head of the HoR, put forward an eight-point political plan to try to reconcile the east of the country with the GNA. Haftar also presented himself to his overseas backers as the man to bring security and hope to Libya and crush ISIS.

All of the countries support him and tolerated him as the legitimate representative of political forces in the east, but his clash with Ageela Saleh, a leading political force in the east, made that claim less tenable.

During Ramadan escalation in violence and the attendant rise in civilian casualties, the LNA shelled a civilian hospital in Tareeq al-Shouq, destroying an intensive care unit. The hospital had been earmarked to take a leading role in the event of a coronavirus outbreak in Libya.

Haftar dismissed the UN-brokered Skhirat political agreement, representatives from throughout the country came together to negotiate this agreement, which represents a unique opportunity to both addresses the immediate suffering of the Libyan people and build a democratic civil state through national consensus. In doing so they have demonstrated their commitment, as true leaders, to place the Libyan people and Libyan State above narrow self-interests and readiness to take a difficult decision for the sake of Libya(AlAshry, 2020, May 03).

The dialogue's political track included key players in the Libyan democratization process. The members of the House of Representatives, chosen in a free and fair election that was organized under and recognized by the General National Congress, have a responsibility to respect the democratic rights of the voters and represent their constituencies. The General National Congress managed the transitional process for more than two years. The National Transitional Council led the country through the earliest stages of the transition. Members from all these three legislative bodies made very important contributions to the dialogue process and to the conclusion of this agreement.

Other independent stakeholders participated as well. The armed groups, municipal councils, political parties, tribal leaders, and women's organizations contributed to other elements of the dialogue to promote genuine and stable reconciliation. Laboriously negotiated in 2015, rejecting all the political institutions set up under it and in effect wiping the constitutional slate clean.

Khalifa Haftar's forces carried out artillery shelling using over 80 rockets against the Mitiga Airport in Tripoli and surrounding areas of Soqu Al-Jumua and Bab Benghashir. The forces' rocket attacks on Mitiga Airport led to massive damage, leaving two Airbus planes damaged and out of service after being hit by shrapnel. Firefighters' vehicles and the runway were also damaged, as was the passenger lounge.

One plane (Airbus 320) was preparing for takeoff to Spain to evacuate Libyans. The Libyan Health Ministry said two people were killed and several others injured in the shelling.

This attack comes two days after Haftar's announcement of the Ababil Birds Operation, vowing to rain down rockets on Tripoli and destroy the infrastructure. The attack also came after a rocket attack on Zawiyet Al-Dahmani near the residence of Italian ambassador Giuseppe Buccino and the Turkish embassy on Shatt Road.

Italy took a stand against Khalifa Haftar, saying the attack near Italy's embassy in Tripoli was out of his "arrogance and weakness at the same time"

Italy still believes there is no military solution to the Libyan conflict and we have to stop the war. Ambassador Giuseppe Buccino said the attack wasn't random as "Italy is targeted by Haftar's militias", saying Haftar is becoming more desperate and the attacks are evidence for his losses on the ground.

Operation IRINI aims to monitor the arms embargo in Libya and is under the oversight of Italian leadership and will be very integrated, transparent, and balanced in its work. It won't be a naval mission only or work freely but also include air surveillance missions to monitor movements on the land.

Moreover, Henry Wooster the United States Deputy Assistant Secretary of State for the Maghreb and Egypt, said the US is seeking to end the conflict in Libya and return to political dialogue. He added that Russian interference in the Middle East, that Moscow is attempting to strengthen its presence in Libya, in order to expand its influence in the Mediterranean and on the African continent.

Moscow's support for Haftar's forces has led to the conflict and encouraged him to continue his aggression.

Recently, Haftar's militia groups, backed by Wagner and Sudanese mercenaries, launched an all-out attack in Mashrou and Yarmouk frontlines in southern Tripoli but it ended in failure.

All of the media outlets loyal to Haftar published "our forces had taken control of Abu Salim and Furnaj districts and members of Presidential Council, ministers, and Turkish officers had escaped to Misrata."

Nevertheless, this news was fake news and disinformation in an attempt to weaken the morale of government forces and local residents of Tripoli. Haftar is using a new strategy, using the media to promoting misleading ideas.

The United Nations Support Mission in Libya (UNSMIL) has strongly condemned the bombing by Haftar's militias at the Mitiga International Airport. It reiterated its absolute condemnation of the attacks against civilians and civilian installations, noting that these horrendous attacks have been regularly occurring near or within residential neighborhoods, and this is in accordance with the plans that will end the community.

They stressed that the intense savage bombing merely reflects a series of indiscriminate attacks attributed to Haftar's forces, which have led since the start of this month to the death of more than 15 and the injury of 50 innocent civilians.

The Turkish direction focused on the attack in Libya and on Mitiga Airport constitute war crimes, the Turkish Foreign Ministry said. The Ministry added that Turkey will consider Haftar elements as legitimate targets if the country's interests in Libya are targeted, referring to Haftar's forces attacks on Zawiyet Al-Dahmani and Shatt Road, near the embassy of Turkey in Tripoli.

Furthermore, Ankara will continue to support the legitimate government of Libya; the Government of National Accord, and its institutions, by providing military, financial, and political support.

Turkey is strongly criticizing the United Nations for what it says is the UN's failure to move against Haftar.

Appeals from the European Union to all foreign countries earlier to stop supplying arms and interfering in Libya and let peace talks proceed have gone nowhere (AlAshry, 2020, May 11).

Forces allied with Libya's UN-supported government have wrested control of a key military base on the outskirts of the country's capital from Khalifa Haftar, dealing a significant blow to the renegade general. In 2019 Haftar planned to take Tripoli in a lightning operation, but his forces have been mired in fighting ever since.

This latest operation has made Haftar's eastern-based forces withdraw from the al-Watiya airbase 90 miles south of Tripoli. His retreat, following other recent military reverses, will force those foreign capitals that back him to review the viability of his plan to overthrow the UN-recognized Government of National Accord (GNA).

On the other hand, negotiations over the town of Al-Asaba to hand over peacefully to Libyan Army forces under the command of the Government of National Accord (GNA) failed as pro-Haftar groups refused to pull out. Hence, the social council of Al-Asaba town announced that the town was under GNA's authority when some of GNA units advanced on the town to seize control, pro-Haftar forces rejected the withdrawal and opened fire on the GNA forces.

Violence escalated with the GNA forces retreating to the Jandouba Bridge between Al-Asaba and Gharyan to reorganize themselves after being hit by airstrikes by UAE drones coming from the Al-Jufra airbase, and which killed five Gharyan Protection Force fighters. In addition, the Libyan Air Force targeted a vehicle laden with a UAE armoured vehicle and ammunition in Al-Asaba as GNA forces mobilized forces to attack the town, possibly liberating it.

Libyan Air Force destroyed seven Russian systems in Tarhouna and another one in Al-Wishka. The Libyan Air Force was continuing its surveillance over Tarhouna city as per the military tactics of the Libyan Army operations room.

Two more Pantsir missile systems were destroyed by Libyan GNA forces in the capturing of Al-Watiya airbase when another Pantsir system was destroyed by GNA forces in southern Sirte.

The Libyan Air Force targeted two UAE Nimr armored vehicles and other military vehicles by six airstrikes on Tarhouna, besides the airstrikes on Al-Wishka, leaving behind casualties among Haftar's forces and a number of destroyed ammunition depots.

Turkey's foreign interventions

Turkish support for the GNA is growing, driven by Ankara's desire to secure its energy supplies. Turkey knows there is coming to a crisis in resources and energy and they want to control the Middle East through Libya's resources, Turkey plans to extend the access to Mediterranean gas fields, which has included the supply of both drones and Syrian mercenaries forces.

Last November, Turkey defied the UN arms embargo and signed a treaty with the GNA in return for Libyan permission to access Mediterranean gas fields. It has since been supplying military support to the GNA. The bilateral treaty has been sharply criticized by Greece as being in breach of international law and in violation of Greek sovereignty.

Turkey claims that the GNA remains by law the UN-recognised government, and they have to find a way to stop the supply of arms and mercenaries to Haftar by the United Arab Emirates, Egypt, and Russia. France also unofficially backs Haftar, regarding him as a bulwark against terrorism in the Sahel.

On the other hand, Turkey has caused concern in France and the UAE, because they take an interest in the country's southern oilfields.

Turkey has reaffirmed that Haftar's elements will be legitimate targets for its armed forces if they attack any of its interests in Libya.

Haftar's response has been to target Turkish forces and interests in all Libyan cities. Turkey's reply to Haftar's statement has mirrored the defeat of his forces on the ground, even though Haftar and his supporters are trying to escalate the conflict in Libya.

Haftar's Air Force Chief Saqr Al-Jaroushi has said, "our warplanes will carry out the largest aerial campaign in Libyan history against Turkish positions and interests in all Libyan cities," and vowed painful hours ahead to "Erdogan and his loyalists," saying that if they don't surrender, "they will be annihilated."

Russian foreign interventions

Russia had sent at least eight warplanes to Haftar, MiG 29s, and two Sukhoi 24s and flown into the eastern region from the Russian-controlled Hmeimim Air Base in Syria, escorted by two SU-35 Russian airforce jets. Russian has not issued any comment or official statements regarding this development, however, it appears that they will support Haftar's forces to carry out the largest aerial campaign in Libyan history to target Turkish interests in Libya. Haftar's forces have shut down oil ports, but the GNA has vowed to bring the perpetrators behind the shutdown of oil ports, valves, and other oil-related apparatuses to justice, adding this step will have severe consequences on Libyans and will lead to deficits in state revenue, let alone the outages of electricity due to shortages of fuel and gas (AlAshry, 2020, May 23).

Libya's internationally recognised government recaptured Tripoli's main airport but driving an eastern commander's forces from the capital ahead of what appeared to move towards talks on a truce. Following a month of gains for the Government of National Accord (GNA) as Turkish drone strikes helped it drive the eastern-based Libyan National Army (LNA) of Khalifa Haftar from much of its foothold in the northwest.

The LNA driven from almost all its ground in the capital, the next rounds of fighting to focus on the areas to the south and southeast of Tripoli around Gharyan, held by the GNA, and Tarhouna, held by the LNA.

Russia had sent at least 14 warplanes to an airbase held by eastern forces. this air flight warplane had struck near Gharyan, the first acknowledged use of warplanes by eastern forces since Washington said Russia had supplied the new MiG 29 and Su-24 jets.

It was the first time Russian armed forces were identified in Libya.

Although the Wagner Group purportedly enjoys Russian state backing, the Kremlin had initially stopped short of deploying official military assets to Libya. US Army General Stephen said "For too long, Russia has denied the full extent of its involvement in the ongoing Libyan conflict," Townsend, who leads AFRICOM. "We watched as Russia flew fourth-generation jet fighters to Libya — every step of the way."

Prime Minister Ahmed Maiteeg of Libya's internationally-recognized Government of National Accord (GNA) arrived in Moscow for talks on stop parties have agreed to restart the ceasefire, respond to that the Libyan Army under the command of the Government of National Accord (GNA) has seized full control on Qasir Benghashir onwards since Haftar's forces left their positions in Qasir Benghashir, Sabea, and Souq Al-Khamis, fleeing to Tarhouna and Bani Walid. GNA forces also seized control of Qasir Benghashir roundabout, Al-Ahyaa Al-Bariya, and Kazirma, let alone the control of GNA forces over Khallatat, Khalla, and Yarmouk Camp, which all were positions for Haftar's forces.

The US general noted that neither Haftar's Libyan National Army (LNA) nor private military contractors could "arm, operate and sustain these fighters without state support they are getting from Russia. Adding Wagner group already has up to 1,200 mercenaries in Libya.

We can call Hafter now Russia's man, Moscow has sought to expand its influence in the Middle East and North Africa, and supported that mission through military escapades. In Syria, Moscow deployed its armed forces to prop up the Assad regime, a move that has ensured its place as a regional stakeholder. the objective that Russian President Vladimir Putin wants to control Europe and possibly even deep-rooted influence and control in the wider MENA region also he wants the logistical and geo-strategical advantage he is attempting to achieve.

Another side with Tunisia's parliament speaker Rachid Ghannouchi said neutrality on Libya is meaningless, adding that a political solution is the safest way to end insecurity and chaos in Libya. Adding "Libya's neighbors cannot live in carelessness. If there is a fire at your neighbor, you cannot be neutral; extinguishing the fire is a duty and necessity, so passive neutrality makes no sense". Moreover, Tunisia's vision is that a political solution in Libya is the safest way to overcome insecurity and chaos.

In the end the refusal of some Tunisian opposition parties of his communication – as speaker of parliament – with the internationally recognized Libyan government headed by Fayez al-Sarraj, Ghannouchi stressed that his communication "did not exceed the Tunisian diplomacy rules."

This trend is in support of Turkey to the reconciliation government to eliminate Russia. Also, Russian-Turkish ties have thawed in recent years, the countries back opposing parties in Syria and Libya. The Turkish government threatened to strike Haftar's forces if they continued to attack diplomatic missions in Tripoli, where the UN-backed government is based. Libya is rich in energy sources, migrants can be leveraged in negotiations with Turkish wants that power.

America's attempts to calm the situation through peaceful intervention using the United Nations Children's Fund (UNICEF) and the Libyan government expressed grave concern over reports regarding the killing of civilians in Tripoli by explosive land mines laid by Haftar's militias in the homes of those displaced from areas that were under Haftar's control south of the capital.

They found in civilian homes in the areas of Ain Zara and Salah al-Din in Tripoli. Residents who returned to their homes in these areas have been killed or injured by explosive devices and mines that were placed inside or near their place of residence. responding to that UNICEF's Special Representative in Libya, Abd al-Rahman Ghandour, emphasized that "all parties to the conflict have to respect their obligations under international humanitarian law and international human rights law."

The Libyan Interior Ministry mechanisms to recruit individuals from backup forces who have been fighting on and around Tripoli frontlines. Moreover, they aimed to put in place a program for backup forces in order to have them join state institutions after the end of the war, adding that Defense and Interior Ministries bear the biggest responsibility for the involvement of those forces in their employment programs, urging for providing the necessary financial support by relevant state authorities for this plan. This is the time to built state security and defence institutions and in the second step, they need a better economy and more financial assistance for security and military projects in the country.

UNSMIL emphasized in a statement that the resumption of dialogue constitutes a response by the parties to the desire and calls of the overwhelming majority of Libyans who long for a return to a safe and dignified life as quickly as possible. it was mention before acceptance by the Government of National Accord and Haftar's forces of the resumption of talks on the ceasefire and associated security arrangements based on the draft agreement submitted by UNSMIL to the parties during the Joint Military Commission talks (5+5) last February.

UNSMIL hopes that the response of the parties coincides with the cessation of hostilities and a reduction in the use of incitement and hate speech in order to reach a solution, also they are hoping to a resumption of the JMC talks will be marked by a return to calm and a humanitarian truce to pave the way for a lasting ceasefire agreement; enable the competent authorities to focus on addressing the repercussions and threat of the COVID-19 pandemic.

In the end, we can be said that the conflict is still in Libya, and no one can stand in front of it unless the conflicting forces retreat from Libya, and we also want the two governments to leave Libya, we want democracy state (AlAshry, 2020, June 03).

The war between Turkey and Egypt

Egypt's president warned that an attempt by Turkey-backed forces in Libya to attack the strategic city of Sirte would cross a "red line" and trigger a direct Egyptian military intervention into the conflict. Egypt intervenes in neighboring Libya with the intention of protecting its western border with the oil-rich country, and to bring stability, Egypt wants conditions for a cease-fire, to Libya. On the other side, Turkey said Haftar's forces in eastern Libya need to withdraw from the strategic city of Sirte for a lasting ceasefire and accused France of "jeopardizing" NATO security by backing him.

Turkey has forged strong ties with GNA head Fayez al-Sarraj, they sent sophisticated drones and air defense systems that helped him repel Haftar's recent offensive, this concerned Egypt and make Egypt's president afraid. France jeopardizing NATO's security by supporting Haftar, whose forces have been conducting an offensive to take the capital Tripoli since last year. The French government is supporting an illegitimate warlord and jeopardizing NATO security, Mediterranean security, North African security, and Libya's political stability.

El-Sissi spoke while inspecting Egypt's air force and commando units stationed in the Sidi Barrani airbase in the country's western region along the porous desert border with Libya, Egypt is ready to provide arms and training for Libyan tribes to "defend their country." He also will support the tribal leaders.

Sirte would open the gate for the Tripoli-allied militias to advance even farther eastward, to potentially seize control of vital oil installations, terminals, and oil fields that tribes allied.

But Turkey's Foreign Minister Mevlut Cavusoglu said that Hifter's forces have lost the chance to engage in a political solution to the conflict because Hifter ignored previous calls for a peaceful solution, It's impossible for Hifter to win.

Donald Trump has joined the calls for a ceasefire in Libya amid concerns that Egypt would be willing to send ground troops into the country to prevent a rout of its ally Haftar.

Egypt's president has announced before an initiative to end nearly a decade of civil war in

Libya, whose siege of the capital, Tripoli collapsed this week. The aims of the initiative to stop the ceasefire this meant to pave the way for elections. He called for peace talks in Geneva and the exit of all foreign fighters from Libya. Also, there can be no stability in Libya unless peaceful means to end the crisis are found, which include the unity and integrity of the national institutions.

The results of the initiative establish an elected presidential council, with representatives from Libya's three regions, ruling for an 18-month transition period until elections are held. It prescribes the unification of all financial and oil institutions, and the disbanding of militias to give state forces a monopoly overpower.

Aguila Saleh, speaker of the country's Tobruk-based House of Representatives Support that initiative, on the other side there were no representatives of the UN-recognised government of national accord (GNA) based in Tripoli. They want to continue fighting to recapture the city of Sirte from Haftar's forces, who had seized it in January.

Western powers are urging forces loyal to the GNA not to exploit its new military advantage by pushing deep into the east but instead to allow peace talks to resume with the aim of creating a new government of national unity.

The standoff came as a Greek helicopter, operating under the aegis of a European Union operation to enforce a UN arms embargo, moved to interrupt a Turkish cargo ship bound for Libya. the Greek helicopter linked by the Greek frigate Spetsai approached the Turkish cargo ship, prompting, this is a good chance for Turkish to defense, according to that highlights the risk in allowing Greece to take a prominent role in the EU's arms embargo enforcement since Greece is not seen by Turkey as a neutral party, but it's opponent.

Greece has angrily rejected a Turkish claim to exclusive drilling rights in the Mediterranean, and they formally asked for Turkish behaviour to meet the EU foreign affairs ministers. On the other side, the next day Greece signed a rival exclusive drilling agreement with Italy, from that day the aims of the Turkish to take Stake from the Mediterranean.

US military command in Africa warned that Russia, which supports Haftar, was pouring fighter planes into the country, and possibly seeking to establish a permanent airbase. Also, the US needs Turkish president, Recep Tayyip Erdoğan, with quick and good-faith negotiations are now required to implement a ceasefire and relaunch the UN-led intra-Libyan political talks.

The United Nations mission in Libya said it was horrified by the reported discovery of mass graves in the town of Tarhouna after the internationally recognized government recaptured it from eastern-based forces. We need International law requires that the authorities conduct prompt, effective, and transparent investigations," it said in a statement.

In addition, the Government of National Accord (GNA), which is recognized by the United Nations, retook control of Tarhouna after the eastern-based Libyan National Army (LNA) of Khalifa Haftar pulled out and set up a committee to investigate the discovery of mass graves, but it has not yet said how many bodies have been found so far.

Turkish response the United States play a more active role in Libya, both in achieving a ceasefire and in political talks, Turkish Foreign Minister Mevlut Cavusoglu said.

Turkey supports Fayez al Serraj's internationally recognized Government of National Accord

(GNA), whose forces have in recent weeks repelled a 14-month assault on Tripoli by Khalifa Haftar's Libyan National Army (LNA).

The LNA is backed by the United Arab Emirates, Egypt, and Russia. While Washington has said it opposes Haftar's offensive, it has not thrown its support behind the GNA. It has also lambasted Russian involvement in support of Haftar.

Libya's conflict has taken a new turn. In a series of rapid victories, the GNA has, with Turkish support, suddenly brought most of northwest Libya back under its control, dashing Haftar's bid to unite the country by force with help from Egypt, the United Arab Emirates, and Russia.

While the United States has said it opposes Haftar's offensive, it has not thrown its support behind the GNA. It has also lambasted Russian involvement, a stance reiterated.

Egypt has also called for a ceasefire starting as part of a wider political initiative, which was welcomed by Russia and the UAE. Turkey dismissed it as an attempt to save Haftar following the losses he suffered on the battlefield (AlAshry, 2020, June 21).

Turkey's intervention is a "new phase of Libya's conflict"

Turkey has taken control of Libya and there are attempts by the superpower to return Haftar's to the political scene, but the conflict has entered a new phase, with foreign interference reaching unprecedented levels, including in the delivery of sophisticated equipment and the number of mercenaries involved in the fighting. At the same time, the international community uses every opportunity to unblock the political dead-end.

At the beginning of Ramadan, the situation was very difficult for the beginning of the conflict, then became quiet since 10 June, with UN-recognized Government of National Accord (GNA) forces 25 km from the Mediterranean coastal city of Sirte, on the other hand, the UN is very concerned by an alarming military build-up around that city, including a high level of direct foreign interference in violation of a UN arms embargo, Security Council resolutions and commitments made at the Berlin International Conference on Libya six months ago.

As a result, the oil blockade imposed in January 2020 by renegade commander Khalifa Haftar's forces under the Libyan National Army in the central and eastern parts caused a $6.5 billion loss. Also, almost 30,000 people have been forced to flee their homes due to continuing fighting in Tripoli's southern suburbs and Tarhouna, bring the total of internally displaced persons in Libya to more than 400,000. Ending with there have been 1,342 confirmed cases of COVID-19 with 38 deaths.

Restart oil production after a six-month shutdown

The Libyan National Oil Company has announced the resumption of oil production and exports after a nearly six-month shutdown that has cost the country $6bn (£4.7bn) in lost revenues and deepened the country's civil war.

The oilfields have been shut since January 2020 and in the past, it's under the control of Haftar, then, a group of Russian mercenaries employed by the Wagner Group.

But the resumption of production, with safety and security this is, would be a sign that progress has been made in UN-led discussions on the distribution of Libyan oil revenues between the east and west of the country, as well as a future professional security force to protect the oil fields.

The oil revenues are gathered by the NOC, but then distributed to the Tripoli-based central bank. this is under the supervision of the Government of National Accord, Fathi Bashagha he resumption of oil production and said, "Oil belongs to all Libyans, and its revenues must be managed transparently and distributed fairly in different regions, and not be a source of sectarian blackmail or political rivalries,".

This production as a result of the fighting between the east and the west after the GNA, backed by Turkish-supplied forces and air defenses, decisively lifted Haftar's siege of Tripoli two months ago. Moreover, the eastern forces have warned Turkey not to try to enter the coastal port of Sirte.

Also, Turkey will protect the oil with a deal a professional, loyal force is established to protect the oilfields, and prevent militia such as the PFG repeatedly hijacking the oil fields to make political and economic demands.

The Acting Special Representative of the UN Secretary-General in Libya, Stephanie Williams, met with the Speaker of Libya's Tobruk-based House of Representatives, Aqila Saleh, in Geneva and discussed the need to intensify efforts to find an inclusive political solution to the Libyan crisis, added, revealing that the officials also welcomed the National Oil Corporation's announcement of lifting the force majeure on oil exports after nearly 6 months of suspension.

Williams and Saleh stressed the necessity to avoid any obstacles in oil flow "as it belongs to all Libyans; and urged that revenues expenditures be managed transparently and professionally,". this statement because they are afraid of Turkey and they want to prevent a new humanitarian and economic catastrophe in Sirte and the Oil Crescent.

The role of Russia

Russia and Turkey are working on an immediate ceasefire agreement for the conflict in Libya. Lavrov Russian Foreign Minister said the Libyan National Army (LNA), which Russia backs, is ready to sign a ceasefire document and hopes that Turkey will manage to convince the country's internationally recognized Government of National Accord (GNA) to do the same. He is saying this because Turkey is controlling the region, and there is no room for a government during a period of happiness for its forces Turkey and Italy agree Libya needs a political solution Turkey and Italy's defense ministers agreed on the need for a political solution to Libya's conflict, according to readout by the Turkish defense ministry.

Turkey, with the second-largest military in NATO, backs the internationally recognized GNA government in Libya's conflict while eastern Libyan commander Khalifa Haftar is backed by the United Arab Emirates, Egypt, and Russia, that point they have relations between some NATO members have soured over Libya as Turkey has accused France of backing Haftar's forces. Paris denies this and accused Turkish warships of aggressive behavior, an incident when a French frigate under NATO command tried to inspect a cargo ship suspected of smuggling arms to Libya in violation of a U.N. embargo.

Besides, the European Union recognizes the GNA but there are differences between member states. Italy, whose state-controlled oil and gas major Eni company is the biggest foreign oil producer in Libya, has sent troops to train GNA security forces.

European countries worry about Libya because of its energy supplies because they have the biggest station power in the region and the role as a major source of undocumented migration to Europe (AlAshry, 2020, July 13).

Turkey controls Libya

Turkish company will run a fleet of floating power generators is sending a technical team to Libya to propose to supply electricity to the west of the North African nation. They will send the team to Libya within weeks and could start supplying power to western Libya within 30 days. The Turkish firm specializes in producing and selling electricity from ships anchored off the coast. It sells power to more than 10 countries that cannot meet power demand from their onshore plants, including Lebanon and several African nations. The company, which operates 25 floating plants with a combined output of 4,100 megawatts (MW), could supply power through the ports of Tripoli West, al-Khoms, and Misrata.

Turkey and Russia have agreed to keep pushing for a ceasefire in Libya, but Ankara said the leader of the eastern forces was not legitimate and his forces must withdraw from key positions for any credible deal to emerge. Turkey made an agreement with Russia to work on a credible and sustainable ceasefire in Libya," President Tayyip Erdogan's top security adviser Ibrahim Kalin told Reuters.

The deal must be based on a return to the Libyan frontlines in 2015, requiring Haftar's forces to pull back from the Mediterranean city of Sirte, gateway to Libya's eastern oilfields, and Jufra, an airbase near the centre of the country. For the ceasefire to be sustainable, Jufra and Sirte should be evacuated by Haftar's forces

On the other hand, the United States has sent warplanes to Jufra via Syria to support Russian mercenaries who are fighting alongside Haftar's Libyan National Army (LNA).

Turkey accuses France of supporting Haftar politically, having previously given him military assistance to fight Islamist militants.

France's respond foreign ministry rebuffed U.S. assertions that a European Union naval mission to enforce a U.N. weapons embargo for Libya was biased and not serious, saying Washington should itself be doing more to stop the flow of weapons.

In the second cooperation between Erdogan and US, Trump agreed to work more closely in Libya to ensure lasting stability in the country — even though he knows that Turkey supports the internationally recognized Government of National Accord in Libya. President Trump originally supported the Haftar government, but when Haftar's forces weakened, he was now in solidarity with Turkey to rearrange reconciliation.

The House of Representatives based in the eastern port of Tobruk wants Egypt to support Libya to stave off what it described as a Turkish invasion and occupation. They claim that Turkey has a plan to seize Libya and they have the growing stakes, where battle lines solidified earlier this month near the city of Sirte after the GNA and Turkey repelled a yearlong assault on Tripoli by the eastern-based Libyan National Army (LNA).

There will be a further escalation in the region that could risk igniting a direct conflict in Libya among the foreign powers that have already poured in weapons and fighters in violation of an arms embargo. There is also escalation between the LNA, backed by the United Arab Emirates, Russia, and Egypt and Turkey with the U.S.

Egyptian President el-Sisi has already warned his country's army might enter Libya if the GNA and its Turkish allies renew an assault on Sirte. Tribal leaders told Sisi at a meeting in Cairo that they authorized him and the Egyptian army to intervene in their country to counter what they described as the "Turkish invasion and terrorism".

Turkey is backed by Qatar and wants to control the Muslim Brotherhood in the region and to place the region under Turkey and Qatar.

In the past, Russia supported Haftar, but now they have moved to support Turkey — these are the interests between those countries who do not care about the Libyan people, they just want oil. And so the war continues for years and years, and there is no solution for reform.

In the end, we find that the region is burning with fire, the Turkish president provokes the superpowers to control Libya and threatens to escalate into a wider conflict (AlAshry, 2020, August 01).

Libya conflict recovers by a ceasefire

International calls for a ceasefire and a demilitarized zone around Sirte, the GNA said its head Fayez al-Sarraj had issued instructions to all military forces to immediately cease fire and all combat operations in all Libyan territories.

According to that many countries welcomed the ceasefire push, including Egypt, the UAE, and Saudi Arabia. Qatar, which is aligned with Turkey and the GNA, also praised the move. Sisi praised both ceasefire calls as "an important step on the road to achieving a political settlement".

GCC Secretary-General Nayef Falah Mubarak al-Hajraf called on all parties to adhere to this constructive step, to urgently engage in political dialogue, and to work through the mediation of the United Nations to reach a permanent and comprehensive solution to end the fighting and conflict in Libya.

Libya's internationally recognized government in Tripoli announced the ceasefire and the leader of a rival parliament in eastern Libya also appealed for a halt to hostilities.

Now the foreign countries are discussing some negotiations for a cease-fire and arranging the papers so that everyone can take a piece from the cake in Libya.

First, the new deal, the Interior Minister of the Libyan Government of National Accord (GNA) Fathi Bashagha with Qatari and Turkish Defense Ministers discussed that vigilance was very important as war can break again in Libya at any moment to control the country no one can come again. Qatar and Turkey will ramp up cooperation in all fields, especially in security, showcasing the mechanisms of his ministry's work and its aims to boost the capabilities of its personnel.

Turkish Defense Minister Hulusi Akar said his government is assisting Libya upon the invitation of the GNA, which was recognized by the United Nations, adding that Ankara will continue standing with our Libyan brothers and sisters in the future, with which we share a common history and culture of 500 years (Reuters, August 2, 2020).

This corporation with Qatari Defense Minister on Libyans to bridge the gap among them to allow their country to be stable and secure. The Turkish presidential Ibrahim Kalin said Germany's call for a demilitarized solution in Sirte and Jufra could be accepted by Ankara as a preliminary approach, the only solution lies in unity in the international community's stance on Libya.

In addition, Turkey and Qatar are present in Libya in an effort to support a political solution in the war-weary country. Turkey was concerned that military elements had been building up in the Libyan cities of Sirte and Jufra for a year and this posed a threat to the country's peace and territorial integrity.

Ankara administration did not seek any military solutions anywhere in Libya and did not want to come face to face with any foreign country, as we know Egypt was a neighbour of Libya she could adopt a constructive role to resolve the conflict or can cooperate with us because we have the presence of mercenaries from Russia's Wagner Group and other mercenaries the United Arab Emirates (UAE) brought from countries such as Sudan, Niger, and Chad was a source of concern for Turkey.

Second, the cooperation with Erdogan and Vladimir Putin did a deal to tackled developments in Libya this cooperation between two countries could help one another in Libya.

On first Russia supported warlord Haftar despite Moscow denying such claims, noting that the Russian administration sought to act as a mediator between the conflicting sides in Libya but now they shift the cooperation with Erdogan. The objective in Libya is to ridding Sirte and Jufra of weapons and mercenaries could be a good idea to stop clashes and this could be a window of opportunity for a political solution in the country, adding this to the process had to be conducted in a fair and transparent.

The third cooperation between the Chairman of the National Oil Corporation (NOC), Mustafa Sanalla at the NOC's HQ, and the German Foreign Minister, Heiko Maas, who arrived in Tripoli he deals with the featured members of NOC senior staff, highlighted the impact of the illegal blockade on oil facilities, in addition to Germany's efforts to solve the Libyan crisis.

They discussed the matters of concern were the economic and environmental damages and the risks arising from the oil shutdown, in terms of public safety, as the oil sites are still occupied by armed groups and foreign mercenaries. They are adding financial transparency in parallel with the restoring of security arrangements.

The German part Foreign Minister emphasized the need to bring the oil blockade crisis to an end as soon as possible. He stressed his country's support for the NOC's efforts to resume production, underscoring the NOC's role in preserving the unity of Libya, now it is Germany's turn to control Libya because it found that Turkey would take all the land, including oil so that

Germany needs to evacuate oil facilities from all manifestations of military presence and make them demilitarized buffer zones, and not to use the oil sector as a political bargaining chip.

Now Haftar finds himself in loss and under pressure agreed to reopen the oil fields and ports after seven months of forced closure that caused losses worth $ 8.368 billion. We find that there is no end to the issue of war in Libya.

Libya's Prime Minister Fayez Al Sarraj Stepping Down.

Libya's Prime Minister Fayez al Sarraj announced he will hand over his duties to the next executive authority at the end of October. Sarraj is head of the Government of National Accord (GNA), based in Tripoli, while eastern Libya and much of the south is controlled by Khalifa Haftar's Libyan National Army (LNA).

According to the UN, Sarraj made good progress in agreeing by a way to unify Libya's fragmented state and prepare for elections. In early October 2015, the United Nations envoy to Libya, Bernardino León, proposed a National Unity Government for Libya, to be led by the Presidential Council of Fayez al-Sarraj, as prime minister, three deputies from the country's eastern, western, and southern regions, and two ministers.

However, this national unity government was rejected by the internationally recognized legislature in Tobruk and the rival government in Tripoli. Sarraj, and six members of the Presidential Council and proposed cabinet arrived in Tripoli on March 30 2016.

The civil war has drawn in regional and international powers with the United Arab Emirates, Egypt and Russia supporting the LNA and Turkey supporting the GNA. With Turkey's help, Al-Sarraj and his internationally recognized government were able to control western Libya and quash a yearlong offensive on the capital by eastern commander Khalifa Haftar.

However, Tripoli has since fallen into political infighting, and Sarraj has also faced pressure from a protest movement against corruption and poor services. Saraj has come under pressure while setting the stage for his exit after the Geneva talks. The warring sides will be urged to agree on a new presidential council structure that unifies the country's duelling administrations and scheduled elections.

Additionally, tensions between Turkey and Greece, a country increasingly backed by France, a non-eastern Mediterranean state, have considerably escalated. France also recently sent warships to the region in a show of support to Athens, all of that because Libya opened the way for Turkey to control it. This decision will be expected to be welcomed by Haftar's and his support Egypt and the United Arab Emirates while facilitating talks to unify the conflict-torn North African country that sits on the continent's highest oil reserves. Haftar also opens a way to Parliament Speaker Ageela Salah, who has proposed a political initiative to unify the country's institutions and is now leading political talks for the eastern camp.

As mentioned, there are tensions between the forces of the West. As such, Greece opened a dialogue with Turkey as both countries' diplomats met at NATO headquarters in Brussels with the aim of reducing tensions.

Washington also urged calm from both countries, two NATO allies, offering its mediation to address their differences. Serraj's departure could lead to new infighting among other senior GNA figures, and between the armed groups from Tripoli and Bashagha's coastal city of Misrata that wield control on the ground. Experts said this is a wrong decision and it's not the time ultimately, as it will leave the GNA as an entity, and western Libya a bit degraded.

An LNA blockade of energy exports since January 2020 has deprived the Libyan state of most of its usual revenue, worsening living standards and contributing to protests.

After Sarraj announced his intention to step down by the end of October, Erdogan told reporters in Istanbul, "A development like this, hearing such news, has been upsetting for us," adding that Turkish delegations may hold talks with Sarraj's government in the coming week. "With these meetings, God willing we will turn this issue towards the direction it needs to go," Erdogan said. "The US backs Turkish political position in the Libyan civil war in order to limit Russian influence in the region." But France, Russia, and the UAE might try to spoil this new political arrangement, "I do not guess that they could." says Bulovali (Alashry, September 23, 2020).

New Cooperation between EU and US in Libya

The European Union removed an east Libyan powerbroker from its sanctions blacklist to encourage peace efforts and ensure the EU plays a central role in any negotiated settlement in Libya.

The de-listing of speaker Saleh was agreed upon in light of his recent constructive engagement in support of a negotiated political solution to the Libyan crisis. The parliament in eastern Libya no longer faces EU travel bans and asset freezes imposed four years ago, as European powers see a chance to reassert their role in Libya – which has been in turmoil since the first war in 2011 after the fall of Gaddafi and the second period after the ceasefire in August 2020 and to counter growing Turkish and Russian military involvement.

The good situation with the EU supports the internationally recognized Government of National Accord (GNA) based in the capital Tripoli. The EU now sees Saleh as a pivotal figure in a push to bring the two sides of the Libyan conflict together.

The United Nations mission has the same role in Libya; warring sides have agreed to resume military talks next week after meeting in Egypt hoping the step could pave the way towards a lasting ceasefire. The Egypt talks addressed confidence-building measures, security arrangements, and the role of the Petroleum Facilities Guard, which is supposed to protect the energy infrastructure.

The recommendations include prisoner swaps and releases, and expediting the reopening of air and land transport links, and would be presented to military delegations.

The UN and The European Union-led process have run in parallel with other tracks held by factions within both the GNA and LNA and between outside powers involved in the conflict.

The US is concerned about Libya and the troubled Sahel region to the south of the Sahara with Algeria. The US is alarmed by the threat posed by Islamist militant groups in North Africa.

On the same side, Algeria is weighing a more active military role outside its own borders. In addition, the Pentagon chief Esper voiced support for expanding military relations with Algeria.

On the other hand, the UN has accused outside countries, including those who have formally backed its ceasefire process, of breaking an arms embargo to supply the sides with weapons and fighters. This cooperation came as a result of relations between NATO allies Turkey and France having deteriorated over conflicting policies in Libya, and Turkey's dispute with Greece over energy resources.

France has supported Greece in the east Mediterranean, joining military exercises with Italy, Greece, and Cyprus amid conflicting Greek-Turkish claims to continental shelves in areas of exploration for oil and natural gas.

For its part, Ankara accuses Paris of politically backing Libya's Haftar against the Tripoli-based government, having previously given him military assistance to fight Islamist militants.

Turkey and France also almost came to blows in June 2020 after a French warship attempted to inspect a Turkish vessel as part of a UN arms embargo against Libya. From that point, Turkey had thwarted French hope for Haftar to capture the Libyan capital by lending military support for the Government of National Accord (GNA). France was the country provoking Greece the most in the eastern Mediterranean and urged Paris to cooperate with Turkey to achieve regional stability.

On the other hand, foreign countries are discussing some negotiations for a ceasefire and arranging the papers so that everyone can take a piece from the cake in Libya.

The Interior Minister of the Libyan Government of National Accord (GNA) Fathi Bashagha with Qatari and Turkish Defense Ministers discussed that vigilance was very important as war can break out again in Libya at any moment. Qatar and Turkey will ramp up cooperation in all fields, especially in security, showcasing the mechanisms of his ministry's work and its aims to boost the capabilities of its personnel.

Turkish Defense Minister Hulusi Akar said his government is assisting Libya upon the invitation of the GNA, which was recognized by the UN, adding that Ankara will continue standing with our Libyan brothers and sisters in the future, with whom we share a common history and culture of 500 years.

In the end, many situations in Libya are matters of concern, including the economic and environmental damages and the risks arising from the oil shutdown, in terms of public safety, as the oil sites are still occupied by armed groups and foreign mercenaries. Efforts are aimed at adding financial transparency in parallel with the restoring of security arrangements.

The US and EU must emphasize the need to bring the oil blockade crisis to an end as soon as possible and support the NOC's efforts to resume production to underscoring its role in preserving the unity of Libya. Furthermore, Libya needs to evacuate oil facilities from all manifestations of military presence and make them demilitarized buffer zones, and not use the oil sector as a political bargaining chip (Alashry, October 3, 2020).

From War to Democracy: New Elections in Libya By February 2021

Libya will go to democracy and freedom with new national elections. The two warring sides agreed to a ceasefire last week to start a new role for Libya. Libya has been split since 2014 between factions based in the capital Tripoli, in the west, and in the city of Benghazi, in the east.

Last week a truce was agreed in Geneva by the Tripoli-based Government of National Accord (GNA) and Khalifa Haftar's eastern-based Libyan National Army (LNA). The political talks have started online and will move to Tunis on Nov. 9. The United Nations was imperative to agree on arrangements to hold elections as soon as possible, including by forming a new unified leadership to oversee them. This step needs the governments to have a clear focus – preparing for the elections.

In addition, progress to end an eight-month oil blockade and reopening internal transport routes, and involvement of figures from across Libya's political spectrum are in progress.

Libya has suffered from the war from the 2011 'Arab Spring' and the fall of Gaddafi when the protests and thought out Gaddafi. People had endured just over forty years of Muammer Gaddafi's rule, which involved limits on freedom of speech, and a heavy and violent police state. Libyans had grown tired and frustrated with living under a tightly controlled and corrupt dictatorship and they still do, in the same way. These protests quickly evolved into a rebellion and a civil war between Gaddafi loyalists, and those who wished to oust his government, and fighting would go on for several more years. This fighting also involved NATO military intervention, which bombed military sites but also collaterally civilian areas.

Since 2011, Libya has gone through several government changes, which has led to a long stretch of both political and economic instability. So maybe the new elections can control the country again not like in the past with the General National Congress (GNC) who were elected in July 2012, with the primary goal of establishing a new constitution for Libya.

In addition, the two main political parties who formed this Congress were deeply divided on key issues and failed to reach any real compromises. These two parties were the National Forces Alliance, divided into a predominantly liberal group, and the Justice & Construction Party, a group associated with the Muslim Brotherhood. These divisions were happening; Libya's security situation grew worse and worse with the second civil war was triggered. The second situation with the House of Representatives (HoR) was elected, on the other side, the Islamist groups rejected the election results and continued to support the old GNC. Also, the GNC voted itself in as a replacement and declared the HoR government dissolved and took this declaration as a threat.

The Libyan people have lived with instability and violence for nearly a decade, and they're now facing ever-worsening living conditions without health care, inflation of the prices, economic instability, poverty, and the worst with an electricity crisis and Water. As a result, both governments are corrupt, and they cannot continue with the way things are. Interventions from the UN with the Commission of 10 agreed in the Ghadames meeting to form a military sub-committee to supervise the withdrawal of all forces and mercenaries from the frontlines. The Commission also agreed to locate its headquarters in Ouagadougou Conference Halls in Sirte.

The Commission of 10 agreed to meet in mid-November in Brega with the two chiefs of the Petroleum Facilities Guard (PFG) and the Head of the National Oil Corporation (NOC) to discuss the reformation of PFG. Moreover, the committees will focus on the withdrawal of foreign mercenaries and heavy weapons until all forces return to their previous positions and the area to be covered by the joint force after the withdrawal of the forces will be from south Soukna, all across Libya will be tasked with securing the area from which the forces will pull out, adding that all forces will be withdrawing from the regions, cities, and towns in which there were armed conflicts across the country; starting with Sirte and Jufra.

All of that it is hoped will open the floor for new elections with twenty-nine elected mayors from cities and regions across Libya and elections to be held by February 2021, the Transitional Constitutional Declaration said, stressing that HNEC is able to hold parliamentary elections within a period of 120 days. Following the transitional Constitutional Declaration including the needs to speed up the holding of parliamentary elections end of February 2021, the Presidential Council has to provide the material support required to hold parliamentary elections, UNSMIL must accept full responsibility for these elections and the next elected House of Representatives shall exercise its functions for two years, without extension.

The goal of that is going to be to firmly set the roadmap for national elections because that is the one way that the Libyan people can restore their sovereignty and exercise their right to elect their representatives(Alashry, November 5, 2020).

US Blacklist Libyan Militia, Leader After Russia Stopped UN Sanctions.

The United States unilaterally blacklisted Libya's Kaniyat militia and its leader Mohamed al-Kani. The Kaniyat militia has tortured and killed civilians during a cruel campaign of oppression in Libya, despite Russia last week preventing a U.N. Security Council committee from imposing sanctions over human rights abuses by the group.

The United States and Germany proposed that the U.N. Security Council's 15-member Libya sanctions committee impose an asset freeze and travel ban on Kaniyat militia and al-Kani. This will be imposed under the Global Magnitsky Act, which allows the U.S. government to target human rights violators worldwide by freezing assets and prohibiting Americans from doing business with them.

On the other hand, Russia said it could not approve the sanctions because it wanted to see more evidence first that they had killed civilians and give evidence about what happened in the city 12 bodies from four unmarked graves in Tarhouna, adding to the scores of corpses already discovered since June, as we know Government of National Accord (GNA), had for years been controlled by the Kaniyat militia run by the local Kani family, which fought alongside Khalifa Haftar's eastern-based Libyan National Army (LNA).

In addition, the United Nations Libya envoy pressed the U.N. Security Council to blacklist anyone who obstructs peace efforts after the warring parties agreed on a ceasefire and Libyan participants in political talks set a date for elections.

The council has tools at its disposal including preventing obstructionists from jeopardizing this rare opportunity to restore peace in Libya. Last month the two sides in the country's war – the internationally recognized Government of National Accord (GNA) and Khalifa Haftar's eastern-based Libyan National Army (LNA) – agreed with a ceasefire and Libyan participants in political talks last week set Dec. 24, 2021, as the date for elections.

The United States and Germany wrote in their sanctions proposal that international human rights groups, known as UNSMIL, has "received reports of hundreds of human rights abuses perpetrated by the al-Kaniyat militia against private individuals, state officials, captured fighters, and civil society activists in Tarhouna, under Mohammed al-Kani's leadership, has reportedly carried out enforced disappearances, torture, and killings at Tarhouna Prison conducted on September 13, 2019, the proposal read. The United States investigated the corruption issues allegations undoubtedly threaten the integrity of the Libyan political situation. Additionally, the failure to reveal the results of the investigation around these allegations and excluding those involved in the bribery will undermine the political situation process in its entirety.

This will put the credibility of this political situation or any future stability in jeopardy with potentially dire consequences on future general elections as well as attaining peace and stability in the country. The United Nations has a moral and ethical obligation to continue the elections and announce the results. Recommendations of the Secretary-General of the United Nations and the United Nations Support Mission in Libya:

Continue the investigation and announce the mission and take all measures to help reveal the truth.

Declare the results of the investigation publicly announce the members of the dialogue involved in acts of corruption and exclude them from the remaining dialogue sessions.

Inform the public about the investigation results.

Prevent anyone who involved in corruption issues from running for sovereign positions, whether in the Presidential Council or the government.

Recommendations of the Office of the Public Prosecutor in Libya:

- Take the necessary legal measures and start an urgent criminal investigation into the incident.
- Refer those involved to the national justice system in accordance with the law.
- Publicly announce the results of the investigation and the procedures that will follow (AlAshry, December 16, 2020).

Conclusion: prosectes for National Consensus

The war in Libya will not end because there are many interactions between America and the superpowers that want to control the region the main reason for Israel's tendencies to dominate the Middle East and to destroy the country

On the other hand, Russia wants control, it has taken control of Syria and wants to expand in Libya. Turkey has recently emerged and has supported the Muslim Brotherhood through Qatar and Iran and wants to control the Middle East and eliminate Egypt. But Egypt took its support from the UAE and Saudi Arabia to secure its external borders. There is another group of superpowers, France, Italy, and Germany they want only the oil.

You can see there is something hidden It is the arms trade, when conflict increases, the agencies sell arms this is the most important goal to sell a share of oil to buy weapons.

In future scenarios, the two governments will be eliminated, and other conflicting parties will emerge, which will be formed by America, to increase the conflict. This goal is that the Middle East is always in a state of delay and wars. This increases the power of America and Israel and weakens the Middle East.

The war will remain in Libya for petroleum smuggling, arms sales, and illegal immigration.

The conflict never ends

Glossary

Abdul Rahman al Swehli. The chairman of the GNA High Council of State. He is from Misrata in northwestern Libya and previously supported Libya Dawn.

Ageela Saleh Issa. The president and speaker of the Libyan House of Representatives.

Ahmed Maetig. The deputy prime minister–designate of the GNA and the vice-chairman of the GNA Presidency Council.

(ARSC). An Islamist militant group formed in 2015 that has ties to Ansar al Sharia.

Ajdabiya. A city located on the road to eastern Libya's largest cities and ports.

Al Bunyan al Marsous (BAM). A coalition of primarily Misratan militias that formally submits to the GNA's Presidency Council as commander in chief but operates independently in practice. BAM forces captured Sirte city from ISIS in 2016 with US air support.

Al Qaeda. The network of Salafi-jihadi groups.

Ansar al Sharia. A Salafi-jihadi group established during the 2011 Libyan revolution.

AQIM. See Al Qaeda in the Islamic Maghreb.

ARSC. See Ajdabiya Revolutionaries Shura Council.

Benghazi Defense Brigades (BDB). A militia coalition comprised of Islamist-leaning military officers and Salafi-jihadi fighters.

Benghazi. The second-largest city in Libya.

BRSC. See Benghazi Revolutionaries Shura Council.

da'wa. The obligation to call others to the Islamic faith.

Derna. A coastal city in northeastern Libya with longstanding ties to Salafi-jihadi networks.

Fayez al Serraj. The prime minister–designate of the Government of National Accord (GNA) and the chairman of the GNA's Presidency Council. He previously represented Tripoli as a member of the Tobruk Parliament.

Fezzan. A region in southwestern Libya.

General National Congress (GNC). A rump Islamist parliament. It was Libya's legislature from 2012 until the election of the House of Representatives in 2014.

GNA. See Government of National Accord.

GNC. See General National Congress.

Government of National Accord (GNA). A UN-backed unity government established by the Libyan Political Agreement in 2015.

High Council of State (HCS). A consultative body comprised of former GNC members under the 2015 Libyan Political Agreement.

House of Representatives (HoR). A formerly internationally recognized legislature based in Tobruk in eastern Libya.

Islamic State of Iraq and al Sham (ISIS). The network of Salafi-jihadi individuals and groups affiliated with the group led by Abu Bakr al Baghdadi.

Khalifa Haftar. Field Marshal Haftar commands eastern Libya's largest fighting force, the Libyan National Army. He defected from the Gaddafi regime in the 1980s.

Kufra. A district in southeastern Libya.

Libya Dawn. A defunct coalition of Islamist, Misratan, and other western Libyan forces.

Libyan Investment Authority. The body responsible for overseeing Libya's sovereign wealth fund.

Libyan National Army. A coalition of military units, local and tribal militias, and Salafi fighters led by Field Marshal Khalifa Haftar.

Libyan Political Agreement (LPA). A partially implemented UN-brokered deal signed by Libyan political factions in December 2015 to create the GNA unity government.

LPA. Libyan Political Agreement. Misratan Third Force. A force that secured oil sites, military installations, and population centers in southwestern Libya between 2014 and 2017.

Muammar al Gaddafi. The late dictator of Libya. Gaddafi took power in a military coup in 1969 and ruled until his death during the 2011 revolution.

National Salvation Government (NSG). The rump government associated with the former GNC Parliament. It stepped down in 2016 but has sought to regain power in Tripoli.

National Transitional Council (NTC). The internationally recognized council that led the Libyan opposition during the 2011 revolution.

NOC. Libyan National Oil Corporation.

NSG. National Salvation Government.

Oil Crescent. A region in north-central Libya that contains the majority of the country's oil reserves and two major export terminals.

Operation Dignity. An operation launched by Khalifa Haftar in 2014 in Benghazi.

Operation Libya Dawn. An operation by Islamist and Misratan militia groups that began in summer 2014 to capture Tripoli.

Sabratha. A human trafficking hub in northwestern Libya.

Saif al Islam al Gaddafi. The heir apparent of late Libyan dictator Muammar al Gaddafi.

Salafism. An ideology whose followers seek to return to the fundamentals of Islam as practiced righteously by the earliest generation of Muslims (the Salaf).

Sirte. A city on the central Libyan coast that ISIS governed from 2014 to 2016. It is Muammar al Gaddafi's hometown.

Tripoli. Libya's capital and home to one-sixth of the country's population.

UNSMIL. A special mission established in September 2011 to support Libya's transitional authorities.

Ghassan Salamé. Lebanese academic is a head of UNSMIL.

Zintan. A city-state in northwestern Libya. Zintani forces temporarily seized Tripoli as part of Operation Dignity in 2014.

Libya Conflict Timeline: 1951-2020

1951 Libya achieves independence from Italy.

1969 King Idris is ousted in a coup led by Colonel Muammar Gaddafi.

1975 Libya occupies the Aouzou strip, an area of northern Chad adjacent to the southern Libyan border.

1980 Libya intervenes in a civil war in northern Chad to back President Goukouni Oueddei against the French-backed forces of Hissein Habré.

1986 The US bombs Libyan military facilities in Tripoli and Benghazi over the alleged involvement of Libya in bombing a nightclub in West Berlin which led to the deaths of US military personnel.

1988 An airliner is blown up over the Scottish town of Lockerbie allegedly by Libyan agents.

1990 Chad and Libya decide to go before the International Court of Justice (ICJ) over the Aouzou strip. ICJ rules in favour of Chad in 1994.

1992 The UN imposes sanctions on Libya in line with the suspected involvement of Libyans in the Lockerbie bombing.

2003 The UN Security Council lifts sanctions against Libya after the Lockerbie bombing.

2006 The US restores full diplomatic relations with Libya.

2011 February Violent protests break out in Benghazi and spread to other cities in the wake of the Arab Spring.

2011 March The UN Security Council authorizes a no-fly zone over Libya led by the North Atlantic Treaty Organization (NATO).

2011 October Gaddafi is captured and killed in ambiguous circumstances. Following the death of Gaddafi, NATO ends operations in Libya on 31 October 2011.

2012 July the General National Congress (GNC) is elected in a popular vote and handed power by the National Transitional Council (NTC) in August 2012.

2012 October the GNC elects Ali Zeidan as prime minister.

2014 February the GNC refuses to dissolve after its power expires.

2014 March the GNC deposes Ali Zeidan and elects businessman Ahmed Maiteeq as prime minister.

2014 May General Khalifa Haftar launches Operation Dignity against Islamist militias in Benghazi.

2014 May Pro-Dignity forces storm the GNC building demanding the dissolution of the GNC.

2014 June Prime Minister Maiteeq steps down following the Supreme Court's decision that his appointment is unlawful.

2014 July UN staff pulls out from Libya given the deteriorating security situation.

2014 August United Arab Emirates jets fly from military bases in Egypt to conduct airstrikes against Dawn forces in Tripoli.

2014 August Operation Dawn forces mainly made up of Berber factions and Tripoli- and Misrata-based militias seize control of the Tripoli International Airport.

2014 November The Libyan Supreme Court rules that the 25 June elections are unconstitutional and formally dissolves the House of Representatives (HoR), which ignores the ruling and continues operating in Tobruk.

2014 November the HoR confirms its support for Operation Dignity for the first time.

2015 January Libyan army and Tripoli-based militia declare a partial cessation of hostilities agreement in UNmediated talks in Geneva.

2015 February the Islamic State affiliates in Libya seize control of the town of Nawfaliyah in central Libya. The same day they release a video depicting the beheading of 21 Egyptian Copts.

2015 December the HoR and GNC along with their respective governments, sign the Libyan Political Agreement (LPA) in Skhirat, Morocco in a move to resolve their disputes.

2016 January the UN declares a new interim government, the Government of National Accord (GNA), which the Tobruk and Tripoli parliaments refuse to recognize.

2016 March the UN-backed government of GNA sails into Tripoli.

2016 May the Unity government leads a military campaign to retake the town of Sirte from the occupation of the Islamic State group.

2016 July the UN Security Council adopts Resolution 2298 providing for Libya's category 2 chemical weapons to be transferred and destroyed outside of the country.

2016 September General Haftar's Libyan National Army (LNA) seizes key oil export terminals in the East.

2 February 2017 Italian Prime Minister Gentilono and Libyan counterpart Fayez-al Sarraj sign a Memorandum of Understanding to curb migration.

2017 March General Haftar's forces regain control of two major oil ports of Ras Lanuf and Es Sider weeks after it was captured by the Benghazi Defence Brigades.

2017 May General Haftar meets the head of the Presidential Council of Libya for talks in Abu Dhabi.

2017 May the Prosecutor of the International Criminal Court tells the UN Security Council in a briefing that she is considering launching an investigation into alleged migrant-related crimes.

2017 May Following heavy fighting in Libya, Libya's Ansar al-sharia announces its dissolution in a communiqué.

2017 December the UN moves to evacuate thousands of African migrants following disclosure of slave auctions outside of Tripoli.

2018 July - Haftar claims that his forces are fully in control of Derna.

2019 April - Haftar Libyan National Army advances on Tripoli.

2020 June - UN-backed government drives Haftar forces out of Tarhouna

References

Abbas, M. (2019, January 10). Where is the international community from the scandals of smuggling Turkish weapons to Libya?. Retrieved February 02, 2021, from https://www.masrawy.com/news/news-videos/details/2019/1/10/1494336/%D9%85%D8%B5%D8%B7%D9%81%D9%89-%D8%A8%D9%83%D8%B1%D9%8A-%D8%A3%D9%8A%D9%86-%D8%A7%D9%84%D9%85%D8%AC%D8%AA%D9%85%D8%B9-

Abdalla, M., & Garber, K. (2018). Is there a doctor in the house? The challenge of primary health care in Libya". Brookings. Retrieved February 11, 2021, from https://www.brookings.edu/blog/futuredevelopment/2018/12/10/is-there-a-doctor-in-the-house-the-challenge-of-primaryhealth-care-in-libya/

Admin, H. (2013). Global NATO and the Catastrophic Failure in Libya: Lessons for Africa in the Forging of African Unity. Retrieved February 01, 2021, from https://monthlyreview.org/product/global_nato_and_the_catastrophic_failure_in_libya/

Africa News Portal. (2018, January 12). ISIS in Sinai faces the challenge of survival. Retrieved February 11, 2021, from https://www.afrigatenews.net/article/%D8%AF%D8%B1%D8%A7%D8%B3%D8%A9-%D8%AA%D9%86%D8%B8%D9%8A%D9%85-%D8%AF%D8%A7%D8%B9%D8%B4-%D9%81%D9%8A-%D8%B3%D9%8A%D9%86%D8%A7%D8%A1-%D9%8A-%D9%88%D8%A7%D8%AC%D9%87-%D8%AA%D8%AD%D8%AF%D9%8A-%D8%A7%D9%84%D8%A8%D9%82%D8%A7%D8%A1/

Agence France-Presse. (2014, August 18). Splits emerge between Libyan Islamists and jihadists. Retrieved February 01, 2021, from https://news.yahoo.com/splits-emerge-between-libyan-islamists-jihadists-183000425.html

Ahlmasrnews. (2019, April 5). The events of Libya .. What happened between Haftar and Guterres in Benghazi? Retrieved February 02, 2021, from https://www.ahlmasrnews.com/823745

Aimade, W., & McMahon, C. (2018, June 20). Oil battle Returns Libya to the brink. Retrieved February 11, 2021, from http://en.minbarlibya.org/2018/06/20/oil-battle-returns-libya-to-the-brink/

Akhbarelyom. (2019, July 17). Mutual accusations between the army and al-Sarraj of bombing residential neighborhoods in Tripoli.(17 July2019). Retrieved February 02, 2021, from https://akhbarelyom.com/news/newdetails/2877453/1/%D8%AD%D9%81%D8%AA%D8%B1--%D8%AD%D8%B5%D9%88%D9%84-%D8%A7%D9%84%D8%AC%D9%8A%D8%B4-

%D8%A7%D9%84%D9%84%D9%8A%D8%A8%D9%8A-
%D8%B9%D9%84%D9%89-%D8%A3%D9%8A-
%D8%A3%D8%B3%D9%84%D8%AD%D8%A9-%D8%A3%D9%85%D8%B1%D9
%8A%D9%83%D9%8A%D8%A9-%D8%A7%D9%84%D8%B5%D9%86%D8%B9--
%D9%85%D8%AD%D8%B6-%D9%87%D8%B1%D8%A7%D8%A1-

Al Ashry, M. (2020, May 04). Why the European Union sent statement calls for a humanitarian truce in Libya? Retrieved January 31, 2021, from https://www.mediamonitors.net/why-the-european-union-sent-statement-calls-for-a-humanitarian-truce-in-libya/

Al Jazeera. (2018, March 01). Libya embargo VIOLATIONS: UN panel to report findings to UNSC. Retrieved February 11, 2021, from https://www.aljazeera.com/news/2018/03/libya-embargo-violations-panel-report-findings-unsc-180301080019627.html

Al-Qaddaf, M. (1975). The Green Book. Retrieved February 01, 2021, from http://openanthropology.org/libya/gaddafi-green-book.pdf

AlAlashry, M. (2019, July 5). Why Attack On Libya Detention Center. Retrieved February 11, 2021, from https://www.eurasiareview.com/05072019-why-attack-on-libya-detention-center-oped/

AlAshry, M. (2019, December 05). 'Time Is Right' For US: Haftar Must Stop Tripoli Operation Warning Of Russian Meddling In Libya - OpEd. Retrieved February 02, 2021, from https://www.eurasiareview.com/19112019-time-is-right-for-us-haftar-must-stop-tripoli-operation-warning-of-russian-meddling-in-libya-oped/

AlAshry, M. (2019, December 08). Why Did Greece Expel Libyan Ambassador? - OpEd. Retrieved February 02, 2021, from https://www.eurasiareview.com/09122019-why-did-greece-expel-libyan-ambassador-oped/

AlAshry, M. (2019, December 12). UN Security Council Warns Libya To Stop, After Arms Embargo Breaches - OpEd. Retrieved February 02, 2021, from https://www.eurasiareview.com/12122019-un-security-council-warns-libya-to-stop-after-arms-embargo-breaches-oped/

AlAshry, M. (2019, December 26). Libya At Risk: Arrival Of Mercenaries Raise Fears Of Prolonged War - OpEd. Retrieved February 02, 2021, from https://www.eurasiareview.com/27122019-libya-at-risk-arrival-of-mercenaries-raise-fears-of-prolonged-war-oped/

AlAshry, M. (2019, May 30). Khalifa Haftar: Is he still the strongest man in Libya? Retrieved February 02, 2021, from https://www.libyanexpress.com/khalifa-haftar-is-he-still-the-strongest-man-in-libya/

AlAshry, M. (2019, November 29). It's Time To Protect The Refugees In Tripoli - OpEd. Retrieved February 02, 2021, from https://www.eurasiareview.com/29112019-its-time-to-protect-the-refugees-in-tripoli-oped/

AlAshry, M. (2019, September 19). Germany Organizes Libya Conference To Shore Up Arms Embargo. Retrieved from https://www.eurasiareview.com/19092019-germany-organizes-libya-conference-to-shore-up-arms-embargo-oped/

AlAshry, M. (2020, April 13). UAE Gives Libyan Army An Israeli Air Defense System? - OpEd. Retrieved January 31, 2021, from https://www.eurasiareview.com/13042020-uae-gives-libyan-army-an-israeli-air-defense-system-oped/

AlAshry, M. (2020, April 16). UN Libya Mission 'Alarmed' By Rise In Violence, Says Risk Of New Waves Of Displacement - OpEd. Retrieved January 31, 2021, from https://www.eurasiareview.com/17042020-un-libya-mission-alarmed-by-rise-in-violence-says-risk-of-new-waves-of-displacement-oped/

AlAshry, M. (2020, August 01). How Did Turkey Gain Control Of Libya? - OpEd. Retrieved January 31, 2021, from https://www.eurasiareview.com/01082020-how-did-turkey-gain-control-of-libya-oped/

AlAshry, M. (2020, September 23). Why Is Libya's Prime Minister Fayez Al Sarraj Stepping Down? – OpEd. Retrieved January 31, 2021, from https://www.eurasiareview.com/23092020-why-is-libyas-prime-minister-fayez-al-sarraj-stepping-down-oped/

AlAshry, M. (2020, October 03 New Cooperation Between EU And US In Libya – OpEd. Retrieved January 31, 2021, from https://www.eurasiareview.com/03102020-new-cooperation-between-eu-and-us-in-libya-oped/

AlAshry, M. (2020, November 05). From War To Democracy: New Elections In Libya By February 2021 – OpEd. Retrieved January 31, 2021, from https://www.eurasiareview.com/05112020-from-war-to-democracy-new-elections-in-libya-by-february-2021-oped/

AlAshry, M. (2020, December 16). Why Did US Blacklist Libyan Militia, Leader After Russia Stopped UN Sanctions? – OpEd. Retrieved January 31, 2021, from https://www.eurasiareview.com/16122020-why-did-us-blacklist-libyan-militia-leader-after-russia-stopped-un-sanctions-oped/

AlAshry, M. (2020, February 07). Libya Situation A Scandal - OpEd. Retrieved January 31, 2021, from https://www.eurasiareview.com/07022020-libya-situation-a-scandal-oped/

AlAshry, M. (2020, February 24). Libyan Crisis: Deploy Warships To Enforce Libya Arms - OpEd. Retrieved January 31, 2021, from https://www.eurasiareview.com/24022020-libyan-crisis-deploy-warships-to-enforce-libya-arms-oped/

AlAshry, M. (2020, January 06). Why Did Turkey Support Libyan Government? - OpEd. Retrieved February 02, 2021, from https://www.eurasiareview.com/06012020-why-did-turkey-support-libyan-government-oped/

AlAshry, M. (2020, January 12). Putin, Erdogan Urge Libyan Parties To Start Ceasefire - OpEd. Retrieved February 02, 2021, from https://www.eurasiareview.com/13012020-putin-erdogan-urge-libyan-parties-to-start-ceasefire-oped/

AlAshry, M. (2020, January 19). Did Berlin Conference End Libya's War? - OpEd. Retrieved February 02, 2021, from https://www.eurasiareview.com/20012020-did-berlin-conference-end-libyas-war-oped/

AlAshry, M. (2020, January 21). Berlin conference: A first step from war to peace. Retrieved February 02, 2021, from https://www.libyanexpress.com/berlin-conference-a-first-step-from-war-to-peace/

AlAshry, M. (2020, July 13). Turkey Intervention Is 'New Phase Of Libya's Conflict' - OpEd. Retrieved January 31, 2021, from https://www.eurasiareview.com/13072020-turkey-intervention-is-new-phase-of-libyas-conflict-oped/

AlAshry, M. (2020, June 03). Russia, America, Turkey: Why Conflicting Parties In Libya? - OpEd. Retrieved January 31, 2021, from https://www.eurasiareview.com/04062020-russia-america-turkey-why-conflicting-parties-in-libya-oped/

AlAshry, M. (2020, March 05). Why Did UN Envoy Ghassan Salame Quit? - OpEd. Retrieved January 31, 2021, from https://www.eurasiareview.com/05032020-why-did-un-envoy-ghassan-salame-quit-oped/

AlAshry, M. (2020, March 26). Libya Records First Covid-19 Case - OpEd. Retrieved January 31, 2021, from https://www.eurasiareview.com/26032020-libya-records-first-covid-19-case-oped/

AlAshry, M. (2020, May 03). Haftar Ends Skhirat Political Agreement: Tripoli Government Rejects Rebel Ceasefire Offer, What's Next? - OpEd. Retrieved January 31, 2021, from https://www.eurasiareview.com/04052020-haftar-ends-skhirat-political-agreement-tripoli-government-rejects-rebel-ceasefire-offer-whats-next-oped/

AlAshry, M. (2020, May 11). Haftar Show Weakness, Turkey Threatens Retaliation: What Is Next Step? - OpEd. Retrieved January 31, 2021, from https://www.eurasiareview.com/11052020-haftar-show-weakness-turkey-threatens-retaliation-what-is-next-step-oped/

AlAshry, M. (2020, May 23). Who Will Survive In The End? UN-Backed Libyan Forces Or General Haftar - OpEd. Retrieved January 31, 2021, from https://www.eurasiareview.com/23052020-who-will-survive-in-the-end-un-backed-libyan-forces-or-general-haftar-oped/

AlAshry, M. S. (2019, August 21). Middle East Countries Must Cooperate To Support Stability In Libya. Retrieved February 02, 2021, from https://www.eurasiareview.com/21082019-middle-east-countries-must-cooperate-to-support-stability-in-libya-oped

AlAshry, M. S. (2019, June 1). Most Wanted Terrorist' Deadly Militant Hisham Ashmawi Extradited To Egypt From Libya. Retrieved February 02, 2021, from https://www.eurasiareview.com/01062019-most-wanted-terrorist-deadly-militant-hisham-ashmawi-extradited-to-egypt-from-libya-oped/

AlAshry, M. S. (2019, June 11). Trump Officials Snub Strongman Haftar: US Shifts Course On Libya – OpEd. Retrieved February 02, 2021, from, https://www.eurasiareview.com/11062019-trump-officials-snub-strongman-haftar-us-shifts-course-on-libya-oped/

AlAshry, M. S. (2019, November 8). Libyan Refugees in Crisis – OpEd. Retrieved February 02, 2021, from, https://www.eurasiareview.com/08112019-libyan-refugees-in-crisis-oped/

AlAshry, M. S. (2019, October 28). Finally: US Kills IS Leader Abu Bakr Al-Baghdadi – OpEd. Retrieved February 02, 2021, from, https://www.eurasiareview.com/28102019-finally-us-kills-is-leader-abu-bakr-al-baghdadi-oped/

AlAshry, M. S. (209, July 5). Why Attack On Libya Detention Center. Retrieved February 02, 2021, from, https://www.eurasiareview.com/05072019-why-attack-on-libya-detention-center-oped/

AlAshry, M., By, & -. (2020, June 21). The war between Turkey and Egypt is coming soon. Retrieved January 31, 2021, from https://www.mediamonitors.net/the-war-between-turkey-and-egypt-is-coming-soon/

Alfasi, K. (2016). Libya's Post-Qadhafi Challenges. Retrieved February 02, 2021, from https://www.washingtoninstitute.org/policy-analysis/libyas-post-qadhafi-challenges

Alghad. (2018, May 15). Tears and joy as the remains of Egyptians victims of ISIS in Libya reach their church. Retrieved February 11, 2021, from https://www.alghad.tv/author/26/

Alghad. (2018, November 12). Libya .. a history of chaos from Gaddafi's death to the Palermo meetings. Retrieved February 08, 2021, from https://www.alghad.tv/%D9%84%D9%8A%D8%A8%D9%8A%D8%A7-%D8%AA%D8%A7%D8%B1%D9%8A%D8%AE-%D8%A7%D9%84%D9%81%D9%88%D8%B6%D9%89-%D9%85%D9%86%D8%B0-%D9%88%D9%81%D8%A7%D8%A9-%D8%A7%D9%84%D9%82%D8%B0%D8%A7%D9%81%D9%8A-%D8%AD%D8%AA/

Ali, L. (2018, June 25). Is ISIS's media machine reeling Monday,. Retrieved February 11, 2021, from https://www.youm7.com/story/2018/6/25/%D9%87%D9%84-%D8%AA%D8%B1%D9%86% D8% AD% D8% AA-% D8% A7% D9% 84% D8% A2% D9% 84% D8% A9-% D8% A7% D9% 84% D8% A5% D8% B9% D9% 84% D8% A7% D9% 85% D9% 8A% D8% A9-% D9% 84% D8% AF% D8% A7% D8% B9% D8% B4-% C2% BB-% D8% AF% D8% B1 % D8% A7% D8% B3% D8% A9-% D8% AC% D8% AF% D9% 8A% D8% AF% D8% A9-% D9% 84% D9% 85% D8% B1% D8% B5 % D8% AF-% D8% A7% D9% 84% D8% A3% D8% B2% D9% 87% D8% B1 / 3848094

Ali, M. (2018, December 18). Libyan anti-immigration agency official: Gangs force infiltrators to join ISIS,. Retrieved February 02, 2021, from https://www.vetogate.com/3381691/%d9%85%d8%b3%d8%a6%d9%88%d9%84-%d8%a8%d8%ac%d9%87%d8%a7%d8%b2-%d9%85%d9%83%d8%a7%d9%81%d8%ad%d8%a9-%d8%a7%d9%84%d9%87%d8%ac%d8%b1%d8%a9-%d8%ba%d9%8a%d8%b1-%d8%a7%d9%84%d8%b4%d8%b1%d8%b9%d9%8a%d8%a9-%d8%a7%d9%84%d9%84%d9%8a%d8%a8%d9%8a--%d8%b9%d8%b5%d8%a7%d8%a8%d8%a7%d8%aa-%d8%aa%d8%ac%d8%a8%d8%b1-%d8%a7%d9%84%d9%85%d8%aa%d8%b3%d9%84%d9%84%d9%8a%d9%86-%d8%b9%d9%84%d9%89-%d8%a7%d9%84%d8%a5%d9%86%d8%b6%d9%85%d8%a7%d9%85-%d9%84%d8%aa%d9%86%d8%b8%d9%8a%d9%85-%d8%af%d8%a7%d8%b9%d8%b4-%d8%a7%d9%84%d8%a5%d8%b1%d9%87%d8%a7%d8%a8%d9%89

Ali, M. (2019, May 13). France calls for an immediate cease-fire in Libya. Retrieved February 02, 2021, from https://www.218tv.net/%D9%81%D8%B1%D9%86%D8%B3%D8%A7-%D8%AA%D8%AF%D8%B9%D9%88-%D9%84%D9%88%D9%82%D9%81-%D9%81%D9%88%D8%B1%D9%8A-%D9%84%D8%A5%D8%B7%D9%84%D8%A7%D9%82-%D8%A7%D9%84%D9%86%D8%A7%D8%B1-%D9%81%D9%8A-%D9%84%D9%8A/

Aljazeera. (2013, July 3). Car blast targets army checkpoint in Benghazi. Retrieved February 01, 2021, from https://www.aljazeera.com/africa/

Almasryalyoum. (2019, April 10). The Libyan army controls Ain Zara and advances towards the center of Tripoli. Retrieved February 02, 2021, from https://www.almasryalyoum.com/news/details/1386767

Almasryalyoum. (2019, April 11). The Libyan army orders the arrest of Fayez al-Sarraj and al-Suwahili. Retrieved from https://www.almasryalyoum.com/news/details/1387271

Almasryalyoum. (2019, June 20). The Libyan army declares war on all Turkish interests, ships and products. Retrieved February 02, 2021, from https://www.almasryalyoum.com/news/details/1408729

Almayadeen. (2019, March 22). The Libyan army controls the south of Sebha. Retrieved February 02, 2021, from https://www.almayadeen.net/news/politics/932679/%D9%85%D8%B5%D8%AF%D8%B1-%D8%B9%D8%B3%D9%83%D8%B1%D9%8A--%D8%A7%D9%84%D8%AC%D9%8A%D8%B4-%D8%A7%D9%84%D9%8A%D8%A8%D9%8A-%D9%8A%D8%B3%D9%8A%D8%B7%D8%B1-%D8%B9%D9%84%D9%89-%D8%BA%D8%AF%D9%88%D8%A9-%D8%AC%D9%86%D9%88%D8%A8-%D8%B3%D8%A8%D9%87%D8%A7

Alshadeedi, H., & Ezzeldine, N. (2019). Libyan Tribes in the Shadow of War and Peace". Netherlands Institute of International Relations. Retrieved February 11, 2021, from https://www.clingendael.org/sites/default/files/2019-02/PB_Tribalism.pdf.

Amin, E. (2018, December 31). ISIS, expands in southern Libya. Retrieved February 11, 2021, from https://aawsat.com/home/article/1526121/%C2%AB%D8%AF%D8%A7%D8%B9%D8%B4%C2%BB-%D9%8A%D8%AA%D9%85%D8%AF%D8%AF-%D9%81%D9%8A-%D8%AC%D9%86%D9%88%D8%A8-%D9%84%D9%8A%D8%A8%D9%8A%D8%A7

Amina, Z. (2018). 'You Exile them in their Own Countries': The Everyday Politics of Reclaiming the Disappeared in Libya. *Middle East Critique, 27*, 247-259. doi:https://doi.org/10.1080/19436149.2018.1475855

Amnesty International. (2017). Libya's Dark Web of Collusion. Retrieved February 11, 2021, from https://www.amnesty.org/en/documents/mde19/7561/2017/en/.

Apap, J. (2017). Political developments in Libya and prospects of stability. Retrieved February 08, 2021, from https://www.europarl.europa.eu/RegData/etudes/BRIE/2017/603959/EPRS_BRI(2017)603959_EN.pdf

Arabic. (2018, July 07). Map of the Libyan oil conflict between local and international players. Retrieved February 11, 2021, from https://arabic.sputniknews.com/arab_world/201807071033609815-%D8%A7%D9%84%D9%86%D9%81%D8%B7-%D9%84%D9%8A%D8%A8%D9%8A%D8%A7-%D8%B5%D8%B1%D8%A7%D8%B9/

Arafat, A. (2018, June 19). The Brotherhood and ISIS Libya with one hand. Retrieved February 11, 2021, from http://www.soutalomma.com/Article/817009/%D8%A7%D9%84%D8%A5%D8%AE%D9%88%D8%A7%D9%86-%D9%88%D8%AF%D8%A7%D8%B9%D8%B4-%D9%84%D9%8A%D8%A8%D9%8A%D8%A7-%D8%A5%D9%8A%D8%AF-%D9%88%D8%A7%D8%AD%D8%AF%D8%A9-%D9%87%D9%83%D8%B0%D8%A7-%D9%83%D8%B4%D9%81%D8%AA-%D9%83%D8%AA%D8%A8-%D8%B3%D9%8A%D8%AF-%D9%82%D8%B7%D8%A8

Arraf, S. (2017, July). Libya: A Short Guide on the Conflict. Retrieved February 01, 2021, from https://www.geneva-academy.ch/joomlatools-files/docman-files/Lybia%20A%20Short%20Guide%20to%20the%20Conflict.pdf. The Geneva Academy, Geneva

Arturo, V. (2017). Islamic State's Re-organization in Libya and Potential Connections with Illegal Trafficking. Retrieved February 02, 2021, from https://extremism.gwu.edu/sites/g/files/zaxdzs2191/f/Varvelli%20IS%20Reorganization%20in%20Libya%20and%20Trafficking.pdf

Asaad, K. (2018, June 23). Derna: The last castles in eastern Libya that are intractable to Haftar fall. Retrieved February 11, 2021, from https://www.ida2at.com/derna-the-last-strongholds-of-eastern-libya-fall/

Asaeid. (2018, January 07). Kani Brigade launch offensive On GARABULLI, then withdraw. Retrieved February 08, 2021, from https://www.marsad.ly/en/2018/01/07/kani-brigade-launch-offensive-garabulli-withdraw/

Ashour, O. (2015, August). Between ISIS and a failed state: The saga of Libyan Islamists. Retrieved February 01, 2021, from https://www.brookings.edu/wp-content/uploads/2016/07/Libya_Ashour_FINALv.pdf

Ashry, M. (2020, January 06). Why Did Turkey Support Libyan Government? - OpEd. Retrieved February 02, 2021, from https://www.eurasiareview.com/06012020-why-did-turkey-support-libyan-government-oped/

Assad, A. (2016, February 11). Libya's attorney general receives financial Corruption files. Retrieved February 11, 2021, from https://www.libyaobserver.ly/news/libya%E2%80%99s-attorney-general-receives-financial-corruption-files

Assad, A. (2018, November 20). Libya's parallel central bank admits printing 9.7 million dinar banknotes in Russia. Retrieved February 11, 2021, from https://www.libyaobserver.ly/economy/libyas-parallel-central-bank-admits-printing-97-billion-dinar-banknotes-russia

Assad, A. (2019, November 19). Misrata municipality condemns UN'S Pick-and-choose sanctions in Libya. Retrieved February 08, 2021, from https://www.libyaobserver.ly/news/misrata-municipality-condemns-uns-pick-and-choose-sanctions-libya

Associated Press, A. (2015, March 27). Qaddafi Vows to Fight to 'Last Drop of Blood'. Retrieved February 01, 2021, from https://www.foxnews.com/world/qaddafi-vows-to-fight-to-last-drop-of-blood

Barakat, M. (2018, April 30). Khalifa Haftar leads a military operation to liberate Derna from ISIS. Retrieved February 11, 2021, from Khalifa Haftar leads a military operation to liberate Derna from ISIS

BBC News. (2015, July 28). Libya trial: Gaddafi son sentenced to death over war crimes. Retrieved February 08, 2021, from https://www.bbc.com/news/world-africa-33688391

BBC News. (2015, October 23). Benghazi attack: Six die as Mortars hit libya protest. Retrieved February 08, 2021, from https://www.bbc.com/news/world-africa-34622897

BBC News. (2020, January 22). Why is Libya so lawless? Retrieved February 08, 2021, from https://www.bbc.com/news/world

BBC. (2012, July 18). Libya election success for secularist Jibril's bloc. Retrieved February 01, 2021, from https://www.bbc.com/news/world-africa-18880908

BBC. (2015, August 14). Libya chaos: Islamic State battles militias IN SIRTE. Retrieved February 08, 2021, from https://www.bbc.com/news/world-africa-33936291

BBC. (2019, April 15). Is the Sisi-Haftar meeting an introduction to "Egyptian forces in Libya"? Retrieved February 02, 2021, from https://www.bbc.com/arabic/inthepress-47936484

Bender, J. (2015, November 30). ISIS now has a 'colony' in an oil-rich Libyan city just 400 miles from Italy. Retrieved February 08, 2021, from https://www.businessinsider.com/isis-now-controls-key-libyan-city-2015-11

Benstead, L., & Kjærum, A. A. (2019, May 3). Libya's Security Dilemma." The Washington Post. WP Company. Retrieved February 02, 2021, from https://www.washingtonpost.com/news/monkey-cage/wp/2014/04/07/libyas-security-dilemma/..

Blanchard, C. (2018). Libya: Conflict, Transition, and U.S. Policy. Retrieved January 31, 2021, from https://fas.org/sgp/crs/row/RL33142.pdf

Booth, R., & Taylor, D. (2014, November 04). Libyan troops sent home after sexual assault allegations. Retrieved February 01, 2021, from https://www.theguardian.com/uk-news/2014/nov/04/lansley-criticises-ministry-defence-serious-failure-libyan-military-training

Boserup, A., & Collombier, V. (2018). Militarization and Militia-tization Dynamics of Armed Group Proliferation in Egypt and Libya. Retrieved February 11, 2021, from https://www.iai.it/sites/default/files/menara_wp_17.pdf.

Boyle, F. A. (2013). *Destroying Libya and World Order: The Three-Decade U.S. Campaign to Terminate the Qaddafi Revolution Paperback*. Clarity Press.

Brahimi, A. (2017, May 25). Why Libya is still a global terror threat. Retrieved February 11, 2021, from https://www.theguardian.com/ commentisfree/2017/may/25/libya-global-terror-threatmanchester-attack-gaddafi.

Bronner, E., & Sanger, D. (2011, March 12). Arab League Endorses No-Flight Zone Over Libya. Retrieved February 01, 2021, from https://www.nytimes.com/2011/03/13/world/middleeast/13libya.html

Casciani, D. (2017, May 24). Manchester attack: The libya-jihad connection. Retrieved February 11, 2021, from https://www.bbc.com/news/uk-england-manchester-40037830

Chivvis, C., & Martini, J. (2014, March 17). Libya After Qaddafi. Retrieved February 02, 2021, from https://www.rand.org/pubs/research_reports/RR577.html

CNN. (2020, August 30). Benghazi Mission Attack Fast Facts. Retrieved February 01, 2021, from https://edition.cnn.com/2013/09/10/world/benghazi-consulate-attack-fast-facts/index.html

Cody, E. (2011, March 20). Arab League condemns broad bombing campaign in Libya. Retrieved February 01, 2021, from https://www.washingtonpost.com/world/arab-league-condemns-broad-bombing-campaign-in-libya/2011/03/20/AB1pSg1_story.html

Cole, P., & McQuinn, B. (2015). *The Libyan Revolution and its Aftermath*. New York: C HURST & CO PUB.

Coughlin, C. (2012, December 02). Al-Qaeda 'intensifying efforts to establish new base in Libya'. Retrieved February 01, 2021, from https://www.telegraph.co.uk/news/worldnews/al-qaeda/9717206/Al-Qaeda-intensifying-efforts-to-establish-new-base-in-Libya.html

Council, A., & Atlanticcouncil. (2017, July). Libya: From Intervention to Proxy War. Retrieved February 01, 2021, from https://issuu.com/atlanticcouncil/docs/libya_from_intervention_to_proxy_wa

Cowell, A., & Erlanger, S. (2011, March 10). France Becomes First Country to Recognize Libyan Rebels. Retrieved February 01, 2021, from https://www.nytimes.com/2011/03/11/world/europe/11france.html

Coyne, C., Estelle, E., & Gambhir, H. (2016, February 4). ISIS's campaign in Libya. Retrieved February 08, 2021, from http://www.iswresearch.org/2016/02/isiss-campaign-in-libya-january-4.html?m=0

CPJ. (2015, November 17). CPJ concerned for safety of photojournalist missing in Libya. Retrieved February 04, 2021, from https://cpj.org/2015/11/cpj-concerned-for-safety-of-photojournalist-missin.php

Crisis Group. (2011, August 11). Libya: Ensuring a Smooth and Peaceful Transition into the Post-Qaddafi Era. Retrieved February 01, 2021, from https://www.crisisgroup.org/middle-east-north-africa/north-africa/libya/libya-ensuring-smooth-and-peaceful-transition-post-qaddafi-era

Crisis Group. (2016, August 11). Holding Libya Together: Security Challenges after Qadhafi. Retrieved February 01, 2021, from https://www.crisisgroup.org/middle-east-north-africa/north-africa/libya/holding-libya-together-security-challenges-after-qadhafi

Crisis Group. (2016, July 26). The libyan political dialogue: An incomplete consensus. Retrieved February 04, 2021, from https://www.crisisgroup.org/middle-east-north-africa/north-africa/libya/libyan-political-dialogue-incomplete-consensus

Çubukçu, A. (2013). The Responsibility to Protect: Libya and the Problem of Transnational Solidarity. *Journal of Human Rights, 12*(1), 40-58. doi:DOI: 10.1080/14754835.2013.754291

Dejevsky, M. (2015, February 16). A Libyan front in the war on Isis may not be all it seems. Retrieved February 08, 2021, from https://www.theguardian.com/commentisfree/2015/feb/16/libyan-front-war-isis-murder-21-egyptian-christians-middle-east

Deutsche Welle. (2019, May 13). European Union: Haftar attack on Tripoli is a threat to world peace. Retrieved February 02, 2021, from https://www.dw.com/ar/%D8%A7%D9%84%D8%A7%D8%AA%D8%AD%D8%A7%D8%AF-%D8%A7%D9%84%D8%A3%D9%88%D8%B1%D9%88%D8%A8%D9%8A-%D9%87%D8%AC%D9%88%D9%85-%D8%AD%D9%81%D8%AA%D8%B1-%D8%B9%D9%84%D9%89-%D8%B7%D8%B1%D8%A7%D8%A8%D9%84%D8%B3-%D8%AA%D9%87%D8%AF%D9%8A%D8%AF-%D9%84%D9%84%D8%B3%D9%84%D9%85-%D8%A7%D9%84%D8%B9%D8%A7%D9%84%D9%85%D9%8A/a-48724239

DeWaal, A. (2013, January 04). The African Union and the Libya Conflict of 2011. Retrieved February 01, 2021, from https://sites.tufts.edu/reinventingpeace/2012/12/19/the-african-union-and-the-libya-conflict-of-2011/

Dilloway, S., & Akhtar, S. (2015). Final report of the Panel of Experts established pursuant to resolution 1973 (2011). Retrieved February 01, 2021, from https://www.securitycouncilreport.org/atf/cf/%7B65BFCF9B-6D27-4E9C-8CD3-CF6E4FF96FF9%7D/s_2015_128.pdf

Dobbs, L. (2012). Displaced Libyans return to rebuild Gaddafi's hometown; face needs. Retrieved February 08, 2021, from http://www. unhcr.org/news/stories/2012/4/4f8c2e7b6/displaced-libyansreturn-rebuild-gaddafis-hometown-face-needs.html

DW. (2019, April 15). A plane of Haftar forces was shot down near Tripoli. Retrieved February 02, 2021, from https://www.dw.com/ar/%D8%A5%D8%B3%D9%82%D8%A7%D8%B7-%D8%B7%D8%A7%D8%A6%D8%B1%D8%A9-%D8%AA%D8%A7%D8%A8%D8%B9%D8%A9-%D9%84%D9%88%D8%A7%D8%AA-%D8%AD%D9%81%D8%AA-%D8%B1-%D9%82%D8%B1%D8%A8-%D8%B7%D8%B1%D8%A7%D8%A8%D9%84%D8%B3/a-48322303

Eaton, T. (2020, October 06). Libya's war Economy: Predation, profiteering and state weakness. Retrieved February 11, 2021, from https://www.chathamhouse.org/publication/libyas-war-economy-predation-profiteering-and-state-weakness

The Economist. (n.d.). Despite everything, it's still a success. Retrieved February 01, 2021, from http://www.economist.com/node/21562944

El-Shenawi, E. (2015, February 16). Egypt strikes back, but how far Will ISIS fight go? Retrieved February 08, 2021, from https://english.alarabiya.net/en/perspective/analysis/2015/02/16/Egypt-strikes-back-but-how-far-will-it-go-

El-Tayeb, M. (218, December 25). Libya .. the country of great chaos. Retrieved February 11, 2021, from https://www.afrigatenews.net/article/%D9%84%D9%8A%D8%A8%D9%8A%D8%A7-%D8%A8%D9%84%D8%AF-%D8%A7%D9%84%D9%81%D9%88%D8%B6%D9%89-%D8%A7%D9%84%D8%B9%D8%A7%D8%B1%D9%85%D8%A9/

Elbalad. (2019, April 6). Surprise .. Terrorist Oases Massacre: We sat 11 months in the desert without anyone knowing us, and members of our camp exiled us because of ISIS. Retrieved February 02, 2021, from https://www.elbalad.news/3772533

Elbasset, A. (2019, June 13). The Libyan army is intensifying its operations in the capital. Retrieved February 02, 2021, from Tripoli. https://www.afrigatenews.net/article/%D8%A7%D9%84%D8%AC%D9%8A%D8%B4-%D8%A7%D9%84%D9%84%D9%8A%D8%A8%D9%8A-%D9%8A%D9%83%D8%AB%D9%81-%D8%B9%D9%85%D9%84D9%8A%D8%A7%D8%AA%D9%87-%D9%81%D9%8A-%D8%A7%D9%84%D8%B9%D8%A7%D8%B5%D9%85%D8%A9-%D8%B7%D8%B1%D8%A7%D8%A8%D9%84%D8%B3/

Eljarh, M. (2014, July 22). Libya's Islamists Go for Broke. Retrieved February 01, 2021, from https://foreignpolicy.com/2014/07/22/libyas-islamists-go-for-broke/

Eljarh, M. (2014, November 06). The Supreme Court Decision That's Ripping Libya Apart. Retrieved February 01, 2021, from https://foreignpolicy.com/2014/11/06/the-supreme-court-decision-thats-ripping-libya-apart/

Eljarh, M. (2019, April 09). Libya: The Lesser of Two Evils. Retrieved February 01, 2021, from https://www.atlanticcouncil.org/blogs/menasource/libya-the-lesser-of-two-evils

Enabbaladi. (2019, July 6). Hifter: The Libyan army obtained any American-made weapons "pure nonsense". Retrieved February 02, 2021, from https://enabbaladi.net/archives/294461

Engel, P. (2015, November 30). ISIS is preparing a 'BACKUP' capital in case its major center in Syria falls. Retrieved February 08, 2021, from https://www.businessinsider.com/isis-sirte-libya-2015-11

Ensor, J. (2018, June 08). UN sanctions six human traffickers in Libya in global first. Retrieved February 11, 2021, from https://www.telegraph.co.uk/news/2018/06/08/un-sanctions-six-human-traffickers-libya-global-first/

Erdbrink, T., & Sly, L. (2011, August 22). In Libya, Moammar Gaddafi's rule crumbling as rebels enter heart of Tripoli. Retrieved February 01, 2021, from https://www.washingtonpost.com/world/middle-east/libyan-rebelsconverging-on-tripoli/2011/08/21/gIQAbF3RUJ_story.html

Eremnews. (2020, June 17). ISIS claims responsibility for an attack on Egyptian forces in the Sinai. Retrieved February 02, 2021, from https://www.eremnews.com/news/world/2266925

Essam, M., & Arfaoui, J. (2013, June 13). Libya: Ultimatum Issued to Militias. Retrieved February 04, 2021, from http://allafrica.com/stories/201306140650.html

Fabbrini, S. (2014). The European Union and the Libyan crisis. Retrieved January 31, 2021, from https://www.researchgate.net/publication/263326293_The_European_Union_and_the_Libyan_crisis

Fisher, M. (2011, October 20). How Qaddafi Fooled Libya and the World. Retrieved February 01, 2021, from https://www.theatlantic.com/international/archive/2011/10/how-qaddafi-fooled-libya-and-the-world/247078/

Fitzgerald, M. (2014, June 24). Libyan renegade general Khalifa Haftar claims he is winning his war. Retrieved February 01, 2021, from https://www.theguardian.com/world/2014/jun/24/libyan-renegade-general-khalifa-haftar-war

Fitzgerald, M. (2015, August 25). Is civil war likely? Retrieved February 01, 2021, from https://www.economist.com/pomegranate/2014/08/25/is-civil-war-likely

Furness, M., & Trautner, B. (2020). Reconstituting social contracts in conflict-affected mena COUNTRIES: Whither Iraq and Libya? *World Development, 135*, 105085. doi:10.1016/j.worlddev.2020.105085

Gartenstein, D. (2015, February). Ross and Nathaniel Barr, "Dignity and Dawn: Libya's Escalating Civil War", International Centre for Counter-Terrorism. Retrieved February 01, 2021, from https://www.icct.nl/download/file/ICCT-Gartenstein-Ross-Barr-Dignity-and-Dawn-Libyas-Escalating-Civil-War-February2015.pdf

Gazzini, C. (2020, March 10). Crisis Group Role. Retrieved February 08, 2021, from https://www.crisisgroup.org/who-we-are/people/claudia-gazzini

Ghaddar, A., & Lewis, A. (2016, April 28). Libya outlines ambitious plans to restore oil output. Retrieved February 01, 2021, from https://www.reuters.com/article/us-libya-oil-production-idUSKCN0XP25R

Ghobara, A. (2018, June 23). Libya's Wealth in the Crosshairs … Chronology of the conflict over the Crescent Petroleum. Retrieved February 11, 2021, from https://www.afrigatenews.net/article/%D8%AB%D8%B1%D9%88%D8%A7%D8%AA-%D9%84%D9%8A%D8%A8%D9%8A% D8% A7-% D9% 81% D9% 8A-% D9% 85% D8% B1% D9% 85% D9% 89-% D8% A7% D9% 84% D8% B3% D9% 84% D8% A7 % D8% AD-% D9% 83% D8% B1% D9% 88% D9% 86% D9% 88% D9% 84% D9% 88% D8% AC% D9% 8A% D8% A7-% D8% A7 % D9% 84% D8% B5% D8% B1% D8% A7% D8% B9-% D8% AD% D9% 88% D9% 84-% D8% A7% D9% 84% D9% 87% D9% 84 % D8% A7% D9% 84-% D8% A7% D9% 84% D9% 86% D9% 81% D8% B7% D9% 8A /

Good, C. (2011, March 21). Obama's Answer to the Question, 'Why Libya?' Retrieved February 01, 2021, from https://www.theatlantic.com/politics/archive/2011/03/obamas-answer-to-the-question-why-libya/72811/

Hamada, A., Sökmen, M., & Zaki, C. (2020). Investigating The Libyan Conflict and Peace-Building Process: Past Causes and Future Prospects. Retrieved February 11, 2021, from https://erf.org.eg/wp-content/uploads/2020/03/1383.pdf

Harchaoui, J. (2019, October 31). Libya's monetary crisis. Retrieved February 11, 2021, from https://www.lawfareblog.com/libyas-monetary-crisis

Hassan, R. (2018, October 27). Egyptian executed in Sinai because of "his cooperation with the security services". Retrieved February 08, 2021, from https://www.eremnews.com/news/arab-world/2266667

Heba, M. (2019, May 13). Ghassan Salama calls for a truce in Libya: The military solution is difficult. Retrieved February 02, 2021, from https://www.almasryalyoum.com/news/details/1396868

Hehir, A. (n.d.). The Permanence of Inconsistency: Libya, the Security Council, and the Responsibility to Protect. *International Security, 38*(1), 137-159.

Hossam, M. (2016, January 22). Economic repercussions of the war on Libya. Retrieved February 04, 2021, from https://almesryoon.com/

Human Rights Watch. (2013, May 4). Libya: Reject 'Political Isolation Law. Retrieved February 01, 2021, from https://www.hrw.org/news/2013/05/04/libya-reject-political-isolation-law.

Human Rights Watch. (2018). Libya: Events of 2018. Retrieved February 11, 2021, from https://www.hrw.org/worldreport/2019/country-chapters/libya

Human Rights Watch. (2020, October 28). Libya: Ensure Gaddafi Son's Access to Lawyer. Retrieved February 01, 2021, from https://www.hrw.org/news/2011/12/21/libya-ensure-gaddafi-sons-access-lawyer

Ibrahim, A. (2018). NOC deplores handover of oil ports to parallel institution, saying 'Haftar Is acting like criminal Jadran. Retrieved February 12, 2021, from https://www.libyaobserver.ly/news/noc-deplores-handover-oil-ports-parallel-institution-saying-%E2%80%9Chaftar-acting-criminal-jadran%E2%80%9D.

Imam, M., Abba,,., & Wader3, M. (2014). Libya In The Post Ghadaffi Era. *The International Journal of Social Sciences and Humanities Invention, 2*(2349-2031), 1150-1166. doi:file:///C:/Users/Laptop/Downloads/223-Article%20Text-431-1-10-20171230.pdf

The Independent. (2012, January 18). Nato accused of war crimes in Libya. Retrieved February 01, 2021, from https://www.independent.co.uk/news/world/africa/nato-accused-war-crimes-libya-6291566.html

International Crisis Group. (2018). After the Showdown in Libya's Oil Crescent. Retrieved February 11, 2021, from https://www.crisisgroup.org/middle-east-north-africa/north-africa/libya/189- after-showdown-libyas-oil-crescent.

International Crisis Group. (2018, October 25). The Prize: Fighting for Libya's Energy Wealth. Retrieved February 01, 2021, from https://www.crisisgroup.org/middle-east-north-africa/north-africa/libya/prize-fighting-libya-s-energy-wealth.

International Crisis Group. (2018, September 24). After the Showdown in Libya's Oil Crescent. Retrieved February 11, 2021, from https://www.crisisgroup.org/middle-east-north-africa/north-africa/libya/189-after-showdown-libyas-oil-crescent

The International Crisis Group. (2019). Search. Retrieved February 02, 2021, from https://www.crisisgroup.org/search?text=Libya

International Foundation for Electoral Systems. (2018, December 8). New survey on libyan voters' attitudes toward political situation and future elections. Retrieved February 11, 2021, from https://www.ifes.org/surveys/new-survey-libyan-voters-attitudes-toward-political-situation-and-future-elections

International organization for migration. (2019). Retrieved February 11, 2021, from https://www.iom.int/

Ispi. (2017, September 27). How much of a threat is the Islamic state in Libya? Retrieved February 08, 2021, from https://www.ispionline.it/it/pubblicazione/how-much-threat-islamic-state-libya-14357

Jebnoun, N. (2015). Beyond the mayhem: Debating key dilemmas in Libya's statebuilding. *Journal of North African Studies, 20*(5), 823-864. doi:https://doi.org/10.1080/13629387.2015.1068697

Jonathan, M. (2019). Origins of the Libyan conflict and options for its resolution. Retrieved February 12, 2021, from https://www.mei.edu/sites/default/files/2019-

Jstor. (2015). V. filling The Vacuum: ISIS'S Libyan wilayat (2014-2015). Retrieved February 4, 2021, from https://www.jstor.org/stable/pdf/resrep03718.10.pdf

Juha, M. (2018, December 2). Who is the real founder of ISIS? Retrieved February 11, 2021, from https://24.ae/article/476808/

Kamal, A. (2019, April 18). Recep Tayyip Erdogan with the Emir of Qatar, Tamim bin Hamad Al Thani, why Qatar and Turkey support the reconciliation forces in Libya ... Experts explain. Retrieved February 02, 2021, from https://arabic.sputniknews.com/arab_world/201904181040567484-%D8%AE%D8%A8%D8%B1%D8%A7%D8%A1-%D8%A3%D8%B3%D8%A8%D8%A7%D8%A8-%D8%A7%D9%84%D8%AF%D9%88%D8%AD%D8%A9-%D8%A3%D9%86%D9%82%D8%B1%D8%A9-%D8%B7%D8%B1%D8%A7%D8%A8%D9%84%D8%B3/

Khaled, A. (2019, April 11). The city of Zintan declares its support for Khalifa Haftar. Retrieved February 02, 2021, from https://www.eremnews.com/news/maghreb-news/1768135

Lacher, W. (2012, February). The Libyan Revolution and the Rise of Local Power Centres. Retrieved February 01, 2021, from https://www.iemed.org/observatori-en/arees-danalisi/arxius-adjunts/anuari/med.2012/lacher_en.pdf

Lacher, W. (2019, April 18). The UN wants to End Libya's civil war. Here's the big challenge they face. Retrieved February 04, 2021, from https://www.washingtonpost.com/news/monkey-cage/wp/2015/11/05/why-libya-isnt-just-divided-but-fragmented/

Lacher, W., & Al-Idrissi, A. (2015, June). Capital of Militias: Tripoli's Armed Groups Capture the Libyan State. Retrieved February 01, 2021, from https://issat.dcaf.ch/Learn/Resource-Library2/Policy-and-Research-Papers/Capital-of-Militias-Tripoli-s-Armed-Groups-Capture-the-Libyan-State

Ladjal, T. (2016). Tribe and state in the history of modern Libya: A ... Retrieved February 2, 2021, from https://www.cogentoa.com/article/10.1080/23311983.2016.1183278.pdf

Lederer, E. (2018, June 07). UN adds 6 traffickers and smugglers to LIBYA sanctions list. Retrieved February 11, 2021, from https://apnews.com/33fa5811cfa3406ebab0cf094ca946ff

Lee, J. (2018, February 4). Qaddafi's Long Gone, But Libya's Oil Still Struggles. Retrieved February 11, 2021, from https://www.bloomberg.com/opinion/articles/2018-02-04/qaddafi-s-long-gone-but-libya-s-oil-still-struggles.

Lewis, A. (2018, July 16). How unstable is Libya's oil production? Retrieved February 11, 2021, from https://www.reuters.com/article/us-libya-oil-explainer-idUSKBN1K61Y6

Lewis, A. (2018, March 29). Libya won't stabilize unless shadow economy smashed: U.N. envoy. Retrieved February 11, 2021, from https://www.reuters.com/article/us-libya-security-un-idUSKBN1H51FE

Li Xia, A. (2019, October 30). Libya's Tripoli airport reopens after 2-month closure. Retrieved February 02, 2021, from http://www.xinhuanet.com/english/2019-10/30/c_138513539.htm

Libya Business News. (2015, January 16). Dramatic measures to Plug budget Deficit: Libya business news. Retrieved February 11, 2021, from https://www.libya-businessnews.com/2015/01/17/dramatic-measures-to-plug-budget-deficit/

Libya Crude Oil Production1973-2020 Data: 2021-2023 Forecast: Historical: Chart. (n.d.). Retrieved February 01, 2021, from https://tradingeconomics.com/libya/crude-oil-production

Libya Ethnic Groups. (n.d.). Retrieved January 31, 2021, from https://study.com/academy/lesson/libya-ethnic-groups.html

Libya Herald. (2017, August 27). NOC calls for more arrests of fuel smugglers. Retrieved February 11, 2021, from https://www.libyaherald.com/2017/08/26/noc-calls-for-more-arrests-of-fuel-smugglers/

Libya Observer. (2018). UN envoy to LIBYA: More than 20 million pieces of arms are held by. Retrieved February 04, 2021, from https://www.libyaobserver.ly/news/un-envoy-libya-more-20-million-pieces-arms-are-held-libyans

Libya Population 2021 (Live). (n.d.). Retrieved January 31, 2021, from https://worldpopulationreview.com/countries/libya-population/.

Libya. (2021, January 28). Retrieved January 31, 2021, from https://www.britannica.com/place/Libya

Libyan Constitution. (2011). Constitute. Retrieved February 01, 2021, from https://www.constituteproject.org/

Libya's Economic Update - October 2019. (n.d.). Retrieved February 01, 2021, from https://www.worldbank.org/en/country/libya/publication/economic-update-october-2019

Lindsay Benstead, A. (2019, May 03). Libya's security dilemma. Retrieved January 31, 2021, from https://www.washingtonpost.com/news/monkey-cage/wp/2014/04/07/libyas-security-dilemma/

Maha, M., & Amzein, A. (2013, June 19). Huge explosion flattens Benghazi police station – no casualties reported. Retrieved February 01, 2021, from https://www.libyaherald.com/2013/06/19/huge-explosion-flattens-benghazi-police-station-no-casualties-reported/

Mahdi, M. A. (2017). A reading of the causes of armed conflict In Libya and its Possible Paths. Retrieved February 04, 2021, from https://www.sis.gov.eg/Newvr/34/9.htm

Mahmoud, N. (2019, April 14). Tensions on all sides … How can Egypt secure its inflamed borders? Retrieved February 02, 2021, from https://www.skynewsarabia.com/middle-east/1242764-%D8%AA%D9%88%D8%AA%D8%B1%D8%A7%D8%AA-%D8%A7%D9%84%D8%AC%D9%87%D8%A7%D8%AA-%D8%A7%D9%84%D8%A7%D9%94%D8%B1%D8%A8%D8%B9-%

Mangan, F., & Murtaugh, C. (2016, October 11). Security and Justice in Post-Revolution Libya. Retrieved February 02, 2021, from https://www.usip.org/publications/2014/09/security-and-justice-post-revolution-libya

Mashali, H. (2019, April 18). Thwarting the infiltration of 36 people from different governorates into Libya through Salloum. Retrieved February 02, 2021, from https://www.youm7.com/story/2019/4/20/%D8%A5%D8%AD%D8%A8%D8%A7%D8%B7-%D8%AA%D8%B3%D9%84%D9%84-36-%D8%B4%D8%AE%D8%B5%D8%A7%D9%8B-%D9%85%D9%86-%D9%85%D8%AD%D8%A7%D9%81%D8%B8%D8%A7%D8%AA-%D9%85%D8%AE%D8%AA%D9%84%D9%81%D8%A9-%D8%A5%D9%84%D9%89-%D9%84%D9%8A%D8%A8%D9%8A%D8%A7-%D8%B9%D9%86/4214672

Masrawy. (2019, July 2). Libyan Wise Men": Egypt is the first support for the re-establishment of the state and the return of stability. Retrieved February 02, 2021, from https://www.masrawy.com/news/news_publicaffairs/details/2019/7/2/1594123/-%D8%AD%D9%83%D9%85%D8%A7%D8%A1-%D9%84%D9%8A%D8%A8%D9%8A%D8%A7-%D9%85%D8%B5%D8%B1-%D8%A7%D9%84%D8%B3%D9%86%D8%AF-%D8%A7%D9%84%D8%A3%D9%88%D9%84-%D9%84%D8%A5%D8%B9%D8%A7%D8%AF%D8%A9-%D9%82%D9%8A%D8%A7%D9%85-%D8%A7%D9%84%D8%AF%D9%88%D9%84%D8%A9-%D9%88%D8%B9%D9%88%D8%AF%D8%A9-

%D8%A7%D9%84%D8%A7%D8%B3%D8%AA%D9%82%D8%B1%D8%A7%D8%B1-

Matthew Herbert, M. (2018, February 14). Analysis | Italy claims it's found a solution to Europe's Migrant Problem. Here's why italy's wrong. Retrieved February 11, 2021, from https://www.washingtonpost.com/news/monkey-cage/wp/2017/09/25/italy-claims-its-found-a-solution-to-europes-migrant-problem-heres-why-italys-wrong/

McGregor, A. (2014). Tripoli Battles Shadowy Qaddafists While Tribal Rivals Fight Over Southern. *Jamestown Foundation,* (12). Retrieved February 1, 2021, from vailable at: https://www.refworld.org/docid/52f20b9c4.html [accessed 1 February 2021]

McGregor, A. (2016, September 20). Autonomy Campaign in Cyrenaica Brings Libya's Oil Industry to a Halt. Retrieved February 01, 2021, from https://jamestown.org/program/autonomy-campaign-in-cyrenaica-brings-libyas-oil-industry-to-a-halt/

Micallef, M., & Reitano, T. (2018, February 01). The anti-human smuggling business and Libya's political end game. Retrieved February 11, 2021, from https://globalinitiative.net/the-anti-human-smuggling-business-and-libyas-political-end-game/

Middle Gate. (2014, August 1). Dignity and Dawn: Libya's Escalating Civil War".Al-Wasat, "Tadhaahoraat dhakhma fi Benghazi tahtef dhad Ansar al-Sharee'a. Retrieved February 01, 2021, from http://alwasat.ly/news/libya/26952.

Mohammed, E. (2013, April 30). Militiamen besiege Libya's Justice Ministry. Retrieved February 01, 2021, from https://www.usatoday.com/story/news/world/2013/04/30/militiamen-besiege-libyas-justice-ministry/2122979/

Mohammed, M. (2019, February 7). Libyan Fields: One on the south and one on the west. Retrieved February 02, 2021, from http://egypt.gov.eg/arabic/home.aspx

Mohsan, A. (2017, March 3). Libya crisis: Head of Islamist Tripoli government fired. Retrieved February 04, 2021, from https://www.bbc.com/news/world-middle-east-32137285.

Murray, R. (2015, April 04). Libya: A tale of two governments. Retrieved February 01, 2021, from https://www.aljazeera.com/news/2015/4/4/libya-a-tale-of-two-governments

Muscato, C. (n.d.). Retrieved January 31, 2021, from https://study.com/academy/lesson/libya-ethnic-groups.html

Nayed, A. (2017). Extremism, Trauma, and Therapy," Radical Engagement: Essays on Religion, Extremism, Politics, and Libya. Retrieved February 08, 2021, from https://www.kalamresearch.com/pdf/Radical-Engagements.pdf

News.UN. (2015, August). ISIS is committing more violence in Libya and worried about the militants' increasing allegiance to the organization. Retrieved February 08, 2021, from https://news.un.org/ar/audio/2015/08/334642

OHCHR. (2014, September 4). Overview of Violations of International Human Rights and Humanitarian Law during the Ongoing Violence in Libya [EN/AR] - Libya. Retrieved January 31, 2021, from https://reliefweb.int/report/libya/overview-violations-international-human-rights-and-humanitarian-law-during-ongoing

OHCHR. (2015, March). Human Rights Defenders under Attack. Retrieved February 08, 2021, from http://www.ohchr.org/Documents/Countries/LY/HumanRightsDefendersLibya.pdf

Ohchr. (2017). International Legal Protection of Human Rights in Armed Conflict. Retrieved February 4, 2021, from https://www.ohchr.org/Documents/Publications/HR_in_armed_conflict.pdf

Oil becomes the key battleground in Libya's civil war. (2020, February 18). Retrieved January 31, 2021, from https://www.nsenergybusiness.com/features/libya-oil-blockades/

Omagu, D., & Odigbo, J. (2017). Democracy and the struggle for democratisation in Libya. *Socialscientia Journal of the Social Science and Humanities, 2*(1), 30-46.

Opec News. (2017). Libya facts and figures", Vienna,. Retrieved February 11, 2021, from https://www.opec.org/opec_web/en/about_us/166.htm

Pack, J., Smith, R., & Mezran, K. (2019, November 13). The origins and evolution of ISIS in Libya. Retrieved February 08, 2021, from https://www.atlanticcouncil.org/in-depth-research-reports/report/the-origins-and-evolution-of-isis-in-libya-2/

Pattison, J. (2013). *Humanitarian intervention and the responsibility to protect: Who should intervene?* (1st ed., Vol. 37). Oxford: Oxford University Press. doi:https://www.jstor.org/stable/24480624?seq=1#metadata_info_tab_contents

Pedde, N. (2017, June 1). The Libyan Conflict and Its Controversial Roots - Nicola Pedde, 2017. Retrieved February 01, 2021, from https://journals.sagepub.com/doi/full/10.1007/s12290-017-0447-5

Phillips, J. (2018, July 17). Spanish charity accuses Libyan coastguard of leaving a woman and toddler to die in the Mediterranean. Retrieved February 11, 2021, from https://www.telegraph.co.uk/news/2018/07/17/spanish-charity-accuses-libyan-coastguard-leaving-woman-toddler/

Porsia, N. (2017, February 20). The kingpin of Libya's human TRAFFICKING MAFIA. Retrieved February 11, 2021, from https://www.trtworld.com/magazine/libya-human-trafficking-mafia-in-zawiya-301505

Pusztai, W. (2015, August 21). News from the Middle east and North AFRICA: The Arab Weekly. Retrieved February 08, 2021, from http://www.thearabweekly.com/?id=1617+.

Radsch, C. (2015, April 22). Treating the internet as the enemy in the Middle East. Retrieved February 04, 2021, from https://cpj.org/2015/04/attacks-on-the-press-treating-internet-as-enemy-in-middle-east.php

Ramy, M. (2019, May 13). French Presidency: An upcoming gathering of Hifter and Macron in Paris. Retrieved February 02, 2021, from https://www.218tv.net/%D8%A7%D9%84%D8%B1%D8%A6%D8%A7%D8%B3%D8%A9-%D8%A7%D9%84%D9%81%D8%B1%D9%86%D8%B3%D9%8A%D8%A9-%D9%84%D9%82%D8%A7%D1-%D9%85%D8%B1%D8%AA%D9%82%D8%A8-%D9%8A%D8%AC%D9%85%D8%B9-%D8%AD%D9%81%D8%AA%D8%B1/

Raval, A. (2017, November 13). Libya's oil guardian coaxes ravaged industry into recovery. Retrieved February 01, 2021, from https://www.ft.com/content/f8d6f892-c85c-11e7-ab18-7a9fb7d6163e

Reliefweb. (2015, July). Libya Multi-Sector Needs Assessment. Retrieved February 08, 2021, from https://reliefweb.int/sites/reliefweb.int/files/resources/JMW_reach_lby_report_libya_multi_sector_needs_assessment_aug_2015.pdf

Reuters. (2020, August 27). Libya's Tripoli government imposes COVID-19 curfew after protests escalate. Retrieved January 31, 2021, from https://www.reuters.com/article/us-libya-security/libyas-tripoli-government-imposes-covid-19-curfew-after-protests-escalate-idUSKBN25N1WO

Sahiounie, S. (2020, November 19). The UN is failing in Libya. Who is to blame? Retrieved February 01, 2021, from https://theduran.com/the-un-is-failing-in-libya-who-is-to-blame/

Samer, A. (2019). Libya's Haftar Orders "Harsh Response" after Surprise Loss of City. Retrieved February 11, 2021, from https://www.bloomberg.com/news/articles/2019-06-29/libya-s-haftar-orders-harsh-response-after-surprise-loss-of-city

Sanalla, M. (2017, June 19). How to Save Libya From Itself? Protect Its Oil From Its Politics. Retrieved February 01, 2021, from https://www.nytimes.com/2017/06/19/opinion/libya-and-another-oil-curse.html

Sarieldin, N. (2015, February). The Battle for Benghazi. Retrieved February 01, 2021, from https://www.swp-berlin.org/fileadmin/contents/products/comments/2015C08_srd.pdf

Sawani, Y. (2020, March 01). Gaddafi's Legacy, Institutional Development, and National Reconciliation in Libya. Retrieved February 02, 2021, from https://online.ucpress.edu/caa/article-abstract/13/1/46/109267/Gaddafi-s-Legacy-Institutional-Development-and?redirectedFrom=fulltext

Search. (n.d.). Retrieved January 31, 2021, from https://www.crisisgroup.org/search

Sengupta, K. (2012, July 07). Armed federalists shut down Libya oil terminals ahead of vote. Retrieved February 01, 2021, from https://www.independent.co.uk/news/world/africa/armed-federalists-shut-down-libya-oil-terminals-ahead-of-vote-7920590.html

Shaarawy, I. (2020, September 07). Oil Politics Fueling Libya's Conflict: Egypt Oil & Gas. Retrieved February 02, 2021, from https://egyptoil-gas.com/features/oil-politics-fueling-libyas-conflict/

Shennib, G., & Bosalum, F. (2013, July 29). Islamist party office attacked as Libya violence persists. Retrieved February 01, 2021, from https://www.reuters.com/article/us-libya-benghazi/islamist-party-office-attacked-as-libya-violence-persists-idUSBRE96S0XT20130729

Shuaib, A. (2012, October 22). Civilians flee besieged former Gaddafi stronghold in Libya. Retrieved February 01, 2021, from https://www.reuters.com/article/us-libya-clashes-idUSBRE89L11B20121022

Shuaib, A. (2012, September 09). Gaddafi son's Libya trial to be delayed by five months: Official. Retrieved February 01, 2021, from https://www.reuters.com/article/us-libya-saif-trial/gaddafi-sons-libya-trial-to-be-delayed-by-five-months-official-idUSBRE8880F720120909

Sputnikhttps. (2018, November 30). Leaked documents reveal serious scenes about the war in Sinai. Retrieved February 08, 2021, from https://arabic.sputniknews.com/arab_world/201811301037108696-%D8%A7%D9%84%D8%AD%D8%B1%D8%A8-%D8%B3%D9%8A%D9%86%D8%A7%D8%A1-%D9%88%D8%AB%D9%8A%D9%82%D8%A9/

Stephen, C. (2013, June 13). Libya: Tensions between government and militias come to a head. Retrieved February 01, 2021, from https://www.theguardian.com/world/2013/jun/13/tensions-government-militia-libya-shield-benghazi

Stephen, C. (2013, September 09). US consulate attack in Benghazi: A challenge to official version of events. Retrieved February 01, 2021, from https://www.theguardian.com/world/2013/sep/09/us-consulate-benghazi-attack-challenge

Stephen, C., & Wintour, P. (2018, July 02). Four Libya oil ports closed amid corruption allegations. Retrieved February 11, 2021, from https://www.theguardian.com/world/2018/jul/02/four-libya-oil-ports-closed-amid-corruption-allegations-allies-khalifa-haftar

Synovitz, R., & Solash, R. (2011, March 01). World Powers Heap Pressure On Qaddafi. Retrieved February 01, 2021, from https://www.rferl.org/a/libya_protests/2322692.html

Tarkowski, S., & Omar, M. M. (2015, January 12). Stakeholders of Libya's 17 February Revolution,. Report - United States Department of Justice. Retrieved February 1, 2021, from https://www.justice.gov/eoir/page/file/989511/download

Taylor, A., & Tharoor, I. (2019, May 02). Here are the key players fighting the war for Libya, all over again. Retrieved February 02, 2021, from https://www.washingtonpost.com/news/worldviews/wp/2014/08/27/here-are-the-key-players-fighting-the-war-for-libya-all-over-again

Thomas, H. M. (2019, May 15). The conflict in Libya. Retrieved February 08, 2021, from https://www.usip.org/publications/2019/05/conflict-libya

Toaldo, M., & Fitzgerald, M. (2016, May 19). A quick guide to Libya's main players. Retrieved February 11, 2021, from https://www.ecfr.eu/mena/mapping_libya_conflict

Trauthig, I. K. (2019, April). Assessing the Islamic State in Libya. Retrieved February 08, 2021, from file:///C:/Users/Laptop/Downloads/inga_trauthig_islamic_state_libya%20(1).pdf

Tuncer, C. (2017). Analysis of the Libyan crisis within the framework of the internationalization of the state concept. Retrieved February 2, 2021, from http://www.openaccess.hacettepe.edu.tr:8080/xmlui/bitstream/handle/11655/3295/10140586.pdf?sequence=2&isAllowed=y

Ukessays. (2017, April). The reasons behind the libya crisis. Retrieved February 04, 2021, from https://www.ukessays.com/essays/history/the-reasons-behind-the-libya-crisis-history-essay.php

UN Security Council. (2019, November 19). U.S. department of the Treasury. Retrieved February 08, 2021, from https://home.treasury.gov/news/press-releases/sm551

United Nations Support Mission In Libya. (2018). Desperate and Dangerous: Report on the human rights situation of migrants and refugees in Libya - Libya. Retrieved February 02, 2021, from https://reliefweb.int/report/libya/desperate-and-dangerous-report-human-rights-situation-migrants-and-refugees-libya

United Nations Support Mission In Libya. (2018). The Libyan National Conference Process - Final Report. Retrieved from https://unsmil.unmissions.org/sites/default/files/ncp_report_jan_2019_en.pdf

United Nations Support Mission In Libya. (2019). The Libyan National Conference Process. Retrieved February 2, 2021, from https://unsmil.unmissions.org/sites/default/files/ncp_report_jan_2019_en.pdf

Waal, A. (n.d.). African roles in the Libyan conflict of 2011. International Affairs, 89(2), 365-379. doi:https://doi.org/10.1111/1468-2346.12022

Wai, Z. (2014). The empire's new clothes: Africa, liberal interventionism and contemporary world order. *Review of African Political Economy, 39*(131). doi:https://doi.org/10.1080/03056244.2014.928278

Watkins, T., Alley, T., & Valley, S. (1982). USA The History of the Development of Libyan Gas and Oil Resources. Retrieved February 02, 2021, from https://www.sjsu.edu/faculty/watkins/libyanoil.htm.

Wehrey, F. (2014). Ending Libya's Civil War: Reconciling Politics, Rebuilding Security. Retrieved February 01, 2021, from https://carnegieendowment.org/2014/09/24/ending-libya-s-civil-war-reconciling-politics-rebuilding-security-pub-56741

Wehrey, F. (2016, February 17). Why Libya's Transition to Democracy Failed. Retrieved February 02, 2021, from https://carnegieendowment.org/2016/02/17/why-libya-s-transition-to-democracy-failed-pub-62808

Wehrey, F. (2016, February). Breaking News, World, US, DC News and Analysis. Retrieved February 01, 2021, from https://www.washingtonpost.com/?tid=paid_gse_eng_intl&utm_source=google&utm_medium=google&utm_campaign=intl_news_search_global&utm_content=&utm_keyword=washington+post+news&campaignid=8867048116&adgroupid=94815991168&adid=411153870850&gclid=Cj0KCQiA6t6ABhDMARIsAONIYyzGXZ5YJbWxl3aB5_aryJGCIp9SqXiCzQVammy4wgA9dLDvlg5BfAEaAoruEALw_wcB

Wehrey, F. (2017). Insecurity and Governance Challenges in Southern Libya. Retrieved February 02, 2021, from https://carnegieendowment.org/2017/03/30/insecurity-and-governance-challenges-in-southern-libya-pub-68451

Wehrey, F., & Jeffrey, F. (2019). Libya Is Entering Another Civil War. America Can Stop It. Retrieved February 02, 2021, from https://carnegieendowment.org/2019/04/05/libya-is-entering-another-civil-war.-america-can-stop-it-pub-78807

Wehrey, F., & Lacher, W. (2014, October 07). Libya's Legitimacy Crisis. Retrieved February 01, 2021, from https://www.foreignaffairs.com/articles/middle-east/2014-10-06/libyas-legitimacy-crisis

Wehrey, F., & Lacher, W. (2019, June 03). Libya's new Civil War. Retrieved February 11, 2021, from https://www.foreignaffairs.com/articles/libya/2019-05-30/libyas-new-civil-war

Wester, K. (2020). Intervention in Libya. *Cambridge University Press*. doi:10.1017/9781108576666

Wintour, P. (2018, July 11). East Libyan general hands back control of oil ports. Retrieved February 11, 2021, from https://www.theguardian.com/world/2018/jul/11/east-libyan-general-hands-back-control-of-oil-ports

World Bank. (2019). International Bank for Reconstruction and Development and International Finance Corporation and Multilateral Investment Guarantee Agency Country Engagement Note for the State of Libya for the Period 2019-2021. Retrieved February 11, 2021, from http://documents1.worldbank.org/curated/zh/750661550977483586/pdf/Libya-CEN-to-Board-final-01252019-636865562772741763.pdf

Yassin, H. (2018, November 7). ISIS focuses more on rhetoric than on military. Retrieved February 11, 2021, from https://www.alghad.tv/%D9%85%D8%B1%D8%B5%D8%AF-%D8%A7%D9%84%D8%A5%D9%81%D8%AA%D8%A7%D8%A1-%D8%AF%D8%A7%D8%B9%D8%B4-%D9%8A%D8%B1%D9%83%D8%B2-

%D8%B9%D9%84%D9%89-%D9%82%D9%88%D8%A9-%D8%A7%D9%84%D8%
AE%D8%B7%D8%A7%D8%A8-%D8%A3/

Zaptia, S. (2018). Libya's economic reforms have been successful. Retrieved February 08, 2021, from https://www.libyaherald.com/2018/11/24/libyas-economic-reforms-have-been-successful/

Zelin, A. (2014, October). The Islamic State's First Colony in Libya," The Washington Institute for Near East Policy,. Retrieved February 08, 2021, from http://www.washingtoninstitute. org/policy-analysis/view/theislamic-states-first-colony-in-libya.

Zenko, M. (2016, March 22). The Big Lie About the Libyan War. Retrieved February 01, 2021, from https://foreignpolicy.com/2016/03/22/libya-and-the-myth-of-humanitarian-intervention/.

Printed in the United States
by Baker & Taylor Publisher Services